# Global Media Policy in the New Millennium

# Global Media Policy in the New Millennium

**Edited by Marc Raboy**

UNIVERSITY
OF LUTON

press

British Library Cataloguing in Publication Data
A catalogue record for this book is available from the British Library

ISBN: 1 86020 589 5

Published by
University of Luton Press
University of Luton
75 Castle Street
Luton
Bedfordshire LU1 3AJ
United Kingdom

Tel: +44 (0)1582 743297; Fax: +44 (0)1582 743298
e-mail: ulp@luton.ac.uk
www.ulp.org.uk

Cover Design by Gary Gravatt
Typeset in Van Dijck MT and Helvetica
Printed in Great Britain by Thanet Press, Margate, Kent

302.23   RAB

iv

# Contents

# Acknowledgements

This book began as a rather ambitious attempt to launch an intellectual debate with activist intentions. In July 1998, the undersigned convened a Global Media Policy working group within the umbrella framework of the International Association for Media and Communication Research's 21st scientific congress in Glasgow, Scotland. The stated purpose of the working group was "to stimulate reflection, discussion and exchange on the premise that the challenges of globalization demand new, transnational policy approaches aimed at enabling media and communication to better serve what can be termed as a global public interest."

More than seventy participants answered the call by attending the working group's two sessions, and the lively discussions that took place there were highlighted in a "Symposium" of short articles published in the journal *Javnost – The Public* (vol. 5, no. 4, 1998). I thank all of the Glasgow participants, the symposium authors, and *Javnost* editor Slavko Splichal, who opened the pages of the journal to us.

The experience was repeated at the following IAMCR congress in Singapore in July 2000, this time with some sixty scholars in attendance. They too must be thanked. A first session dealt with issues and a second one with strategies for intervention in the area of global media policy. Immediately following the Singapore sessions, a group of us decided to try to push our thinking on these questions further, and the result (complemented by contributions solicited later from other leading scholars) is this book.

I wish to particularly thank Stuart Cunningham, Tom O'Regan and Terry Flew for helping to get the project off the ground, and for securing a crucial editing grant from the Centre for Media Policy and Practice at the Queensland University of Technology, Brisbane.

Manuel Alvarado, definitely academia's most laid-back publisher, made the rest easy by streamlining our negotiations with the University of Luton Press.

Robyn Sussel, of the Signals Design Group (Vancouver), deftly rode shotgun over the manuscript, cybermassaging the authors and their texts and giving

1

real meaning to her signature phrase (after H. G. Wells): "No passion in the world is equal to the passion to alter someone else's draft."

Isabelle Mailloux-Beique helped juggle commas and periods at the proof-reading stage.

Finally, I wish to acknowledge the indirect but essential assistance of Myriam Amzallag, administrative assistant of the Department of Communication at the University of Montreal, who always manages to graciously make impossible tasks seem simply mundane.

*Marc Raboy*

*Montréal, June 2001*

# Media Policy in the New Communications Environment

June 1, 2001. Reuters news agency reports today that the new director-designate of the World Trade Organization, Supachai Panitchpakdi, has declared the urgency of putting in place a global framework for the regulation of electronic commerce. "The development of trade via the Internet is such that it is necessary to establish a clearly defined regulatory framework," he is quoted as stating, adding that the upcoming WTO conference in Qatar would undoubtedly deal with this issue (Reuters 2001).

What's wrong with this picture? Isn't the very *raison d'être* of the WTO based on the premise of doing away with the barriers to trade that inevitably come with regulation and on ending the meddling of states, governments and regulatory authorities in the otherwise smooth machinery of the marketplace? Well, yes and no. Indeed, certain types of intervention – public intervention – are seen by the avatars of global commerce as a hindrance to flourishing markets; and justifying this position as the only reasonable one has long been a substantial ideological undertaking. At the same time, however, and usually with much less fanfare, the corporate community has been a most successful user of the levers of governance in promotion of its own interests.

The WTO now joined a chorus of powerful voices emanating from unlikely quarters over the past five years to call for new global policy measures in communication. One of the first was European telecommunications commissioner Martin Bangemann, author of a high-profile blueprint for communication liberalization that bears his name, who, in September 1997, called for an "international charter" to govern the new world order in global communications.[1] Within days, Bangemann's remarks were endorsed by White House policy adviser Ira Magaziner, who stated that the U.S. believed there was a need for international understanding on information policy issues, "some of which may need to be formal agreements, some informal understandings and common approaches." This project – which may some day soon lead to a global agreement on communication governance – has been developing slowly and steadily, but entirely behind closed doors.[2]

Meanwhile, at the extreme opposite end of the global power grid, communications issues were beginning to appear on the radar screen of the growing world-wide movement for a "different" model of human relations and social development; one that would measure progress in units other than those used to describe the private accumulation of wealth. In the Declaration of the Second People's Summit of the Americas, adopted by some 2,500 delegates in Quebec City on the eve of hemispheric free trade talks in April 2001, one could read: "We want states that promote the common good and that are able to intervene actively to ensure the respect of all human rights... *including the right to communication*..." (Declaration... 2001, emphasis added).

The gap between these various projects was immense; and in between, lay a vast grey area where media policy was – is – being played out in the day-to-day politics of our time. To highlight this, consider the following example that illustrates the unresolved question of who gets to communicate what to whom, on what basis and with what relative degrees of freedom and constraint.

At the height of the anti-free trade demonstrations in Quebec City in April 2001, a continent away, the Seattle Independent Media Centre (which had seen the light of day during the 1999 WTO meeting in Seattle[3]) was visited by U.S. FBI and Secret Service agents bearing a sealed court order. The IMC was directed to supply the FBI with recent user connection logs from its Web server as part of an "ongoing criminal investigation" into possible violations of Canadian law. Apparently, the US agencies were seeking to uncover the source of a posting to the IMC newswire which allegedly included classified information stolen from the Canadian government (JL... 2001).

Although the FBI was officially concerned about only one or two postings, the court order demanded *all* user connection logs for a 48-hour period; in other words, the Internet addresses of every person posting to or even visiting the IMC site during the Quebec City summit. Furthermore, the "sealed" nature of the court order prohibited the IMC from speaking about it publicly. So much for privacy; so much for the First Amendment.

The lack of protection for fundamental freedom indicated by this example, juxtaposed onto the call for new structures to enable and facilitate electronic commerce underscores the policy vacuum in which a new global communications environment is emerging. Age-old issues need to be reframed and refocused, old institutions need to be revamped as new ones are invented, conventional practices need to be retooled. Overarching themes such as corporate concentration, technological convergence and national sovereignty are taking on new meanings, affecting who we are, how we see others and ourselves, how we live and how we interact. One of the great paradoxes of the current age of globalization is that this "we" is at once inclusive and fragmenting: no one is left untouched, but everyone is touched by it differently.[4]

In the age of the single super-power, globalization is the highest stage of capitalism.[5] One of the clichés of this era is that the globalization of communications and the emergence of a world media system have made attempts to regulate media at the national level obsolete. This is still far from a *fait accompli*, and debates over the changing role of the nation-state with respect to media are ongoing everywhere. But one aspect of this issue has attracted much less systematic attention, although it is, arguably, the most crucial aspect to address in the present context.

I am referring to the question of how to transpose the media policy issues that have occupied national agendas at least since the invention of the telegraph to the transnational level where, to all intents and purposes, the most important issues are henceforth being played out. Simply put, the question remains how can we globalize the debate on media policy? This is a structural question. A global media system is developing according to its own logic, requirements, protocols, and rules. Profit is one aspect of this. Insulation from regulatory constraints is another. We already know the shape this system is taking. National governments and groups of states are trying to influence the activities of this transnational system in their own countries or regions as best they can. Only the most powerful can even begin to do this, and only then to the extent that they are havens to important global media players. But global issues require global solutions. Where can one begin looking for these?

This is no easy question to address. It is in some respects so overwhelming that it is not even easy to bring it up, let alone address it seriously. There are no precedents, no traditions for dealing with media policy outside the established political frameworks of national states.[6] Many countries do not even have well anchored national traditions, and where these exist, their legitimacy is challenged and their sovereignty undermined in the new context.

In the political arena, various authors, think tanks, and international organizations have been working on new conceptual notions such as global citizenship and new forms of global governance since the mid-1990s.[7] But as of very recently, questions specific to media and communications in this new context were still not being systematically addressed. One of the main problems is that there is still no appropriate forum in which to discuss such questions.[8]

"Policy," Japanese scholar Tatsuro Hanada points out, "is a medium of control acting upon politics and at the same time a product of the political process" (Hanada 1999). This book is therefore about politics and process as well as policy. Our focus is on *media* policy, although here a word of explanation may be necessary. As the technological boundaries that used to distinguish the different forms of mass communication blur and fall away – now that newspaper content travels across telephone lines, to take one example that would have been considered bizarre only a few years ago – we need a new definitional baseline. Nicholas Garnham provides one when he defines media as "systems for the production, distribution and appropriation of symbolic forms... based on the development and deployment of technologies of communication" (Garnham 2000: 3). *Global media policy* then, refers to the full range of attempts to influence the orientation of these systems, by social actors mobilizing whatever resources they can in order to promote their respective interests.[9]

Media policy is about politics, commerce and technology but it is also about culture. Once again, Garnham is useful. He writes:

> By culture I mean patterns of behaviour which are not merely instinctual, but are endowed with meanings which can be transmitted through space and time beyond the immediate stimulus/response site of action, and a learning process the lessons of which are cumulative and open to criticism and modification in the light of experience. Culture in this sense is crucially dependent upon systems of symbolic communication. (2000: 2-3)

Culture and media, in our day, are thus co-dependent. In Canada, where I live and work, we know something about this. For most of the 20th century, the Canadian state tried using communications policy as cultural policy, to use communications to promote and sustain a symbolic notion of nationhood, an *idea* of Canada (see, for example, Raboy 1990). The result was some noteworthy accomplishments, some interesting experiments in media policy design, and a robust cultural economy. Then, beginning around 1980, things began to fall apart. The state no longer had the funds, the political will, or, increasingly, the political capacity to exercise the authority it did previously. It began to look for new formulas. One solution was to join the globalization bandwagon and seek export markets for cultural industries in the hope that benefits would spin back home; a second, more recent but parallel approach is based on forging transnational alliances with other actors who might have similar goals. The Canadian state thus positioned itself as one actor among others in the cultural-industrial sphere. Canada spearheaded efforts to protect cultural goods and services from the new trade regimes, to promote cultural diversity policies within the United Nations Educational, Scientific and Cultural Organization (UNESCO) and other international fora, to facilitate the building of networks of non-governmental organizations as well as national ministers responsible for cultural policy. Through this work, a somewhat universal (as opposed to "national") concept of cultural diversity as basic to fundamental human rights has begun to emerge. So far, it is difficult to put a finger on substantial concrete results of all this bustle, but clearly a new policy model is emerging, an appropriately hybrid model in which diverse political, economic and civic interests have to collaborate.[10]

A range of seemingly disconnected institutions, issues and practices fall into the domain that we are trying to map. The terrain of media policy-making is shifting.[11] What was still, even a short while ago, a field essentially defined by national legislative and regulatory frameworks and a minimum of international supervision, is now subject to a complex ecology of interdependent structures.

This field is characterized by a number of new developments, the most significant of which is that communications policy is no longer "made" at any clearly definable location, is increasingly the result of a vast array of formal and informal mechanisms working across a multiplicity of sites. Specific policy issues, such as copyright or rules governing property transactions, migrate from one level to another, often typifying the flashpoint of conflicts between jurisdictions.[12] But it is no longer possible to understand, let alone deal with, such issues without referring to the broader context.

Briefly, the global policy "map" can be very schematically categorized according to the following general typology:

—*global organizations*, encompassing bodies that have traditionally been part of the United Nations family such as the International Telecommunication Union (ITU), UNESCO, and newer ones such as the WTO. Most politically-constituted "nations" belong to these organizations, through their official state authorities. Procedures are nominally meant to be inclusive but are actually restricted to government representation. Regarding communications, this sector has been strongly marked by the power shift in recent decades from organizations dedicated to communications and cultural issues such as UNESCO or the ITU to those focusing on commercial or trade issues such as the World Intellectual Property Organization (WIPO) and the WTO.[13]

*multilateral exclusive "clubs"* such as the Organization for Economic Co-operation and Development (OECD) and the G8, which collectively exercise enough economic clout to influence global affairs without having to deal directly with lesser economics politically. More streamlined, and thus more efficient than more cumbersome global organizations like the WTO, these clubs can at the same time afford to put forward a more generous public discourse while promoting specific projects (such as the Global Information Infrastructure or the Okinawa Charter on the Global Information Society, launched by the G7/G8 in 1995 and 2000 respectively). These currently serve as the main testing ground for pro-business proto-global policies, with the extremely important caveat that their decisions are actually binding on no one.

—*regional multi-state groupings*, the most important of which are the European Union (EU) and the North American Free Trade Agreement (NAFTA),[14] each of which represents a distinctly different model. The first is an economic union with a political agenda; the latter a trade zone which nominally has no political ambition. The difference means the E.U. can elaborate common policies in the name of the general community, while NAFTA-type regimes can only constrain the policy-making range of member states. The EU's 1997 protocol on public broadcasting (appended to the Treaty of Amsterdam) stands, at this time, as the only living example of a transnational media policy that aims to supersede economic imperatives.[15]

7

—regardless of their weakened condition, *national states* continue to be the main site of communications and cultural policy-making. Cultural policy agencies in countries such as Canada and France have been fighting rear guard actions against the constraining effects of international trade agreements that these countries have themselves signed. There is an increasing recognition of the need to bring these issues to global fora as a basis for legitimating the maintenance of national sovereignty in cultural matters on an equal footing with trade rules. National governments that wish to do so can still actively regulate important aspects of domestic broadcasting and telecommunications industries, sustain public cultural institutions and subsidize national cultural production. But the extent to which this can continue will require agreement at a supranational level.

—the *transnational private sector* has organized itself to achieve representation in official fora. No longer merely restricted to lobbying, transnational corporations and their associations are increasingly present at the tables where policy decisions are made. Groups such as the Americas Business Forum, the World Business Council for Sustainable Development, the Global Information Infrastructure Commission and the Global Business Dialogue for e-commerce (GBDe)—speaking for the 40 or so largest corporations in the information technology sector—have become a powerful force in setting the global communications policy agenda, especially with respect to Internet, e-commerce and new media issues.[16]

—much less well-resourced and generally further from the centres of power, *civil society organizations* are less present in policy debates, but media issues are becoming, like the environment previously, an important rallying point of grassroots mobilization. Global associations such as AMARC (community radio), Vidéazimut (film and video) the Association for Progressive Communication (Internet activists), and Computer Professionals for Social Responsibility now represent alternative media producers world-wide, while umbrella groups with names like the Cultural Environment Movement, People's Communication Charter and the Platform for Communication Rights are burgeoning.[17]

—finally, amid all this bustle, cutting edge issues such as Internet regulation are increasingly *"transversal"* in that they cut across sites of categorical jurisdiction.[18] Controversies surrounding the creation in 1998 of the Internet Corporation for Assigned Names and Numbers (ICANN) and its subsequent development typify this.[19] At the same time, important issue clusters regarding transnational media and universal themes such as the right to communicate can be said to be *"homeless"* in that they are not being dealt with systematically anywhere.[20]

This complex and multifaceted general structure makes it extremely difficult to intervene effectively in the new policy environment and poses a particular challenge for the development of democratic public life at the global level. At this point, the only actor successful at pursuing an agenda with anything approaching consistency is the transnational private sector. A number of national governments are engaged in rear guard efforts to maintain some semblance of cultural sovereignty in the face of the new rule of international trade regimes. But despite all the talk and some excellent independent reports on culture and cultural policy in recent years, concrete media policy developments at every level are clearly being driven by economic concerns.

In the past two years, restructuring in the communication industries has had a high public profile because of its impact on the mass consumer media that nearly everyone uses (or is subjected to) in one form or another.[21] Mergers (for example, AOL-TimeWarner), high-profile court cases (US vs. Microsoft, the record companies vs. Napster) and mediatized protest (the WTO in Seattle) have come to characterize the pressure points of the global information society. In public discourse, the policy dimension of these issues tends to be subordinated to their spectacular aspects, while less spectacular policy issues – such as copyright, intellectual property, telecom give-aways and spectrum handouts – tend to achieve little public profile and, consequently, low political priority.

This book proposes to explore a number of issues, themes, and case studies that can illustrate and enhance public understanding of the situation that has just been described. Its purpose is to amplify the empirical basis for a critique of the emerging global media policy environment as well as serve as a resource for actors seeking to intervene effectively in the area of media policy. Its target audience includes academics and students specializing in media policy; policymakers, regulators and analysts working in national agencies and international organizations; media professionals, grassroots practitioners and civil society activists. A majority of the authors are members of the Global Media Policy Working Group of the International Association for Media and Communication Research (IAMCR); all of them are among the leading critical communications scholars in the world today.

The book is organized in three sections, loosely identified under the headings "Institutions," "Issues," and "Practices." The range of topics covered is quite deliberately broad and eclectic – the only way to adequately reflect a field whose boundaries are not yet firmly established. Our overall goal is to try to problematize the notion of a global media system, something that our various distinguished contributors often see quite differently.[22] While taking a necessarily broad view, we are seeking to discover and emphasize what is really new about the situation described by such notions as convergence and globalization, not to mention concepts such as media and communications. Our topic selection was made with this in mind. Critics will note that the book has a decidedly "northern" (Euro-Austral-American) bias; but is this not a reflection of the geopolitical, socio-economic and cultural biases of the global media policy system? Where, after all, are the major policy issues of the day being played out, if not in the boardrooms and private clubs of the developed world?

Section I consists of five chapters examining specific institutional settings of contemporary media policy-making. The institutions featured make up a sample, and only a sample, drawn from the much more substantial array that would have to be covered by an exhaustive institutional portrait.[23] Each chapter looks at a different aspect of the emerging institutional framework.

In the opening chapter, Dwayne Winseck looks at how the ideology of "free trade in communications" re-emerged with the collapse of the New World Information and Communication Order debate within UNESCO. This gave way to a transformation in the role and functions of organizations such as the ITU, which has played a regulatory role in international communications since the middle of the 19th century. The WTO's involvement in telecommunications arose partially as a result of this displacement. Winseck's historical review illustrates how an adequate governance regime is crucial to policy reform and infrastructure development, and also raises questions regarding the future of cultural policy and telecom regulation in the age of the Internet. He also debunks the myth of deregulation when he writes that "more aid money now goes into creating governance regimes than to developing the communications networks and services that people will actually use." This is useful to bear in mind as the ITU prepares to organize a World Summit on the Information Society due to take place in 2003.[24]

A rather different aspect of institutional globalization is covered by Daya Kishan Thussu in his chapter on the privatization of Intelsat, the global satellite consortium set up in 1964 as a state-based multilateral organization. Recalling the truism that satellites are the *sine qua non* of global communications, and that access to satellite technology is therefore crucial for any country to connect to the digital world, Thussu illustrates the policy implications of the unprecedented privatization of Intelsat for countries of the global South. Achieved with relatively little public attention, the privatization of Intelsat in 2000 can be seen as part of a broader move towards the militarization of outer space, to the advantage of major defence contractors such as Lockheed Martin.

In chapter 3, Wolfgang Kleinwächter explores some of the new global governance issues posed by the development of the Internet and the challenge to the idea of sovereignty that accompanies the conception of "cyberspace" as a territory. Who will have legal jurisdiction over this territory and its citizens? If the Internet is indeed the first comprehensively global medium, its governing framework may be a harbinger of what is to come. Recalling the history of the global policy framework for Internet governance – still in its infancy, barely five years old! – Kleinwächter describes the unique status of new institutions such as ICANN and the GBDe, and explores general concepts of "trilateralism" and "co-regulation" that are indicated by these new institutional practices. Along the way, his narrative dramatically illustrates the relative weakness of the civil society sector and the overarching presence of the major governments, most notably the US, in this process.

Yet another relatively new institutional level is revealed in the chapter by Katharine Sarikakis, on the European Parliament. As the only functioning supranational institution based on an extension of the operating principles of liberal democracy, the EP experience is rife with ambiguities. For one thing, it is at one and the same time the only elected and the least powerful of the European Union institutions. Can this, the only international democratically elected political organization in the world, stand as a new model for governance? It is probably more prudent to look at the interaction of the range of European institutions in a perspective of democratization and proactive policy intervention. In this respect, Europe's emphasis on keeping media freedom and diversity issues on the political agenda is a unique contribution to the practices of transnational media policy.

The section on institutions closes with the chapter by Ben Goldsmith, Julian Thomas, Tom O'Regan and Stuart Cunningham, on the enduring place of the national in media policy development. Goldsmith *et. al.* demonstrate how national governments in the Euro-Austral-North American sphere continue seeking to promote cultural policy objectives in the rich new weave of what they call "converging media systems." Transnational alliances, multilateral institutions and the fora of international trade negotiations form the backdrop, or setting, for this process. The crucial point is that the state remains the key player.

Moving to the book's second section, there is a shift in register. Here the emphasis switches to issues, rather than institutions. Our general purpose is to sample the range of issues that can be considered component parts of the field that we are trying to map. Many of the chapters in this section reflect a particular area of interest and expertise and are almost personal in their approach. Each of them deals in some respect with a new take on the role of the state.

Terry Flew examines how neo-liberal ideology has influenced the evolution of public policy in an area which in many respects typifies the conventional approach to media policy: broadcasting. Policy approaches to broadcasting have evolved along with broader discourses on communications and citizenship, ideas of the public, and notions of what it means to constitute a public trust. As commercial broadcasting moves to the centre of national systems, the idea of a "social contract" – where industry protection is offered in exchange for regulation – takes shape. But new developments "are moving media regulation away from frameworks that are national, sector-specific and discretionary, towards frameworks that are generic, compatible with international trade law, and legally binding." These put the social contract at risk, and raise unresolved questions about culture, citizenship, and the role of public policy with respect to media old and new.

In his chapter on the regulation of harmful or illegal content, Monroe E. Price presents regulatory lawmaking as an issue of technique, not sovereignty: the key question (once a consensus is reached on normative goals) is what to do and how to do it? In media content regulation, a combination of methods and legal jurisdictions overlap: industry self-regulation, voluntary versus coercive approaches, "cross-national regulatory influence." Price's story belies the new wave argument that today's media "can't" be regulated. His case material shows the important link between national control of content and notions of what is deemed harmful content; as the distinction between information generated within and without a state's boundaries diminishes, "increasingly, practicalities, efficiencies and international agreements, not nationally imposed limitations, will keep such boundaries in place. ... In this sense, all messages, wherever they originate, are domestic in impact and, as a result, fall under the responsibility of the state."

For Robert W. McChesney, "neo-liberalism" rather than "globalization" should be the preferred explanatory term for understanding the global restructuring of media systems. Where media systems in the past were primarily national, a global system, built around a global commercial market, has emerged. This has to be the starting point of understanding the political economy of media: beginning with the global system and then "factor(ing) in differences at the national and local levels." Neo-liberalism, rather than globalization, explains, for example, that the highest quality media fare today is aimed at business consumers. Media are entertainment vehicles rather than institutions of political debate and public education. Meanwhile, recent mergers (such as AOL-Time Warner or Seagram-Vivendi) demonstrate that huge is no longer big enough, and also that global does not necessarily mean American in the same way that it once did (five of the nine major media corporations are American, but all view the global media system as a single market.)

In his chapter on media regulation in post-conflict societies, David Goldberg addresses an aspect of media policy-making that is bound to become increasingly problematic in the new global environment. A new litany of appropriate media practices is an inevitable aspect of the post-cold war international order. As this order evolves and consolidates, it imposes a certain model of media behaviour on the world's most troubled areas, a politically correct stance on communication that is sanctioned by the need to assert moral authority in the face of extreme immorality. But if the so-called "international community" (made up of the most politically authoritative national states and state-based international institutions) is to be checked in any way, a countervailing power of international civil society will need to be developed. Assuming the legitimacy of an international community intervening in the affairs of particular states, how can the action of such a community be made accountable?

In the final chapter of this section, John Hannigan examines some of the policy implications of physical location for the outcroppings of the global media system. Cities welcome the global entertainment economy as a motor for revitalizing urban cores; cultural practices thus becomes less a mode of expression in urban life, and more a locomotive of the urban economy. This begs the question of how to establish a meaningful political power base in the world's major cities, in the context of the international policy vacuum and diminishing national sovereignty? Public access and democratization of cultural life are among the generally unproblematized aspects of this question. If the development of the global entertainment economy does not solve urban problems, does it nonetheless increase access to culture? And what kind of culture? The city is the predominant concrete flashpoint of conflict between abstract conceptions of the global and the local.

In the book's third section, the focus is on alternative practices. Here, we are seeking to show that media policy-making does not take place in a political vacuum. The efforts of both mainstream and alternative media practitioners, scholars and researchers, educators and lobbyists are all part of a common process. This is increasingly so in the context of change, fluidity and uncertainty that characterizes the present time.

Alison Beale argues for the pertinence of gender-conscious research to political economy and policy studies in general, and media policy in particular. Reminding us that every set of theories has its blind spots, Beale writes that "the political economy of communications and culture is not only structured in gendered terms but also researched and regulated using tools of analysis that are gendered." Echoing one of the book's central themes, she points out that while the international women's movement has pressed for gender-sensitive policies internationally, it is within *national* institutions and laws that gains have been made. In issues involving sex-role stereotyping, employment equity and professional codes of conduct, there is still no international media regulation.

Meanwhile, on the ground, media activists are appropriating technological resources, developing skills, and inventing new forms of communication. John D. H. Downing's tale of the rise of the Independent Media Centre movement helps to situate our thinking about media and globalization with respect to the world-wide mobilization around the corporate-driven international free trade agenda. This story unveils a potentially hidden aspect of the global media policy framework: will it aid or hinder the emergence and sustainability of grassroots alternative media? A key unexamined area of the global media policy debate concerns the link between different possible uses of media in the struggle between projects of political emancipation and repression.

A second example of grassroots organizing through media is explored in the chapter by Bram Dov Abramson who focuses on media system design as a policy issue. In the vein of Lawrence Lessig's pioneering work which opened the horizons of thinking about media policy to include the regulatory power of "code," Abramson's study investigates what he terms "policy's broadband bias." On the surface a case study of one media NGO's attempt to undertake virtual conferencing as an alternative model for Internet use, this exploration underscores the complex nature of "communication rights" – both as a topic of policy intervention and as a problematic object in itself.

These examples contribute to what Cees J. Hamelink describes as the civil society challenge to global media policy. The so-called anti-globalization movement, he notes is itself an example of globalization, facilitated in part by communications technologies. Hamelink presents an overview of two opposing agendas, the neo-liberal and the humanitarian, breaking them down to show their discrete elements with respect to media and communications. One of the key distinctions, for Hamelink, is the basic inclusiveness of a human rights-inspired democratic order. Among other things, he raises the issue of the role of researchers in forming an "epistemic community" of knowledge-based support for activist groups (a fringe benefit of books such as this, one might say!).

The final chapter reproduces the founding statement of Voices 21, an informal association of media activists and other individuals who have been trying to place media and communications issues on the agendas of broader social movements. Not coincidentally, several of our authors are among the signatories of the Voices statement, which recapitulates many of the themes and issues raised elsewhere in the book. The bottom line, of both the statement and the book, is that these can no longer be considered narrow or isolated issues; indeed, the future of democratic public life in the new global environment will depend on their resolution.

## Notes

1   An Internet (Alta Vista) search for the term "global communication policy" in March 2000 turned up 400,000 sites, first of which was Bangemann's 1997 speech.

2   See, for example, the Web site of the Global Business Dialogue on Electronic commerce (GBDe): www.gbd.org (discussed in Kleinwächter, this volume). The GBDe describes itself as "a world-wide, CEO-driven effort to strengthen international co-ordination in the development of policies that will promote global electronic commerce for the benefit of business and consumers everywhere" (http://www.gbd.org/media/papers/workplan.html).

3   See Downing (this volume).

4   Like everyone else, I use the term "globalization" as a buzzword. Mine is meant to refer to a situation characterized by the diminishing sovereignty of national states; the increasing integration of the world economy; the technologically-based shrinking of time and space; the passing of received ideas about identity; the emergence of new geographically dispersed yet locally-based global networks; and the establishment of a new framework for global governance.

5   This was noted, prospectively, as early as 1969 by US national security adviser Zbigniew Brzezinski (1969) who pointed out that the United States had become the first society in history to propose a global model of modernity based on universal values and behaviours rooted in cultural productions. For this reason, "globalization" has become a more appropriate descriptive term than "imperialism." I am thankful to Dr. Eric George for this insight.

6   With the notable exception of the New World Information and Communication Order (NWICO) debate within UNESCO during the 1970s, whose story is told in Galtung and Vincent (1993). The UN-UNESCO World Commission on Culture and Development (1995) has more recently generated pockets of discussion on these issues, but official international diplomacy has generally shied away from dealing with media policy issues

since the publication of the provocative "MacBride Report" (UNESCO 1980) led to withdrawal of the United States and Great Britain from UNESCO.

7 The range of emerging literature on this subject is truly vast. In the interest of brevity, let me mention simply, as illustrative examples: The Group of Lisbon (1993); The Commission on Global Governance (1995); and Archibugi et. al. (1998).

8 This problem was first addressed in a pioneering article by Price (1994).

9 See also Thompson (1995), who calls for the invention of a new kind of "publicness."

10 On the complexity of "cultural diversity" as a policy concept in Canada, see Baeker (2000). In this volume, see chapters by Goldsmith et. al., in which further examples of new governance models for "converging media systems" are developed, and Kleinwächter, who refers to these as processes of "trilateralism" and "co-regulation."

11 This is, of course, not unique to media. On the general notion of "global public policy," see Reinicke (1998); on the process of policy "forum-shifting" as it affects international business, see Braithwaite and Drahos (2000).

12 The Canada-U.S. dispute over split-run magazines that wound up before the World Trade Organization in 1999 was a case in point.

13 See Winseck (this volume).

14 Possibly to be superseded by an eventual Free Trade Area of the Americas (FTAA).

15 See Sarikakis (this volume).

16 Examples of initiatives in this regard are abundant. See, for example, AP Online (2000), which begins as follows: "Geneva (AP) – Some of the biggest names in computers and communications have asked the United Nations to help regulate a system they claim will ease the headache and cost of keeping up with software advances, spokesmen said today. (...)"

17 See chapters by Downing, Abramson and Hamelink in this volume.

18 Indeed, the transversality of Internet-related governance issues is rapidly extending the boundaries of the field we have tried to map out in this volume. See, for example, Lessig (1999) and Hamelink (2000).

19 See Kleinwächter (this volume).

20 Hence the importance of initiatives such as Voices 21 (this volume).

21 See McChesney (this volume).

22 See, for example, chapters by Winseck and McChesney in this volume.

23 For an attempt to represent this range schematically, see Appendix I to this book.

24 See http://www.itu.int/wsis/. A coalition of NGOs and other associations of communication activists has been launched to lobby the ITU for input to a promised "civil society" dimension on the WSIS agenda. See http://www.comunica.org/cris/.

# References

AP Online. 2000. UN Asked to Oversee Software System. May 3.

Archibugi, D., Held, D. and Kohler, M. (eds). 1998. *Re-imagining Political Community. Studies in Cosmopolitan Democracy*. Cambridge: Polity Press.

Baeker, G. 2000. Cultural Policy and *Cultural Diversity in Canada*. Report prepared for the Council of Europe Study on Cultural Policy and Cultural Diversity. Ottawa: Strategic Research and Analysis, August.

Braithwaite, J. and Drahos, P. 2000. *Global Business Regulation*. Cambridge: Cambridge University Press.

Brzezinski, Z. K. 1969. *Between Two Ages: Americrica'sa's Role in the Technotronic Era*. New York: Viking Press.

Declaration of the Second People's Summit of the Americas. 2001. Quebec City, April 19. http://www.sommetdespeuples.org/en/une.html.

Galtung, J., and Vincent, R. C. 1993. *Global Glasnost: Toward a New World Information and Communication Order?* Cresskill: Hampton Press.

Garnham, N. 2000. *Emancipation, the Media, and Modernity. Arguments about the Media and Social Theory.* Oxford: Oxford University Press.

Hamelink, C. J. 2000. The Ethics of Cyberspace. London: Sage Publications.

Hanada, T. 1999. Digital Broadcasting and the Future of the Public Sphere. *Studies of Broadcasting* 34: 9-40.

JL for the Seattle IMC Spokescouncil. 2001. Gag Order Lifted; IMC in Free Speech Battle Following FBI/Secret Service Visit. Posted to Cyberjournal.org list, May 11, from http://seattle.indymedia.org/display.php 3?article_id=3013.

Lessig, L. 1999. *Code and Other Laws of Cyberspace.* New York: Basic Books.

Price, M. E. 1994. The Market for Loyalties: Agenda-setting for a Global Communications Commission. *InterMedia* 22, 5: 14-21.

Raboy, M. 1990. *Missed Opportunities: The Story of Canada's Broadcasting Policy.* Montreal and Kingston: McGill-Queen's University Press.

Reinicke, W. H. 1998. *Global Public Policy: Governing without Government?* Washington: Brookings Institution Press.

Reuters. 2001. Le futur directeur de l'OMC veut réguler le commerce en ligne. Le Devoir, June 1.

The Commission on Global Governance. 1995. *Our Global Neighbourhood.* Oxford: Oxford University Press.

The Group of Lisbon. 1993. *Limits to Competition.* Lisbon: The Gulbenkian Foundation.

Thompson, J. B. 1995. *The Media and Modernity. A Social Theory of the Media.* Cambridge: Polity Press.

UNESCO. 1980. International Commission for the Study of Communication Problems (chaired by Sean MacBride). *Many Voices, One World.* London: Kogan Page.

World Commission on Culture and Development. 1995. *Our Creative Diversity.* Paris: World Commission on Culture and Development.

# Part One

# Institutions

# The WTO, Emerging Policy Regimes and the Political Economy of Transnational Communications

## Dwayne Winseck

Electronic mediascapes have been radically altered over the last decade and we now live in a world of instantaneous connectivity. The consolidation of multimedia conglomerates and a greater role for the World Trade Organization (WTO) are reinforcing these trends. However, the more significant fact is that people now have unprecedented access to electronic media. This is especially true as the spectacular growth of the Internet has grown from a few million users a decade ago to 300 million users at the turn of the century (Netwizards 2000). These upheavals appear to point unequivocally to a prominent new feature of our times: a global media system (McChesney 1999).

These changes are impressive, but do they comprise a "global media system?" This chapter suggests that those who focus on the "global media system" tend to place too much emphasis on new technologies, deregulation, and the idea that globalization represents a new historical condition. David Held *et. al.* (1999) refer to those who offer such analysis as "hyperglobalizers," although crucial differences among such analysts turn on whether globalization is positively or negatively valued and the weight given to technology, markets, politics or culture in bringing about these changes. In this analysis, I assume the position of those that Held and his colleagues refer to as the "transformationists," a perspective that rejects the claim that the advent of the global media represents a crucial discontinuity in human history and that focuses on the regularly changing institutional manifestations that globalization has assumed over the long term.

After a brief historical account of the "global media," this chapter analyzes the creation of a new governance framework for telecommunications and information services during the 1990s that is based on three pillars—the WTO, new regulatory agencies, and private interests. Then this analysis assesses the effect of these changes on the "transnational communication system" in contrast to the idealistic illusion of an all-embracing "global media system." This discussion will also assess the role of privatization, competition, communication policy, and the future relationship between communication, democracy, and human rights in a global context.

## A Brief History of the Global Media

The "global media system" is both far less encompassing than commonly assumed and deeper historically than often acknowledged. In fact, any discussion of the "global media" should begin in the late 19th century when a world-wide web of cable communication firms and news agencies emerged as the pre-eminent transnational corporations of their times (Boyd-Barrett 1999; Pike and Winseck 2000).

By the late-19th century, both Britain and the US had embraced a "free trade in cables" policy and were aggressively using such policies to expand access to foreign markets for firms such as All American Cables, the Anglo-American Telegraph Company, the Direct United States Cable Company, the Eastern Extension Telegraph Company, and Western Union among others (Cable Committee 1902: 112; Shreiner 1924: 44-46). These policies were also used to buttress cable cartels and leverage access to domestic markets as a means of obtaining reciprocal privileges for American and British communications firms abroad. Elihu Root, a lawyer for All American Cables, summarized this state of affairs saying "the British and American lines...get what they can for themselves and, where it is possible, break up the monopolies of the rivals, and so far the British Foreign Office has actively assisted the British lines and the American State Department has actively assisted the American lines" (quoted in Shreiner 1924: 80). As a result, British and American cable companies gained monopoly concessions for up to 60 years throughout Latin America. In fact, from 1870 to 1920, Latin America was divvied up among less than a handful of companies and similar conditions prevailed on the rest of the world's main communications routes (Shreiner 1924: 80; Pike and Winseck 2000).

Oliver Boyd-Barrett (1999) has identified similar arrangements among the global news agencies: Reuters, Havas, Wolf, and Associated Press. By the 1860s, these news agencies had world-wide operations linked to the domestic press in numerous countries and within a decade or so such alliances included the cable companies. Yet, this nascent system of global communication was nowhere near universal. Networks connected major cities and were used mainly by business, the press and governments, not the public (Pike and Winseck 2000).

The "global media" went on hiatus after World War I and research in the field was largely reduced to studies on propaganda and people's (in)ability to comprehend foreign news (e.g. Lasswell 1927). The idea of the "global media" was also eclipsed as international agreements consigned each successive new media technology—radio, television, satellite broadcasting, and so on—to operations mainly *within* national boundaries. This state-of-affairs only changed in the 1970s and 1980s as developing countries mounted relatively successful demands for policies at the United Nations Educational, Scientific and Cultural Organization (UNESCO) and the International Telecommunication Union (ITU) that would help achieve a more equitable allocation of communication resources. This push for a New World Information and Communication Order (NWICO) critiqued the dominance of western-based transnational communications conglomerates in the international media system, sought greater access to new and old media as well as advocated more diversified information flows within and among *all* countries. In response, UNESCO and the ITU sponsored major studies of these issues by the MacBride Commission and the Maitland Commission, respectively, and implemented concrete initiatives.[1]

These initiatives included an attempt to achieve a "free *and balanced flow* of information" through a variety of measures including the expansion of developing countries' roles in both organizations, improvements in the equitable allocation of resources held in common (eg radio spectrum and orbital locations for geostationary satellites), and augmented communications infrastructures in developing countries through the creation of the International Program for Development Communication (IPDC) and by supplying technical and financial support to regional news and broadcasting organizations. Of course, the aims of the NWICO were only partially realized, but the initiatives pursued did contribute to creating a global media system that at least tried to reflect the interests of all countries rather than slavishly buttress the dominance of Europe, Japan, and North America (Gerbner, Mowlana and Nordenstreng 1993).

The NWICO soon met its nemeses in those countries that chafed at the idea of creating a new communication order based on equity and the redistribution of power and resources. By the mid-1980s, the NWICO and its supporting agencies (UNESCO and, to a lesser extent, the ITU) were eclipsed as the United States, Britain and Singapore abandoned UNESCO and threatened the same fate for the ITU if it refused to embrace sweeping internal reforms, competition, and privatization as well as a greater role for the General Agreement on Tariffs and Trade (GATT – later the WTO) in telecommunications and information services (Cowhey 1990: 181; US 1996: 17). As a result, "free trade in communication" was revived from its prolonged slumber, the authority of UNESCO and the ITU was redefined and reduced, and debates over the NWICO abandoned. Moreover, by the end of the 1980s, UNESCO had unconditionally re-embraced the "free flow of information" doctrine in its efforts to woo back Britain, Singapore and the United States while a few years later the WTO made it a cornerstone of its nascent global communications policy regime by requiring all its members to permit the "unrestricted movement of information within and across borders" (WTO 1994b: Article 5(c)(e)).

In the wake of the NWICO's demise, a new regime was created – one anchored in the philosophy of an augmented role for the private sector in the Organization for Economic Co-operation and Development (OECD), the ITU, and the WTO as well as through a plethora of self-regulatory initiatives. As the following sections show, these agencies, as well as UNESCO, adopted several new roles to assist in the creation of new communications markets and policy frameworks: (1) *research* covering main trends and access to communications resources in various regions of the world and in support of privatization, competition and the development of new regulatory frameworks in specific countries; (2) *offering support* to developing countries, such as the development of telecentres as community resources to provide people in developing countries greater access to telecommunications services; and finally, (3) *providing financial and technical assistance* to support regulatory and policy-making capacities in developing countries (rather than networks and information services that are now the exclusive domain of the market).

## The Transformation and Privatization of Global Communications Policy

In addition to the demise of the NWICO, several other events recast the governance regime for global telecommunications and new media. The thrust toward regulatory liberalization was accelerated by the break-up of the American Telephone and Telegraph Co. (AT&T) in 1984 during the Reagan administration. After divestiture, AT&T entered global markets and the newly-created Regional Bell Operating Companies (RBOCs) did the same to experiment with broadcasting, cable television, and information services, something they were prohibited from doing in the United States. Across the Atlantic, the impact of these developments were amplified by the privatization of British Telecom (BT) and Cable & Wireless in the mid-1980s and by the advent of competition in telecommunications between 1984 and 1991 in Great Britain. The scope of privatization and liberalization steadily widened thereafter as Australia, Canada, Japan, New Zealand, and the European Union embraced competition in telecommunications between 1990 and 1998 (Cowhey 1990; OECD 1999: 47; US 1996). The debt crisis in Latin America and Africa, the World Bank's structural adjustment policies, and neo-liberal ideology also accelerated privatization and, to a lesser degree, competition in developing countries. By the late 1990s Chile, China, the Congo, Madagascar, Mexico, the Philippines and Uganda had embraced competition while Argentina, Bolivia, Brazil, Costa Rica, Eritrea, Kenya, Kuwait, Nigeria, Peru, Sudan, and Venezuela announced plans to do the same by 2001 (ITU 1999; ITU 1997: 32).

In the face of these changes and threats of withdrawal by the US and Britain, the ITU adopted internal reforms and conceded to an enlarged policy remit for a number of international groups including the WTO and the OECD. It also became a staunch advocate of privatization, competition and regulatory reform. Through internal reforms, ITU membership grew beyond national governments and telecommunications monopolies to include equipment manufacturers, information service providers, and computer systems vendors. This altered context reduced the ITU's focus on telecommunications companies' needs and enlarged the influence of new players on the evolution of new telecommunications networks and the ever-increasing range of services delivered over them – eg virtual private networks, electronic data interchange, e-mail, the Internet, and so on. This helped foster more open network designs that gave users greater flexibility, allowed new services to flourish, and prevented new media such as the Internet from becoming mere appendages of existing telecommunications monopolies (Abbatte 1999: 152-165). Simultaneously, however, these changes also disconnected new services from the ITU's earlier emphasis on public service and development principles. Consequently, the Internet and new services were implemented solely according to the "ability to pay" principle rather than as part of an expanding range of communication services governed by principles of access, rights, and universal service.

The ITU's internal reforms reflected the subordination of conventional communications policy issues to market forces in other ways as well as members of the private sector were endowed with new voting privileges alongside national governments. In addition, by the early 1990s, the number of private members came to out-number governments 450 to 187. The private sector also amassed new power as the ITU convened privately-funded annual colloquia on telecommunications policy and as it created new entities such as the World Telecommunications Advisory Council through which private sector members gained greater access to technical standards committees and the Secretary-General. In stark contrast, efforts to elevate the status of public interest groups in global communication policy were rebuffed by the private sector members now driving the policy agenda at the ITU (Kleinwächter 1999: 10; Tarjanne 1999: 60).

By the early 1990s, the ITU had redesigned itself as an architect of expanded markets. However, this did not mean deregulation, as commonly assumed. Instead, one of the new roles of the ITU, in conjunction with the World Bank, the International Monetary Fund, and even the United Nations Development Program, is to advise governments on privatization and competition, eliminate barriers to media convergence, and promote electronic commerce (ITU 1999; UNDP 2000; Wallsten 1999; Wellenius and Stern 1994). A consensus has emerged that new markets need to be cultivated and that this requires government intervention under the wise tutelage of these bodies. As such, markets do not emerge naturally, but are actively constituted through the agencies at the core of the new governance regime. Reflecting this, one of the biggest ironies of the recent so-called era of deregulation was the massive expansion in the number of national communications regulators world-wide, from ten at the outset of the 1990s to nearly 90 by decade's end. In fact, the design of markets and regulatory regimes is now a burgeoning industry, with specialists being sent to the four corners of the earth by the US Federal

Communications Commission (FCC), the Canadian Radio-television and Telecommunications Commission (CRTC), the UK's Office of Telecommunications Policy (Oftel), the US-based Telecommunications Training Institute and the World Bank, and as countries such as Brazil, Kenya and Zambia import western policy regimes wholesale. In fact, more aid money now goes into creating governance regimes than to developing the communications networks and services that people will actually use (ITU 1999: 5-6; OECD 1999: 237; Hills 1998: 462).

## The WTO and New Policies for Telecommunications and New Media

It is within this context that the WTO adopted several agreements covering telecommunications and information services in the 1990s. There are four cornerstones to the WTO's nascent governance regime for telecommunications and new media: (1) the General Agreement on Trades and Services (GATS) 1994 agreement on enhanced services; (2) the 1996 Singapore Agreement eliminating taxes on information technologies; (3) the 1997 Basic Telecommunications Agreement; and (4) the creation of a Global Electronic Commerce Task Force in 1998 and the ensuing moratorium on the taxation of cyberspace. While these agreements are often seen as the pillars of a radically new governance regime, it can be argued that even the ambitious Basic Telecommunications Agreement (signed by 72 countries) mainly consolidated the status quo among countries that signed it, with the crucial proviso that WTO oversight ensures that countries cannot reverse course and that the future of competition and privatization will proceed according to WTO rules (Drake and Noam 1997). The remainder of this chapter assesses these agreements in relation to the following themes: (1) privatization; (2) regulated competition; and (3) the adoption of new policies for new media.

### *The WTO and Privatization*

Between 1984 and 1999, 110 telecommunication companies were privatized.[2] Some of these were full privatizations, such as British Telecom, while others were partial, such as Malaysia Telecom, Singapore Telecom and many others. More than just sheer numbers, the key questions are why did this spate of privatizations occur at this time and what impact, if any, did the emerging global governance regimes have on these trends?

In fact, the privatization of telecommunications operators was very uneven and took on a myriad of forms that reflected economic conditions, historical experience, and political cultures. For example, the debt crisis which hit Latin American countries the hardest during the 1980s translated into many privatizations across the continent. The connection between a national debt crisis and privatization was highlighted as several foreign banks became part owners in newly privatized public telecommunications operators (PTOs) in return for debt cancellation. In contrast, robust markets and strong states in Asia meant that privatization was pursued less, while greater reliance was placed on the selective introduction of competition. In Africa, privatizations were fewer and more limited in scope, due to the neocolonial overtones of returning state-owned PTOs to foreign operators, especially since they had only been brought under domestic control after independence was gained from the 1960s onwards. Thus, broader political, economic and historical considerations had a much greater impact on telecommunications privatization than did the WTO well into the 1990s.

Yet, many countries did embrace privatization and the WTO as means of attracting the foreign investment needed to build the telecommunications infrastructure that would catapult them into the "global information age." The need for investment was undeniable and government-owned telecommunications monopolies often performed poorly, with lengthy waiting lists and low availability of basic telephone services, let alone more advanced data and Internet services. This was obvious as 60 per cent of all telephone lines remained in the OECD countries, two-thirds of all households world-wide lacked access to telephone service, 43 countries had less than one telephone per 100 people, and as the length of waiting lists was measured in years rather than days (ITU 1998a: 13-15, A8-A10).

Similar figures for the Internet are even starker. By the end of 1999, only three per cent of the world's population had access to the Internet. In 23 countries, an Internet connection was not available and another 58 countries had less than 1000 Internet users each (Netwizards 1999). In contrast, 45 per cent of all Internet users resided in North America, with another 35 per cent living in Europe, followed by Japan with 11 per cent of all users. Indeed, just 20 countries accounted for nine out of 10 Internet users world-wide. The global distribution of Internet users is shown below.

## Global Distribution of Internet Users (July 1999)

Europe
35%

Japan
11%

Asia
6%

Latin America
1.2%

North America
45%

Africa
.9%

Source: Netwizards, 1999.

The promise of greater access to basic telephone service and the Internet depends on a great deal of investment. Analysts estimated that over US$7 billion would be needed in Africa alone to achieve just one telephone line per 100 people, while others claimed that up to US$200 billion would be needed in the last half of the 1990s to achieve modest levels of access to telecommunications service in Africa, Asia, Latin America and Central Europe (Wellenius and Stern 1994). Promoters of the WTO claimed that it would address these needs by reducing foreign ownership limits, that is, bolstering privatization, advancing investment in new services, and creating a "less politicized . . . regulatory environment" (Thompson 1999: 1; Tarjanne 1999: 56).

Nonetheless, the WTO agreements did not compel countries to undertake privatization or to permit foreign ownership. Although there was enormous pressure to adopt such commitments, many countries did not, much to the consternation of the United States. Consistent with existing trends, Latin American countries took the greatest steps to eliminate foreign ownership restrictions. Asian and African countries marginally raised permissible levels of foreign ownership in incumbent PTOs while allowing greater investment in new services (ITU 1998b: 10; GIIC 1997: 88-95).

This less than enthusiastic embrace of privatization through the WTO reflects the fact that privatization has not been an unequivocal success. This is because privatization has often simply substituted a privately-owned monopoly for a state-owned one, and private monopolies are little better than their state-owned counterparts at improving access to telecommunication services (ITU 1998a: 55, A8-A10; Melody 1999: 14). Consequently, a new consensus has emerged that improved access to services depends on a well-designed regulatory framework that establishes clear goals for new telecommunications operators to meet within specific periods. Thus, in Côte d'Ivoire, Ghana and South Africa, and, eventually, in Argentina and Mexico, newly privatized PTOs were required to establish between 225,000 and 2.5 million new subscriber lines within five years (ITU 1998a: 71). These approaches, coupled with the massive expansion of regulatory architectures world-wide referred to above, underlined the transition from the dogma of deregulation in the 1980s and early 1990s to the idea that adequate governance regimes are vital pillars of telecommunications policy reform.

The WTO embraced the new governance paradigm through its Regulatory Reference Paper, a document signed by 55 countries committed to creating a regulatory architecture rooted in several key principles: transparency, interconnection, autonomy, and the fair allocation of scarce resources (WTO 1997b). The Reference Paper was also an exercise in the technocratic management of telecommunications politics. Thus, unlike telecommunications legislation in Canada and the United States, for example, there were no provisions allowing public interventions in the regulatory arena and an absence of normative principles usually associated with communications policy, such as privacy, freedom of expression, access, and diversity. This was not an oversight.

It reflected the persistent, strong opposition to privatization among labour unions, citizens and others, opposition that had become significant enough to halt or postpone privatization in Brazil, Costa Rica, India and elsewhere (Petrazzini 1997). The WTO played a crucial role in this context, as the ITU (1997) noted, by providing "[h]igh level government officials with the opportunity to rely on its negotiations to dismantle domestic political opposition and to move forward with new market strategies that would have otherwise been impossible to implement" (: 12). In essence, the WTO limited democracy in order to help expand markets in telecommunications and information services.

These limits are crucial impediments to the democratization of global communications policy. They are reminiscent of communications policy in the United States and Canada prior to the late 1960s and mid-1970s when the FCC and CRTC only permitted those with a *material interest* to participate in regulatory proceedings until the courts and changing political conditions forced them to allow greater citizen and public interest group participation in the communications regulatory process.[3] Transferring a similar process of political liberalization to the ITU and WTO could offer a step toward progressive global communications policy reform.

## The WTO and Competition

Similar observations can be made with respect to the WTO's impact on competition in telecommunications. As with privatization, the promise was that the WTO would bolster competition, a move that would improve access to telecommunications services. The WTO's case was supported by studies by academics, the OECD and the ITU demonstrating that developing countries that had introduced competition were more effective than those that had retained monopolies at increasing access to basic telephone service as well as to new services such as cellular telephony and the Internet.[4] Moreover, the same studies also indicated that competition had not diminished access in Britain, Canada and the United States, although it was noted that most people now paid higher rates for basic telephone service (ITU 1999: 7-8; OECD 1995; Petrazzini 1997; UNCTAD 2000: 86-96).

Backed by such studies, the 1997 Basic Telecommunications Agreement sought to expand the number of countries formally committed to competition in telecommunications. This was not to be. The agreement mainly reinforced the status quo among the 72 countries that signed it, and only a few countries expanded their embrace of competition (Drake and Noam 1997). One of the biggest ironies was that several countries used the occasion to lock in monopolies for lengthy periods of time as in Jamaica, for example, where the privately-owned affiliate of Cable & Wireless now has the advantage of a national monopoly until 2013 backed by the force of international law (GIIC 1997: 88-95).

Nonetheless, the promotion of competition by the WTO did spur on a huge increase in investment—as promised. The essential questions, though, are by whom and where?

Most of the new investment has come from new competitors in the OECD countries. One-quarter of new investment in the network infrastructures of these countries is now accounted for by competitors, although the overwhelming dominance of incumbent PTOs in terms of subscribers, revenues and market share still persists (OECD 1999: 61-65; FCC 2000: 6-8). Investment also accelerated rapidly in developing countries, with investment between 1995 and 1998 nearly triple that of the previous decade (OECD 1999: 61-65; World Bank 2000).

The capacity of fibre optic cables spanning the globe also increased over 100-fold in the three years following the Basic Telecommunications Agreement (FCC 1999: 5). Much of this investment went into laying new fibre optic cables across the Atlantic between the US and Europe as well as across the Pacific between the US, Japan, China, Hong Kong and Singapore. The most striking feature of these new patterns of network deployment, however, is the concentration of resources in about 150 cities world-wide and the focus on serving large corporate users, governments, and between one per cent and ten per cent of the populations residing in the rich "information suburbs" of these centres (BT 1999; AT&T 2000; Global Crossing 1999; Microsoft 1999a; 1999b; 1999c).

In stark contrast, in Africa a dearth of bandwidth and the continuous delay of the Fiber-optic Link Around the Globe (FLAG) project to knit the continent into the nascent system of globe-straddling fibre optic cables means that countries there continue to route whatever little Internet traffic they have through the former colonial metropolises of Europe (UNCTAD 2000: 94-103). Thus, the evolution of the "global information infrastructure" continues to be marked by stark, albeit changing, patterns of inclusion and exclusion as well as continuities between the colonial flows laid down by the telegraphs and cables in the Imperial era and patterns of information flows in cyberspace today. Mapping out these patterns of inclusion and exclusion reveals that the nodal points on the global communications grid are not confined to New York, Toronto, London, Paris and Amsterdam and similar places but also encompass cities such as São Paulo, Shanghai, Mexico City and Bangkok. Networks are powerful technologies of discrimination, able to switch nodes on and off on the global grid with extraordinary precision. This point is highlighted by AT&T, BT and MCI/WorldCom's goal of connecting 40,000 to 60,000 buildings world-wide that house the demanding and prosperous users of the new global information infrastructure now being put into place (AT&T 2000; BT 1999; WorldCom 1999).

These patterns challenge our thinking about world communications. It is no longer possible to speak of the first and third worlds, or developed and developing countries. Instead, we should think of regions of the world that are hardwired to networks and information flows, and thus "switched on" compared with the vast disconnected, or "switched off" regions of the world

(Castells 1996; Sassen 1999). In the emerging geography of transnational communications and wired cities, nodal points and tributary networks connect not only the wealthy regions of Europe, North America and Japan, but also key business districts scattered across the "developing world." Indicative of this, many of the advanced networks and integrated computer technologies (ICTs) being deployed in the transnational core are also being implemented in the business districts and affluent suburbs of Latin America, Asia and, to a far lesser extent, Africa (BT 1999; FCC 2000: 7; WorldCom 1999).

AT&T, for instance, gained millions of cable system subscribers in Latin America and Asia through its acquisition of Tele-Communications, Inc. (TCI) (AT&T 2000: 47-50). Microsoft has also done the same through alliances and ownership stakes in Globo Cabo, Brazil's largest multimedia conglomerate, Global Crossing and Hong Kong Telecom (Microsoft 1999a; 1999b; 1999c). These arrangements exemplify the growing number of alliances between "global media" players and local and regional players (McChesney 1999) as well as the thrust to bring the "information revolution" to "third world" elites. As Microsoft and Globo Cabo note, they are striving to "accelerate the deployment of advanced broadband and Internet services to millions of Brazilians" (Microsoft 1999b: 2), although their promotional materials indicate that such efforts only apply to 10 per cent of the elites residing in Sao Paulo, Rio de Janeiro and Belo Horizonte. For the vast majority of Brazilians, access to basic telephone services, let alone computers and the Internet, remain far out of reach – a reminder that wealth and living conditions in Brazil are among the most polarized in the world (ITU 1998a: A7, A78; Netwizards 1999).

These patterns of connectivity influence access to the Internet as highlighted by a recent study of world-wide Internet use by Angus Reid (2000). The study looked at entire countries when reporting on Internet use in the transnational core. However, when it turned its gaze to Brazil, China, Malaysia, Mexico, and similar countries, it considered Internet use in just a few key cities, but let these measures represent *all* Internet users in each country. The results were telling, especially when we compare them with national data on Internet users, as is indicated in the table below:

**Wired Cities and Disconnected Countries in the "Global Information Society"**

|  | % of People in Largest City with Internet Access (2000) | % of People in Country with Internet Access (1999) | Teledensity[5] in Largest City (1996) | Rest of country Country Teledensity (1996) |
|---|---|---|---|---|
| Brazil | 21 | .65 | 16.5 | 8.7 |
| Mexico | 28 | .8 | N/A | 9.5 |
| China | 12 | .5 | 19 | 4.3 |
| Malaysia | 23 | 2.5 | 22.4 | 14.2 |
| OECD (Gen. Avg.) |  | 13.5 |  | 49 |

Source: Netwizards, 1999; Angus Reid, 2000; ITU, 1998: A28-A30; OECD, 1999: 74, 86.

The data reveal a striking contrast between the use of the Internet within the wired cities of Brazil, Mexico, China and Malaysia and the rest of these countries and also suggest that the gap between the information rich and poor in these countries is being amplified by new technologies rather than diminished. Internet use within these wired cities is also similar to the extent of Internet use within many European countries and certain regions of North America—in fact, levels of Internet use in the wired cities of Brazil, Mexico and Malaysia are *higher* than the OECD average. This suggests a convergence between the electronic mediascapes of wired cities and the transnational core, while the rest of the world remains characterized by heterogeneity, fragmentation and a persistent paucity of access to both "new" and "old" media.

Of course, we cannot paint a picture of the global media system based solely on Internet use and the availability of broadband networks. However, similar patterns are visible for the old media. Despite all the talk of a global media system, the linchpins of this system – AOL/Time Warner, AT&T, BT, Bertelsmann, Disney/ABC, Microsoft, Viacom/CBS, Vivendi – still derive just 20 to 30 per cent of their revenues from foreign markets and even then the vast majority is from a handful of countries: Britain, France, Germany, Italy and Japan (AT&T 2000; Disney 1999: 34; Time Warner 1999: 27; Viacom 1999). Furthermore, even though "global channels" such as CNN, the BBC, ESPN and MTV are available in 130 countries, less than 1.4 per cent of Asian households, for example, subscribe to CNN, one per cent to the BBC, and .9 per cent to ESPN (Maherzi 1997: 187). In short, these data show that the patterns that we have described with respect to telecommunications, and their implications for global governance, are general across the field of electronic media.

## The WTO and New Policies for New Media

Aside from questions regarding the availability and use of telecommunications and the Internet, there are pressing questions about the impact of the WTO on citizens' and policy-makers' ability to shape how these technologies are used and regulated. There are three significant areas affected by the WTO's telecommunications agreements: universal service, cultural policy, and the regulation of Internet content.

A goal of telecommunication policy has always been universal and affordable access to basic and more advanced services. While many critics of the WTO argued that universal service would be compromised, proponents claimed that it would contribute to universal access and allow countries to establish and maintain universal service policies. In fact, the Basic Telecommunications Agreement explicitly allows "any member . . . to define the kind of universal service obligation it wishes" (WTO 1997b, sec. 3). Yet, at the same time, this right is restricted by the requirement that universal service policies be competitively neutral and only applied to basic telephony rather than a panoply of "luxury services" (McLarty 1998: 56).

This limitation on universal service is underpinned by the distinction drawn between *basic services* and *enhanced services*. Although arcane in its details, the distinction *prevents* the adoption of universal service or any other non-technically oriented policies for enhanced services carried over telecommunication networks, such as electronic databases, the Internet, e-mail and so on (WTO 1994b, Art. 5). The real world consequence is a straitjacket on policy-makers' ability to expand universal service to include changing technologies. As a result, network-based new media services are tethered to the market and removed from the politics of domestic communications policies.

The distinctions between basic and enhanced services, as well as those between services that are *formally* included under the WTO (telecommunications and information services) and those that are not (the cultural industries), also constrain communications and cultural policies for "new" and "old" media. This is especially significant as governments shift from *preventing* to *promoting* media convergence and as cross-media consolidation between AT&T, TCI and MediaOne, AOL and Time Warner, and between Microsoft and cable systems world-wide, for instance, proceed quickly. In particular, how can distinctions between telecommunications and information services *that are included* in the WTO agreements, on the one hand, and cultural industries (broadcasting, film and publishing) *that are not formally included* within the WTO's purview[6] on the other, be maintained when all content is translated into digital bits and sent down the same pipe? Moreover, if the lines cannot be maintained, will all electronic media be swept into the orbit of the WTO through convergence, thus superseding intractable debates over the relationship between culture and trade? In addition, given that basic services can be regulated, while enhanced services cannot, how can cultural policies be retained for film, publishing and television once they are carried over telecommunication networks and conform to the definition of an enhanced service? This is precisely the point made by the United States International Trade Commission (1996) in its assessment of the Basic Telecommunications Agreement:

> . . . the *Annex on the Negotiations on Basic Telecommunications* permits the provision of audiovisual services over telecommunications networks . . . . This, in combination with technological advances, global networking, and the deregulation of information networks, may limit the applicability of audiovisual restrictions on US service suppliers (: 602).

Thus, convergence could sweep the cultural industries into the ambit of the WTO or limit the extension of cultural policies to "enhanced services," thereby constraining the kinds of policies that governments can maintain. Although such issues were avoided during WTO negotiations to defuse a confrontation that might scuttle the Basic Telecommunications Agreement, the United States was emphatic that network-based media and information services will be treated as enhanced services (GIIC 1997: 9, 33).

At the same time that the distinction between basic and enhanced services removes new media from the reach of communications and cultural policies, the same measures that permit the free "movement of information within and across borders" (WTO 1994b, Art. 5(c)(e)) could expand free speech in cyberspace. It is for this reason that Human Rights Watch (1999), among others, applauds China's entry into the WTO and its adoption of the telecommunications agreements. Regulators in Singapore acknowledged this prospect during interviews in 1996. However, this potential to expand communicative freedoms through the WTO collides with reality on several fronts. First, governments bent on regulating cyberspace could claim that the WTO allows them to adopt actions that are "necessary to protect public morals or to maintain public order," although only "where a . . . serious threat is posed to one of the fundamental interests of society" (WTO 1994a, Art. XIV). Whether or not states could invoke these measures, the prospect of the WTO making choices between defending free speech in cyberspace, on the one hand, versus upholding government sanctioned visions of morality and public order, on the other, would explode its veneer of political and cultural neutrality. Yet, despite the tantalizing potential of the WTO faltering on the shoals of morality and claims about public order, such a scenario is remote given that the agency promotes free trade, not free speech. Moreover, it is improbable that those seeking to advance freedom of speech could garner the support of government ministers needed to push such goals through the WTO. Finally, the idea that government efforts to regulate Internet content could be thwarted overlooks the point that censorship is being privatized as multimedia conglomerates—AOL/Time Warner, Bertelsmann, BT, Disney/ABC, France Telecom, Microsoft, MCI/WorldCom, Vivendi and so on—form consortia and adopt "voluntary" global rating systems for Internet content and filtering software that influences who gains access to the desktops of users and who does not (ICRA 1999; Lessig 1999).

## Conclusion

In this discussion, I have suggested that analyses of international communication governance should focus on three things: (1) the historical continuities of the "global media system," (2) the new patterns of inclusion and exclusion visible in the system of transnational mediaspaces and wired cities and, finally, (3) how the emerging system is being shaped by the WTO, ITU, OECD and World Bank, new domestic regulators, and private sector organizations. The impact of the WTO is vital. On the one hand, the WTO has expanded markets and contributed to efforts to wire the world. These efforts have improved access to telecommunications and information services, but it is also true that new networks and services are being deployed in ways that generate new dynamics of inclusion and exclusion that do little to extend the "information revolution" beyond the reach of affluent users in the transnational core and wired cities. The impact of the WTO is even greater in terms of the politics of communication policy and how we think about information and communications. In this respect, there are two central issues.

First, the WTO offers a form of limited democracy that allows policy-makers to bypass domestic political arenas in order to ram through contested policies regarding competition and privatization. The WTO can accomplish this while also constraining the ability of national governments to apply communication and cultural policies to network-based media and information services within their own countries.

Second, the global communications policy environment has been almost severed completely from questions of democracy and human rights thanks to its oversight by a limited democratic institution. This is done as the WTO bypasses United Nations-based organizations such as UNESCO and the ITU that have traditionally considered the cultural and public service aspects of communication issues. As no WTO documents make any reference to communication policy values such as privacy, freedom of expression, pluralism and diversity, this divorce from cultural issues is already quite large and will likely grow even larger in the future. In essence, the WTO conceptually annihilates the qualities of information and communications by segregating them from the values and issues that have made communications/information central to democracy in modern life.

This conceptual dissociation of communications from democracy is not only a theoretical problem. Many countries that signed the WTO telecommunications agreements have not committed to basic human rights documents, such as the Universal Declaration of Human Rights (1948) or the International Covenant on Civil and Political Liberties (1966).[7] At a time when media convergence has become the new holy grail, there is a need for another kind of convergence, one that couples the expansion of communication markets and the potential of new ICTs (Information and Communication Technologies) with basic human rights and democracy. Until that occurs, the most pressing problem with globalization is that it has not gone far enough.

## Notes

1     The first commission, the *International Commission for the Study of Communication Problems*, was initiated by UNESCO and chaired by Sean MacBride (UNESCO 1980) while the second, the *Independent Commission for Worldwide Telecommunications Development*, was organized by the ITU and chaired by Donald Maitland (ITU 1984). Their reports were published in 1980 and 1984, respectively. In general terms, both commissions reflected the ascendancy of developing countries in the United Nations system and their concerns with the unbalanced structure of the system. The MacBride Report was far more ambitious, with a task of analyzing the "totality of communication problems within modern societies," while the Maitland Commission focused on the relationship between telecommunications and development, proposing in the end that "first world" countries direct far greater technical and financial resources to the development of telecommunications infrastructures in the "third world" countries. Taken together, both groups were part and parcel of efforts to create a "New World Information and Communication Order" (NWICO) based on the analysis and advocacy of policies for the development of national communication systems, a set of general principles regarding the operation of the "global media," and the democratization of communications at the global level.

2     This figure includes firms of various sizes, and performing varying roles, (ie some were national carriers, others provided only certain satellite or radio services).

3     See, for example, the *United Church of Christ* (1966) case in the United States.

4　There were, however, numerous exceptions to these generalizations, such as China, Costa Rica and Iran, to name just a few, although the forces of neoliberalism ignored these counter examples as far as possible.

5　Teledensity refers to the number of main telephone lines per 100 households within a country.

6　The WTO agreements *do not* contain a cultural exemption clause and countries *can* include film and television programmes as goods and services covered by the WTO. Indeed, 19 countries have done so with respect to television programming and another 25 have also included commitments covering global news agencies (WTO 1998: 7).

7　hThese include Antigua and Barbuda, Bangladesh, Brunei, Ghana, Indonesia, Malaysia, Pakistan, Papua New Guinea, Turkey, and, if it is ultimately included, which now appears to be almost certain, China (UNDP 1999: 242-245).

# References

Abbatte, J. 1999. *Inventing The Internet*. Cambridge, MA: MIT.

Angus Reid Research. 2000. *Faces Of The Web*. Available at: www.angusreid.com.

AT&T. 2000. *Annual Report 1999*. Available at: www.att.com/ir/pdf/99my.pdf.

Boyd-Barrett, O. 1999. Global News Agencies. In O. Boyd-Barrett & T. Rantanen (eds.). *The Globalization of News*. London: Sage.

British Telecom. 1999. *World Communications Report*. Available at: www.bt.com.

Britain. 1902. *Report of the Interdepartmental Committee on Cable Communications*. London: HMSO.

Castells, M. 1996. *The Information Age (vol. 1)*. Malden, MA: Blackwell.

Cowhey, P. 1990. The International Telecommunications Regime. *International Organization 44*(2): 169-199.

Disney. 1999. *Annual Report*. Available at: www.disney.com.

Drake, W. J. & Noam, E. 1997. The WTO Deal on Basic Telecommunications. *Telecommunications Policy* 21(9/10): 799-818.

Federal Communications Commission. 2000. *Report on International Telecommunications Markets*. Available at: www.fcc.gov.org.

Federal Communications Commission. 1999. *Cable Landing License*. Available at: www.fcc.gov.org.

Fiber-optic Link Around the Globe (FLAG). 1999. *Organizational Structure*. Available at: www.flagltd.com.

Gerbner, G., H. Mowlana and K. Nordenstreng (eds.). 1993. *The Global Media Debate*. Norwood, N.J.: Ablex.

Global Crossing. 1999. *Global Crossing, Softbank and Microsoft Establish Joint Venture to Build Telecom Network Providing Advanced Services Throughout Asia*. Available at: www.globalcrossing.bm.

Global Information Infrastructure Commission. 1997. *The WTO Telecoms Agreement*. Washington, D.C.: Centre for Strategic and International Studies.

Held, D., A. McGrew. D. Goldblatt and J. Perraton. 1999. *Global Transformations*. Stanford, CA: Stanford University.

Hills, J. 1998. Liberalization, Regulation and Development. *Gazette 60* (6): 459-476.

Human Rights Watch. 1999. *Human Rights Watch Envisions Possible Press Freedom Gains in Wake Of WTO Deal*. Available at: www.ifex.org.

International Telecommunication Union. 1999. *Trends in Telecommunication Reform*. Available at: www.itu.org.

International Telecommunication Union. 1998a. *World Telecommunications Development Report*. Geneva: International Telecommunication Union.

International Telecommunication Union. 1998b. *General Trends in Telecommunication Reform*. Geneva: International Telecommunication Union.

International Telecommunication Union. 1997. *World Telecommunications Development Report*. Geneva: International Telecommunication Union.

International Telecommunication Union. 1984. Independent Commission for Worldwide Telecommunications Development (chaired by Sir Donald Maitland). *The Missing Link*. Geneva: International Telecommunication Union.

Internet Content Ratings Association. 1999. *An Invitation to Membership*. Available at: www.icra.org.

Kleinwächter, W. 1999. *Transnational Management of TAP Projects and New Challenges to the International Regulatory Framework*. Paper prepared for the European Commission's Telematics Applications Programme.

Lasswell, H. 1927. *Propaganda Technique in The World War*. London: Paul Kegan.

Lessig, L. 1999. *Code and Other Laws of Cyberspace*. New York: Basic Books.

Maherzi, L. 1997. *World Communication Report*. Paris, UNESCO.

McChesney, R. 1999. Media Convergence and Globalization. In *Electronic Empires*, edited by D. Thussu. London: Edward Arnold.

McLarty, T. 1998. Liberalized Telecommunications Trade in the WTO. *Federal Communications Law Journal* 51(1): 1-59.

Melody, W. 1999. Telecom Reform. *Telecommunications Policy 25*: 7-34.

Microsoft. 1999a. *Annual Report 1999*. Available at: www.microsoft.com.

Microsoft. 1999b. *Globo and Microsoft Announce Strategic Agreements and Investments to Develop New Internet Services in Brazil*. Available at: www.microsoft.com.

Microsoft. 1999c. *Microsoft Partners With Softbank and Global Crossing to Increase Broadband Connectivity in Asia*. Available at: www.microsoft.com.

Netwizards. 2000; 1999. *Internet User Survey*. Available at: www.netwizards.org.

Organization for Economic Co-operation and Development (OECD). 1999. *Communications Outlook*. Paris: OECD.

Organization for Economic Co-operation and Development (OECD). 1995. *Telecommunications Infrastructure*. Paris: OECD.

Petrazzini, B. 1997. Regulating communication services in developing countries. In *Telecoms Reform*, edited by W. Melody. Lyngby, Denmark: Technical University of Denmark.

Pike, R. and Winseck, D. 2000. Monopoly's First Moment in Global Electronic Communication. *Journal of the Canadian Historical Association*. Summer.

Sassen, S. 1999. *Globalization and its Discontents*. New York: The New Press.

Shreiner, 1924. *Cable & Wireless and Their Role In The Foreign Relations of the United States*. Boston: Arno Press.

Tarjanne, P. 1999. Preparing For the Next Revolution in Telecommunications. *Telecommunications Policy 25*: 51-63.

Thompson, B. 1999. Investing in the Global Information Infrastructure. Speech presented to the Global Information Infrastructure Commission Conference, Geneva, Switzerland, October 11. Available at: www.giic.org/events/991011 HBT.html.

Time Warner. 1999. *Annual Report 1998*. Available at: www.timewarner.com.

United Church of Christ. 1966. *Office of Communications of the United Church of Christ v. FCC*, 359 F.2d 994 (DC Cir.).

United Nations Conference on Trade and Development. 2000. *Building Confidence*. Geneva, Switzerland: United Nations.

United Nations Development Programme. 1999. *Human Development Report*. New York: Oxford University.

United Nations Educational, Scientific and Cultural Organization (UNESCO). 1980. International Commission for the Study of Communication Problems, (chaired by Sean MacBride). *Many Voices, One World*. London: Kogan Page.

United States International Trade Commission. 1996. *General Agreement on Trade in Services (GATS) (Investigation No. 332-358)*. Lexis Nexis Database.

United States. 1996. *Future of International Telecommunications Trade Issues*. Washington, DC: US Government Printing Office.

Viacom. 1999. *Annual Report*. Available at: www.viacom.com.

Wallsten, S. J. 1999. *An Empirical Analysis of Competition, Privatization and Regulation in Africa and Latin America*. Washington, DC: World Bank.

Wellenius, B. and P. Stern. 1994. *Implementing Reforms in the Telecommunications Sector*. Washington, DC: World Bank.

World Bank. 2000. *Telecom Projects with Private Participation (1984-1998) (PPI Database)*. Washington, DC: World Bank.

Worldcom. 1999. *1999 Worldcom Annual Report*. Available at: www.wcom.com.

World Trade Organization. 1998. *Audiovisual Services* (s/c/w/40). Geneva: World Trade Organization.

World Trade Organization. 1997a. *Fourth Protocol to the General Agreement on Trade in Services*. Available at: www.wto.org.

World Trade Organization. 1997b. *Regulatory Reference Paper*. Available at: www.wto.org.

World Trade Organization. 1994a. *General Agreement on Trade in Services*. Available at: www.wto.org.

World Trade Organization. 1994b. *Annex on Telecommunications*. Available at: www.wto.org.

# Privatizing Intelsat: Implications for the Global South

## Daya Kishan Thussu

Satellites are the sine qua non of global communications, from television, mobile telephony to e-commerce. Access to satellite technology is crucial for any country to connect with the digital world thus the privatization of Intelsat – the global satellite consortium – has serious policy implications, especially for the global South.

Created in 1964 as an intergovernmental treaty organization, the International Telecommunications Satellite Organization (Intelsat) reflected the spirit of the United Nations (UN) with the objective of improving global communications, particularly between developing and developed economies. It was established to operate a global satellite telecommunications system to provide affordable satellite capacity and reliable international public telephony on a non-discriminatory basis to all areas of the world (von der Weid 1992).

Intelsat became a leader in the development of a new industry – satellite communications – selling wholesale satellite capacity to telecommunications operators and broadcasters in virtually every country of the world. For many Southern countries, the creation of Intelsat ensured that they could have means to connect to each other and the rest of the world. The preamble of the agreement relating to Intelsat, signed in 1971 and entered into force in 1973, says that the organization has been established "to provide, for the benefit of all mankind, through the most advanced technology available, the most efficient and economic facilities possible consistent with the best and most equitable use of the radio frequency spectrum and of orbital space."[1]

Following a massive global shift to privatization of telecommunications in the 1990s, Intelsat endorsed the restructuring of the organization from an intergovernmental co-operative to a fully commercial company in April 1999. The General Assembly, responsible for making policy decisions, approved the proposal that Intelsat should be converted into a corporation at its meeting in Malaysia in October 1999 (*SatNews* 1999). At an historic meeting on November 13-17, 2000, the Intelsat Assembly of Parties, representing all 144 member governments, unanimously approved a plan to privatize Intelsat, under which all assets, liabilities and operations of Intelsat were to be transferred to a private, Bermuda-based holding company, known as Intelsat Ltd., and its 100 per cent-owned subsidiaries. By 2001, Intelsat owned and operated a global satellite system of 19 satellites, bringing both public and commercial networks, video and Internet services to over 200 countries and territories around the world.

## Growth of the Satellite Industry

Economic deregulation and globalization in the 1990s, in conjunction with rapid technological progress, fuelled a huge rise in demand for global telecommunications services of all types, resulting in the phenomenal growth of the satellite industry. More geostationary satellites were launched in that decade than all previous decades combined. The convergence of the telecommunications, computer and media industries and their globalization mean that satellites are now crucial in providing the cheap, dependable, and fast communications services that are essential for international businesses to operate in the global electronic marketplace, especially in such areas as transnational broadcasting, telephony, and financial services. At the beginning of the 21st century, satellites are set to become the "trade routes in the sky" (Price 1999).

According to the 1999 report *2000 State of the Space Industry* released by the International Space Business Council, a US-based trade association, the global space industry drew over US$9 billion in investments for commercial ventures, creating US$87 billion in revenue (*SatNews* 2000a). As many as 50 mergers and acquisitions valued at more than US$55 billion have taken place in recent years, the report says, as corporations recognize the key role of satellites in providing high-speed access to the Internet and television services to customers. One key reason for this growth has been the shift to a digital, wireless world, which has opened up new opportunities for corporations, taking advantage of satellites' ability to reach a geographically diverse customer base and broadcast to multiple locations simultaneously. Combined with dramatic increases in bandwidth requirements, the telecommunications, media, Internet, and entertainment corporations have made satellites an integral part of their communications infrastructure. The global market for satellite-based Internet services grew by more than 300 per cent in 1998-1999, and in international satellite Internet connections, Intelsat is the biggest player (Intelsat 2000). One billion telephones and mobile phone connections now exist world-wide, many of which are connected to the Internet. By 2004, Internet Protocol Telephony could account for up to 40 per cent of all international traffic (ITU 2001).

Electronic commerce over the Internet is an essential development in the emergence of an increasingly borderless global economy. Satellites provide the indispensable communications link and the access to the US Internet backbone for areas of the world that are not served by cable, for example most of the global South.

With growing convergence between the telecommunications and computer industries, the ability of privatized international telecommunications networks to transmit data across borders unhindered by national regulations has become a crucial element in the globalization of financial services, especially banking and insurance, and has contributed substantially to the emerging global electronic economy. The liberal global regime in telecommunications, with fewer restrictions on telecommunications flows and encouragement of investment in infrastructure in the South, aims to create the conditions necessary to enable transnational corporations to penetrate the "emerging markets" of Asia and Latin America, where the potential of the services remains enormous (Thussu 2000).

The quantum leap in satellite communications has been aided and promoted by the US-led neo-liberal ideology that began to dominate the global political arena after the end of the Cold War, leading to the creation of pro-market international trade regimes (Schiller 1998). This is reflected in the policy shifts – from a state-centric view of communications to one governed by the rules of the free market – among major powers and, at their behest, among multilateral organizations such as the International Telecommunication Union (ITU).

## Privatization of Telecommunications

For most of the twentieth century, the state was the key player in the telecommunications sphere, providing a national infrastructure and equipment and regulating international traffic. However, the increase in global telecommunications in the 1980s led to demands from transnational corporations for the reduction of tariffs for international services. State monopolies of post, telegraph and telecommunications (PTT) were forced to give ground to private telecommunications networks. The 1984 announcement of an "open skies" policy by the US Reagan Administration that resulted in the gradual deregulation of the American telecommunications sector, was swiftly followed by other major international players such as Britain and Japan and later by Western European nations (Hamelink 1994; Venturelli 1998). By the end of the century, the majority of PTT's across the globe were privatized or in the process of privatization (ITU 1999; OECD 1999).

The setting up of the World Trade Organization (WTO) in 1995 with a clear agenda for privatization and liberalization – largely dictated by the interests of the US and the companies with global telecommunications operations – gave a boost to telecommunications expansion in the global South. This was facilitated, in part by the 1995 General Agreement on Trade in Services

(GATS), the first multilateral, legally enforceable agreement covering trade and investment in the services sector (which include telecommunications services such as telephone, telegraph, data transmission, radio, TV and news services).

The opening up of the global market in telecommunications services pitted the ITU (whose ethos was based historically on the concept of telecommunications as a public utility), against the pro-market WTO over the regulation of telecommunications. The ITU was forced to play a key part in the shaping of a new, privatized, international communications regime in which the standards of universal public service and cross-subsidization were increasingly replaced by cost-based tariff structures.

One area of controversy was the renewed pressure on the ITU from Western governments to allocate more radio and satellite frequencies to commercial operators. Satellite companies are particularly keen to have appropriate orbital positions (36,000 kilometres above the equator is the optimal location as communications satellites move at the same speed as the earth and cover up to one third of the earth's surface) for maximum commercial exploitation of space. Traditionally, the ITU had administered frequency allocation on a "first come, first served" basis and the 1967 Outer Space Treaty that governed the regulation of the use of space, stated that the exploration and use of outer space should "be carried out for the benefit and in the interests of all countries, irrespective of their degree of economic and scientific development" (Article I cited in Hamelink 1994: 106) while Article II established that outer space "is not subject to national appropriation by claim of sovereignty, by means of use of occupation, or by any other means" (Ibid.).

However, the privatization of the satellite sector and the resulting proliferation of satellite operators obliged the ITU to ensure international standards for network compatibility and its constitution was accordingly amended at the 1998 Plenipotentiary Conference, in Minneapolis, increasing the power of the ITU's private-sector members (MacLean 1999). This shift of policy could also be observed in the way the ITU advised Southern countries to dismantle regulations preventing cross-ownership among broadcasters, cable operators and telecom companies. Since 1990, more than 150 countries have introduced new telecommunications legislation or modified existing regulations. By 1999, 88 countries had fully or partially privatized their telecommunications networks (ITU 1999). Among the global South, Latin America was first to take the road to privatization (Ros and Banerjee 2000).

In essence, the ITU was following the communications agenda set by the world's most powerful nations and the telecommunications corporations based in them. One indication of this was that, following the 1998 Organization for Economic Co-operation and Development (OECD) Ministerial Conference on Electronic Commerce, the ITU began to play a leading role among international organizations in the development of electronic commerce, particularly through standardization activities and working with Southern countries.

The US-based corporations have aggressively lobbied the WTO and the ITU to further liberalize global communications, particularly after the 1996 US Telecommunications Act, promoting the expansion of private US telecommunications corporations to operate globally, with the full support of the US government. The US Federal Communications Commission (FCC) now sees its role more of a "market facilitator" than an industry regulator, pursuing "an aggressive agenda aimed at increasing competition in communications markets around the world. Increased international competition will...open up new market opportunities for American companies" (FCC 1999).

Institutions such as the FCC have consistently promoted the idea that telecommunications "reform" can work only with privatization. An almost mythical status has been given to the efficacy of private initiatives, with the same model being implemented across the developing world, irrespective of the differences in political and economic factors. However, in Asia one of the most spectacular growths in telephony has been achieved under state control, in the case of China, where government-sanctioned and government-led actors have transformed the telecom market. As one commentator notes: "It seems to indicate that government bodies competing with each other maximize welfare better than private ones" (Singh 2000: 891).

## Commercialization of Space

There has been an increasing realization that, despite the continuing expansion of telephone companies and cable-service providers to connect users to higher-speed lines, it would be cheaper for consumers to receive entertainment and information by satellite. Satellite communications also offers the widest possible customer base, given that even in heavily wired Western Europe and North America an estimated 30 per cent of customers live far from major population centres. By 2003, there will be thousands of satellites in low, medium and geostationary orbits, providing universal voice data, multimedia and "Internet in the sky" services across the planet (Wooldridge 1999).

Crucially important is the potential use of satellite communications for e-commerce. Industry estimates show that at current growth rates, 350 million people world-wide will be online by 2005. The FCC estimates that world-wide revenues from commercial fixed and mobile satellites will increase from the 1996 level of US$9.4 billion to US$37.7 billion in the year 2002. As a recent US government report notes "the proliferating forms of e-business and the extraordinary dynamism of the industries that produce information technology products and services are harbingers of a new economic era" (US Government, 2000a).

Within the WTO, the US has been arguing that new regulations should not be imposed upon on-line service providers that might hinder e-commerce. Under US pressure, in 1998, the WTO's Ministerial Conference adopted a declaration committing members to refrain from imposing customs duties on electronic transmissions. The growth of electronic commerce is expected to exceed US$1.4 trillion by the year 2003, according to a 1999 report from the US government, which is keen on enforcing existing agreements and secure new agreements to make electronic commerce "a seamless global marketplace" to ensure "a free flow of commerce" (US Government 1999).

Privatization is seen as a prerequisite for this flow of commerce and increasingly intergovernmental organizations are being privatized. In 1999, Inmarsat (International Marine Satellite), became the world's first international treaty organization to transform itself into a commercial company. Part of the company's attraction to likely investors was that it would be operating in the mobile satellite communications industry, estimated to generate annual revenues of up to US$13 billion by 2002. With privatization, some of the largest national telecommunications businesses in the world, from among Immarsat's former 86 member countries, have become the shareholders and backers of the new company.

The Paris-based, pan-European intergovernmental organization Eutelsat that operates 14 satellites broadcasting more than 500 television channels to over 70 million homes in Europe, the Middle East and North Africa, is also being privatized. According to its Director General, Giuliano Berretta, Eutelsat was to become a completely private entity by 2001 and has already started joint ventures with private operators, ranging from German telecommunications firms, to Brazilian and Russian satellite companies (Thomson 2000). However, in an international context, the most significant change has been the gradual commercialization and privatization of Intelsat.

## Privatizing Intelsat

At the time of Intelsat's creation, commercial satellite communications did not exist and most telecommunications organizations were state-controlled monopolies, operating within a highly regulated environment. As it was the height of the Cold War, the Soviet Union and its allies inevitably saw Intelsat as a US instrument to control satellite communications, while France strongly argued for a French satellite system to cover the francophone world (Snow 1976).

Intelsat operated as a commercial co-operative, providing advanced telecommunications services to its 144 member countries, and indeed to all nations. Its organizational structure had Parties (national governments that had signed the Intelsat treaty), and Signatories (government agencies or, in some cases, private companies designated as their governments' representatives). Each country had one vote in the Assembly of Parties, the body that set policy. Signatories were represented on the Board of Governors in proportion to their investment shares. The Board made most managerial, financial and operational decisions for Intelsat.

In 1971, Intelsat endorsed the landmark UN resolution on space communications, made ten years earlier, that satellite communications should be available to every nation "as soon as practicable on a global and non-discriminatory basis" (Colino 1985). To ensure that the less developed countries could also benefit from satellite technology, Intelsat followed a policy of global price averaging, using revenues from high-traffic routes, such as North America, Europe and Japan, to subsidize the less profitable routes (Gershon 1990: 249). However, Comsat (the Communications Satellite Corporation, a privately-owned corporation with AT&T as its largest stockholder), representing the US and therefore the dominant interests within Intelsat, aggressively pushed for commercial applications of satellite television. Contrary to the 1971 UN resolution, notes Herbert Schiller, the space communications development was affected by decisions "based on market considerations emphasising capital distributions, volumes of international communications and expectations of profitability" (Schiller 1969 [1992]: 190).

As privatization of telecommunications firms accelerated in the 1990s, the ownership structure of Intelsat also began to change, from state-owned enterprises to a mix of private and semi-private corporations. The monopolistic era when a majority of the Intelsat Signatories were both telecommunications service providers and national regulators, gave way to private corporations, as many of the Intelsat Signatories were rapidly moving toward privatization. Among developing countries, especially in Africa, this restructuring was made possible through significant injections of foreign capital investment.

Given this pro-market climate, some companies argued that Intelsat's structure was inhibiting their expansion into new markets. By the 1990s, private satellite organizations were offering many of the interconnectivity services that Intelsat was created to provide and, by 1991, Intelsat was being described as "an obsolete, monopolistic structure that routinely overcharges users and restricts trade in telecommunications services" (Muller 1991).

Although ostensibly a non-profit, international co-operative that provides all countries with access to the global satellite system, Intelsat has really been controlled by a few nations. Eight Western countries account for half the controlling shares, with the US holding the largest investment – 20.42 per cent, followed by Britain. According to its 1999 Annual Report, for three consequent years – 1997, 1998 and 1999 – nearly 15 per cent of Intelsat's revenue was derived from its largest customer, Comsat. No other single customer accounted for more than five per cent of revenue in any of those years (Intelsat 2000). Consequently, Intelsat, like other international organizations, has reflected the concerns of the Western countries that have the power to set and implement the policy agenda.

By the end of the 1980s, Intelsat's near monopoly status was threatened by the growth of regional intergovernmental satellite systems, such as Eutelsat and Arabsat and the increasingly competitive conditions in the international satellite market. A rethinking of global satellite policy was also necessitated by technological reasons – the first fibre optic cable became operational in 1988. The 1984 decision by the Reagan Administration to authorize other private international satellite systems in the US to compete with Comsat, ending its role as the sole provider of international satellite services for the country, led in 1989, to the decision of the FCC to authorize a private company, Pan American Satellite Inc. (PanAmSat) to provide international carrier services between the US and Latin America. This in effect triggered the process of privatization of satellite-based international communications (Frieden 1996). Commercialization received a boost with the end of the Cold War-related space race, as many eastern-bloc countries, including Russia, joined Intelsat. The International Organization of Space Communications (Intersputnik), which was established in 1971 as a rival to Intelsat to provide satellite communications to socialist countries, began to negotiate with Western satellite companies for joint ventures.

Reflecting the strides made by satellite communications globally, Intelsat massively expanded its operations in the 1990s. After an agreement with the UN in 1993 to increase satellite services globally, the pace of development was rapid. In 1997-1998, Intelsat launched five new satellites. In 1998, with revenues exceeding US$1 billion for the first time, the organization transferred a quarter of its satellite fleet to a newly created private commercial company, New Skies Satellites, a global system with five satellites based in the Netherlands. The move was justified by Conny Kullman, the new Director General and Chief Executive Officer of Intelsat, in the organization's 1998 Annual Report: "The creation of New Skies was a fundamental step toward the full commercialization of Intelsat, a goal we consider vital to our continued ability to prosper in an increasingly competitive and dynamic marketplace....Competition breeds innovation and technological advancement, which leads to lower prices and better services for customers. The end result is a more vibrant market for all communications companies, and a confirmation that Intelsat's owners are prepared to undertake fundamental change to maximize value to shareholders and customers alike" (Intelsat 1999).

The passing of the Open-Market Reorganization for the Betterment of International Telecommunications (ORBIT) Act by the US Senate in July 1999, facilitated the rapid privatization of Intelsat. In keeping with the ORBIT Act, in August 2000, the FCC approved Intelsat's application to become an FCC licensee after privatization. This gave Intelsat access to the US market to provide satellite services to, from, and within the United States and thus facilitated the final transition of the last intergovernmental satellite organization to a private entity, promoting competition in the global satellite market (US Government 2000b).

Kullman stated in the organization's 1999 Annual Report: "Privatization will allow us to continue providing state-of-the-art communications links between all parts of the globe, in a pro-competitive manner. It will also free us to expand on our unparalleled success in the satellite communications industry" (Intelsat 2000:1). As its Annual Report affirms, a privatized Intelsat is committed to "helping multinationals be truly global...Our satellite services enable corporate network providers to target global multinational corporations with enterprise-wide solutions" (Intelsat 2000: 8).

## Satellite Communications and Militarization

Apart from the economic aspects, there are concerns about the military and security implications of a privatized satellite industry. These became more pronounced when Comsat, the largest individual shareholder in both Intelsat and the London-based Inmarsat, agreed to merge with Lockheed Martin one of the world's biggest defence corporations in August 1999. The ORBIT act allowed the Lockheed Martin-Comsat merger to proceed, and in September 1999, the FCC approved Lockheed Martin's application to own up to 49 per cent of Comsat and the US Department of Justice cleared the proposed merger without conditions under anti-trust law. In August 2000, Lockheed Martin and Comsat announced the completion of their merger, giving the new business projected revenues of nearly US$1 billion (*SatNews* 2000b). The merger makes Lockheed Martin the largest shareholder of both Intelsat and Inmarsat and the largest owner in New Skies.

More than 70 per cent of satellites launched during the Cold War years were used for defence purposes – both super powers used satellites to spy on each other's nuclear capabilities – and, since the end of the Cold War era, satellite technologies have become an important element in the West's arsenal, particularly deployed in "humanitarian crises."

The satellite imaging industry has also been gradually privatized as a sign of greater civilian-defence co-operation. The US government permits its defence forces to use satellite intelligence from commercial companies. Now the public can buy computer simulators developed for the army or download satellite imaging from the Internet. *Space Imaging*, a US-based company formed in 1994 by Lockheed Martin and Raytheon, is moving into the commercial satellite imaging market, with predictions that the industry is likely to grow by 56 per cent to US$2.5 billion by 2003 (Robinson 1998).

The US already has an extensive international surveillance operation, *Echelon*, run by the US National Security Agency, which uses a combination of spy satellites (such as Orion/Vortex for telecom surveillance and Trumpet to intercept cell-phone calls) and sensitive listening stations to eavesdrop on all international electronic communications around the world – phones, faxes, telexes, e-mail and all radio signals, airline and maritime frequencies.

After Boeing's take-over of Hughes' satellite operations in 2000, the defence role of satellites has increased, given Hughes' expertise in reconnaissance, surveillance and imaging systems, and Boeing's position in integrated space, air and terrestrial information and communications systems. Boeing, the world's largest manufacturer of commercial jetliners and military aircraft, is NASA's leading contractor and is developing the next generation of global positioning system satellites – GPS IIF (*SatNews* 2000c). This is likely to ensure that the already considerable control that the US wields over international communications – both soft entertainment and hard espionage – will strengthen further.

Conscious of the pre-eminent position that the US has in global satellite imaging, the European Union too wants to strengthen its satellite intelligence. A view most forcefully articulated by France – the only European country with its own delivery system capable of putting satellites into space – is that the EU will never have a completely independent foreign and defence policy as long as it is dependent on the US for satellite intelligence.

Satellites are vital in giving up-to-date military intelligence for troops on the ground and provide decision-makers with early warnings, helping to prevent or manage a crisis. Satellites are also useful for security and intelligence agencies to exchange material obtained from informers, terrestrial surveillance, or electronic eavesdropping on terrorists, criminals, and on illegal immigration (Norton-Taylor 2000).

As the proliferation of weapons of mass destruction in "rogue" states in the South becomes a major security concern among Western nations, satellite detection – for example, the use of satellite imaging to verify compliance with the Comprehensive Test Ban Treaty – has become an important component of international verification regimes. It has been proposed that satellite images with sufficient resolution could be used in identifying nuclear test sites, locating, and detecting the occurrence of nuclear explosions (Alden 2000). Although data from commercial satellites is theoretically accessible to all countries of the world, in practice only a few, mainly Western nations and their corporations control these and zealously guard this privilege.

It is well known that the technology extensively employed for weather forecasting, international broadcasting, and instant telecommunications is also used for geo-strategic spying from space. The Global Positioning System (GPS) which can provide one-metre satellite resolution imaging to target fixed objects, was deployed by the US in the 1991 Gulf War. As privatization ensures greater Western investment in the global South paralleled with the deepening economic and political crisis in many developing countries, "Third World threats" may be kept under check by the likes of Lockheed Martin.

## The New Intelsat and the Global South

Privatization has opened up a debate about who will have strategic control of the world's largest commercial geostationary satellite network, raising important questions about telecommunications access for the world's poorer countries: in 2001 more than 60 countries depended entirely on Intelsat for their satellite-based international communications. Intelsat has played a crucial role in bringing satellite technology to the South and there is a concern that unfettered market competition will ignore unprofitable segments. Developing countries may be left out in the cold as competition is permitted and leads to "cream skimming." Economies of scale, coupled with innovations in satellite technology, had made it possible for Intelsat progressively to cut its rates. Developing countries benefitted from its policy of rate averaging – high-density routes, for example between North America and Western Europe, had lower costs per circuit than low-density routes (in which category came much of the developing world). In order to provide services to "thin" routes, Intelsat charged the same rate for all routes, the high-density traffic subsidizing the others. However, the new commercial Intelsat is unlikely to continue this practice.

Given their economic situations, it would be extremely difficult for poorer countries to afford transponder fees or to acquire other commercial satellite services. The satellite industry demands very substantial investment and high risk; only the large corporations will be able to exploit this communications hardware. Three US corporations – Hughes Space and Communications, Lockheed Martin, and Loral – that between them have built 68 per cent of the geostationary communications satellites in orbit, dominate the satellite industry. According to *Via Satellite* magazine, in early 2000 there were 222 Western-built, geostationary, commercial communications satellites in orbit, while 52 more satellites were on order with total industry revenues reaching more than US$69 billion (Fernandez 2000). Deregulation and privatization of the global telecommunications market, coupled with the perceived need for a strong communications infrastructure to open up new regions to the global economy, has resulted in mergers, take-overs and regional alliances between major operators in Latin America, the Middle East, and Asia. The European satellite consortium *Société Européenne des satellites* holds a 34 per cent share of AsiaSat, which provides broadcast and telecommunications services to 53 countries in the Asia-Pacific region, while PanAmSat, the first private satellite service for Latin America, launched three satellites for the Latin American region. In 1999, Loral acquired a Brazilian orbital satellite slot through its local subsidiary *Loral Skynet do Brasil*, while Hughes Space and Communications has investment in Saudi-owned Thuraya Satellite Telecommunications, the commercial company launched by Arabsat.

These trends reflect the unprecedented merger activity and corporate consolidation in the information and communications industries: according to UN figures, the total value of mergers and acquisitions in the telecommunications sector world-wide jumped from US$6.8 billion in 1988 to US$265.8 billion in 1998. In 1998, the top ten telecommunications corporations held 86 per cent of the global market in telecommunications (UNDP 1999). The opening up of global telecommunications services to Southern countries is set to benefit the suppliers of telecommunications hardware. The US$301 billion world-wide communications equipment market is controlled by corporations based in a few, mainly Western, countries. According to the OECD, the total revenues of the communications sector, including telecommunications services, broadcasting services and communications equipment, exceeded one trillion dollars for the first time in 1998 (OECD 1999). Though the availability of new communications technologies could provide the countries of the global South with more efficient telecommunications and broadcasting services, the fact that control of their satellite communications lies in the hands of a few Western consortia raises questions about cultural and economic autonomy.

The biggest beneficiaries of deregulation and privatization have been the transnational corporations (TNCs) that dominate global trade. So powerful are the TNCs that the annual sales of the top corporations exceed the gross domestic product of many developing countries (UNDP 1999). Just two out of the world's largest 100 TNCs, measured in terms of foreign assets, were from the global South, according to the 1999 *World Investment Report* from the United Nations Conference on Trade and Development, while only 26 companies from the South appeared in the *Fortune 500*, the annual list published by the US business magazine *Fortune* of the world's top 500 corporations. Market-based progress is also failing a large section of the world's poor. The 1999 *Human Development Report* of the United Nations Development Programme notes that the income gap between the richest fifth of the world's people and the poorest fifth, measured by average national income per head, increased from 30 to one in 1960 to 74 to one in 1997 (UNDP 1999).

## "Information Poverty"

Although the UN General Assembly endorsed in 1997 the objective of universal access to basic communications for all, the global information and communications disparity in terms of vast differences in access to telecommunications remains. Despite "the right to communicate" being promoted in 1996 by the ITU as a fundamental human right, the organization, which claims to be committed to redress global inequity in telecommunications, admits the existence of an information poverty gap between the North and the South (ITU 1998).

Many developing countries lack affordable access to information resources and their telecommunications systems need technological upgrading. The biggest dilemma they face is that in order to widen access, telephone tariffs need to be reduced and the sector opened to international operators, thus undermining the often subsidized domestic telecoms. As the UN statement on Universal Access to Basic Communications and Information Services proclaims: "We are profoundly concerned at the deepening maldistribution of access, resources and opportunities in the information and communications field. The information and technology gap and related inequities between industrialized and developing nations are widening: a new type of poverty—information poverty – looms" (Ibid.).

According to the ITU, in 1998, nearly 75 per cent of international outgoing telephone traffic and 57 per cent of international incoming traffic was generated in just 23 northern countries. Though mobile telephony offers possibilities of improving telecommunications access in the South, as systems can be installed relatively cheaply and more rapidly than fixed-line networks, frequency constraints and the high level of initial investment in establishing networks can act as barriers (ITU 1999). Limited telecommunications infrastructure has seriously undermined access to the Internet in the developing countries. In 1998, nearly 88 per cent of Internet users were in the North, home to less than 15 per cent of world's population. As the Intelsat Annual Report for 1999 admits: "Some four billion people around the world remain without access to communications services" (Intelsat 2000: 12). This has serious implications for the South's ability to participate in the development of the move to the wireless Internet and e-commerce.

## Notes

1    From www.intelsat.com.

## References

Alden, E. 2000. Curbs Bring U.S. Satellite Industry Down To Earth, *Financial Times*, October 10: 14.

Colino, R. 1985. Intelsat: Facing the Challenge of Tomorrow, *Journal of International Affairs*, 39, 1: 129-146.

Federal Communications Commission. 1999. *A New FCC for the 21st Century*, Available at http://www.fcc.gov/21st_century/.

Fernandez, R. 2000. Via Satellite's Global Satellite Survey, *Via Satellite*, June.

Frieden, R. 1996. *International Telecommunications Handbook*. Boston: Artch House Publishing.

Gershon, R. A. 1990. Global Cooperation in an Era of Deregulation, *Telecommunications Policy*, 14, 3: 249-59.

Hamelink, C. 1994. *The Politics of World Communication – A Human Rights Perspective*. London: Sage.

Intelsat. 1999. *Annual Report 1998*. International Telecommunications Satellite Organization, Washington.

Intelsat. 2000. *Annual Report 1999*. International Telecommunications Satellite Organization, Washington.

International Telecommunication Union (ITU). 1998. *World Telecommunication Development Report 98*. Geneva: International Telecommunication Union.

International Telecommunication Union (ITU). 1999. *Trends in Telecommunication Reform*. Geneva: International Telecommunication Union.

International Telecommunication Union (ITU). 2001. *ITU Internet Reports: IP Telephony*. Geneva: International Telecommunication Union.

MacLean, D. 1999. Open Doors and Open Questions: Interpreting the Results of the 1998 ITU Minneapolis Plenipotentiary Conference. *Telecommunications Policy* 23: 147-158.

Mueller, M. 1999. Intelsat and the Separate System Policy: Toward Competitive International Telecommunications. *Policy Analysis* 150, March 21.

Norton-Taylor, R. 2000. Intelligence Test. *The Guardian*, 20 December: 17.

OECD. 1999. *Communication Outlook 1999*. Paris: Organization for Economic Cooperation and Development.

Price, M. 1999. Satellite Broadcasting as Trade Routes in the Sky. *Public Culture* 11, 2: 69-85.

Robinson, E. 1998. The Pentagon Finally Learns How To Shop. *Fortune*. 21 December: 124-130.

Ros, A. and Banerjee, A. (eds.) 2000. Telecommunications Privatization And Tariff Rebalancing: Evidence From Latin America. *Telecommunications Policy*. 24 (3): 233-252.

*SatNews*. 1999. Intelsat Members Decide To Privatize. *SatNews*. 8 November.

*SatNews*. 2000a. Space Industry Attracts Over $9 Billion Of New Investment - To Increase By More Than 90 Per Cent Over Next Five Years. *SatNews*. 26 June.

*SatNews*. 2000b. Lockheed-Comsat Merger Complete. *SatNews*. 3 August.

*SatNews*. 2000c. Boeing Completes Acquisition Of Hughes' Space And Communications Businesses. *SatNews*. 6 October.

Schiller, H. 1969. *Mass Communications and American Empire*. New York: Augustus M. Kelley. Second revised and updated edition published by Westview Press in 1992.

Schiller, H. 1998. Striving for Communications Dominance - A Half-Century Review. In *Electronic Empires - Global Media and Local Resistance*, edited by D.K. Thussu. London: Arnold.

Singh, J. P. 2000. The Institutional Environment And Effects Of Telecommunications Privatization And Market Liberalization In Asia. *Telecommunications Policy* 24: 885-906.

Snow, M. 1976. *International Satellite Communications: Economic and Political Issues of the First Decade of Intelsat*. New York: Praeger.

Thomson, S. 2000. Berretta's Way. *Cable and Satellite Europe*. November: 18-22.

Thussu, D. K. 2000. *International Communication - Continuity and Change*. London: Arnold.

UNDP. 1999. *Human Development Report*. United Nations Development Programme. Oxford and New York: Oxford University Press.

US Government. 1999. *Towards Digital eQuality*, US Government Working Group on Electronic Commerce. 2nd Annual Report, Washington. Available at http://www.ecommerce.gov.

US Government. 2000a. *Digital Economy 2000*. Department of Commerce, Economics and Statistics Administration. Available at http://www.ecommerce.gov.

US Government. 2000b. *Towards competition in international satellite services: Rethinking the role of Intelsat*. The White House. Available at http://www.whitehouse.gov/.

Venturelli, S. 1998. *Liberalizing the European Media – Politics, Regulation and the Public Sphere*. Oxford: Oxford University Press.

von der Weid, D. 1992. *Development, Democracy and Outer Space*. Geneva: United Nations Non-Governmental Liaison Service.

Wooldridge, A. 1999. Telecommunications – The World in Your Pocket – The Economist Survey, *The Economist*. 9 October.

World Bank. 1998. *Knowledge for Development, World Development Report 1998-1999*. Washington: World Bank Publications.

# Trilateralism, Co-regulation and Governance in the Global Information Society

**Wolfgang Kleinwächter**

G lobalization challenges many of our notions of national governance. Since the time of the Peace of Westphalia (1648), the world's governance systems have been based mainly on the nation-state. The sovereignty of nations is the cornerstone of the contemporary system of international relations. The principle of sovereign equality is the basis of modern international law, codified in the Charter of the United Nations. In the industrial age, the nation-state also became a precondition for the development of a national economy.

As the industrial society systematically transforms into a global information society (GIS), many issues are moving outside of national governance arenas. This "information revolution,"[1] like other revolutions in the past, will undoubtedly have consequences for our various systems of governance. The question remains: will the traditional rules, procedures and institutions that reflected the needs of the industrial age have to be just adjusted and "modernized" to keep pace with the new circumstances, or will the winds of change lead to a totally new global governance system extending beyond the nation-state?

## National Sovereignty and Cyberspace

After the political and industrial revolutions of the 18th and 19th centuries, kingdoms were substituted by representative democracies. National governments and national parliaments together with an independent judiciary became the essential institutions of the governance systems. National parliaments created the legal systems; national governments executed the policies, and courts settled conflicts within the country. If national laws, policies and conflicts took on international dimensions, governments embarked on negotiations with other governments and concluded bi- or multilateral treaties requiring ratification by national parliaments before they were enacted. Although non-governmental actors like private industry or non-governmental organizations (NGOs) have a growing influence in international policy and law-making, international law is de facto an intergovernmental law. International organizations, including the whole system of the United Nations, are nothing more than an arrangement among governments that delegate (a limited number of) rights to them. Sovereignty remained and remains with the nation-state.

Sovereignty of a nation-state is based on two elements: sovereignty over territory and sovereignty over citizens. The principle of "sovereign equality of states" implies that "each state has the right freely to choose and develop its political, social, economic and cultural system."[2] This term encompasses primarily the national government, which acts as the representative of a nation-state. This government has, in principle, all the necessary (political) means to execute this sovereignty.

With the information revolution and the emergence of the Internet, these assumptions are beginning to appear in a different light. Cyberspace is not part of national territory like air space. Internet communications go beyond national borders. Also, cyberspace can not be compared with borderless "outer space." Outer space is not accessible to everyone and only a limited number of government-controlled, sponsored or licensed activities take place in it. Cyberspace is an open place for everyone with no territorial boundaries.

In the past, states adopted national laws for broadcasting and telecommunications or concluded treaties like the international telecommunications conventions where they introduced legal regimes under national control such as licensing of broadcasters, allocation of frequencies, tapping of telephone calls, or interrupting communications with other countries. There is no similar legal arrangement concerning the Internet. If national governments insisted that Internet communications remain within their territory under "sovereign control" like broadcasting and telecommunications, it would stretch their technical and financial capabilities.

For example, while a radio or television transmitter and a public switched telephone network (PSTN) can be controlled by governments, the decentralized Internet system is nearly uncontrollable by traditional means. Messages are sent in distributed packages, which makes tapping difficult; computer addresses do not have a country and city code (like telephone numbers) which complicates the determination of the geographical location of a computer. In addition, there is no central authority over Internet communication.

Not only is territorial sovereignty undermined by the Internet, it also challenges sovereignty over citizens. Individuals do not lose their citizenship if they enter cyberspace, but as "netizens" they have numerous opportunities to escape from national regulations and governmental supervision by changing identities, using servers from outside the country, and bypassing national laws. Within a country, the law defines the rights and duties as well as freedoms and responsibilities of citizens and legal entities. If the execution of national sovereignty in cyberspace becomes nearly impossible, what are the consequences for the political and legal systems of the future?

Furthermore, the Internet stimulates international activities of individuals and private institutions. Transnational corporations and international NGOs are the main beneficiaries of the Internet. They can deepen and broaden their transborder activities. The Internet also allows small organizations without a large bureaucracy the chance to participate in global operations. Private industry institutions, Internet users, consumer groups and citizen's organizations (NGOs) are developing their own policies, independent from national governments and their international organizations, and are building self-regulated global systems with their own sets of norms, rules, and standards.

Against this background, cyberspace becomes an area where actors and subjects with different legal status and different political and economic weight are coexisting in a rather new and widely unregulated manner. It is unclear how cases of conflict can be settled, or behaviour in bad faith corrected. Already the question of whether a problem is a legal issue and which jurisdiction applies, produces confusing answers.

It is true that the Internet does not create a "law free zone." Even if there is neither a "National Internet Law" nor an "International Internet Convention," rational thinking concludes that what is illegal offline, is also illegal online. Even if it is more difficult to fight crimes in cyberspace, the general legal system does not disappear when a netizen enters cyberspace. The Internet is nothing more than a new challenge to further adjust and improve the relevant instruments for dispute settlement, crime investigation, law enforcement etc. There is a greater need for international co-operation among governments and, in some cases, there is a need to redefine old crimes or define new crime categories.

But while this can be done mainly within the traditional political and institutional framework, based on national laws and international conventions, a growing number of new problems are arising that go beyond the "business as usual" of international law and policy- making. The challenge comes when incompatible national legal systems meet in cyberspace. There are numerous cases where different countries have regulated the same issues in different ways, with no international convention to harmonize the varying national approaches. While the different legal systems can easily coexist in the real world with clearly defined territorial borders between them, the Internet, by removing these borders, leads directly to clashes among them. It starts with the "core business" of the Internet, the distribution of content, and leads up to issues like taxation, privacy, data protection, and dozens of others.

The controversial issue of information content illustrates the problem. While in Europe nearly all states have adopted laws that restrict racist and Nazi propaganda, in the US such propaganda is protected as "free speech" by the First Amendment to the US Constitution. If a Bertelsmann bookstore in Germany sold Adolf Hitler's fascist book *Mein Kampf*, it would be punished by a German court. But an Internet user in Germany, regardless of her or his citizenship, can buy the book for US$18 at www.bn.com, the virtual bookshop of Barnes & Noble, a company based in the US (with Bertelsmann AG as a main shareholder). German customs authorities could certainly confiscate the book at the border if it is delivered by mail, but what could the German government do if the whole book can be downloaded from a server based in the US?

With the growth of controversial issues, national courts, and national governments have started to react unilaterally. Courts in Germany and France decided in cases against CompuServe and Yahoo.com that it is the responsibility of the service provider to stop the distribution of content deemed illegal in the two countries (eg pornography and racist propaganda).[3] In other cases, the governments in China or Singapore tried to get critical political propaganda under control via proxy servers and rigid national legislation.

However, the anarchic structure of the Internet, the difficulty in identifying the geographical position of an Internet address, the liberal regime of domain name registration, and the packet switching system for the transport of messages, makes it nearly impossible to translate the above mentioned national court decisions into practice. Critical Web sites that protest the violation of human rights in China and Singapore will not disappear when a minister calls for strong actions or when a court puts an Internet service provider or user in jail. Even if European courts ordered global companies headquartered in the United States to deny access to certain Web sites for users in Germany or France, these Web sites would most certainly reappear on servers operating from a Caribbean or Pacific island. Yahoo.com, after a French court instructed it to shut down Nazi Web sites in November 2000, asked an American court whether the French court had authority to regulate the business of an American company operating on the global market. If the American court denies the authority of the French court, there is no "higher institution" where the cases can be negotiated.

While there is a global consensus that the "information superhighway" needs some "rules of the road," it seems obvious that a nationalistic approach to any kind of Internet legislation and governance will fail. The global Internet needs a global political and regulatory framework. It needs a procedure to develop global policies. It needs an institutional mechanism to execute these policies.

Traditionally, if a global problem appeared that needed an international solution, national governments convened an intergovernmental codification conference to draft an international convention. For example, governments agreed on the Outer Space Treaty in 1966 and the Law of the Sea Convention in the 1980s. They agreed on a number of international conventions to protect the natural environment. And they have been able, after 20 years of controversial negotiations, to establish an International Criminal Court in 1999. But while all these international conventions can be seen as great achievements of contemporary international law, it is hard to believe that this is a usable model for policy and law-making for the Internet.

Firstly, the conventions are legally binding only for the states that have ratified the treaties. Because practically no convention has a one hundred per cent membership of the international community, there are always "holes" in the system. In the case of the Outer Space Treaty, these holes are not fatal as long as the "big players" sign on. What illegal activities can a Pacific Island undertake on the moon? However, a "small hole" in an Internet convention could undermine the whole system.

Secondly, time is a critical factor. One Internet year is seen as seven man-years, and drafting international conventions is a time consuming endeavour. The Human Rights Convention of 1996 was the result of 18 years of hard work in the UN. Negotiations on the Outer Space Treaty started in the early 1960s and the convention was enacted a full ten years later. The Law of the Sea Convention was a 25-year project. If governments would start now to convene an Internet codification conference, it would be a great surprise to have an "Universal Internet Convention" before the year 2015. And there would be no guarantee that all 243 "country code Top Level Domain Names" (ccTLDs, such as .ca, .ch, .uk) and the dozens of new "generic Top Level Domain Names" (gTLDs, such as .net, .org, .com) would fall under such a convention.

The progress achieved with the draft Convention on Cyber Crime is an interesting illustration of this timing difficulty.[4] Since 1989, the Council of Europe has been working to draft an international convention to fight criminal activities concerning computers and the Internet. The Council's Committee of Ministers adopted in 1995 a recommendation to promote legislation against cybercrime. The established working group produced 25 drafts up to March 2000. On April 24, 2001, the Parliamentary Assembly of the Council of Europe adopted the Final Draft in principle. Probably, the Convention will be signed under the Belgian presidency of the European Union in the second half of 2001. It could take another two to five years until the needed number of states has ratified the convention and it is enacted.

## From NWICO to the GIS

The discussion around the development of a global political and legal framework for international communications started in the late 1960s. Third World and Eastern Bloc countries were calling for the establishment of a "New World Information and Communication Order" (NWICO) under the auspices of the UN system. This order was to be "based on the fundamental principles of international law, as laid down in the Charter of the United Nations,"[5] including the principle of "information sovereignty." The efforts within the Paris-based United Nations Educational, Scientific and Cultural Organization

(UNESCO) to elaborate a global regulatory system for international information and communications (in the form of a "NWICO Declaration"), failed. The issue became a hostage of the final stage of the ideological East-West cold war. Furthermore, the longer the debate continued, it became clear that a mainly governmental approach that ignores the growing role of non-governmental actors in the field of information and communications, leads to a dead-end. When the UNESCO "Windhoek Declaration" of 1991 ended the NWICO debate,[6] there was a global consensus that a regulatory system for international information and communications, based on the principle of state "information sovereignty," risked opening the door for governmental censorship and suppression of individual freedoms.

## The New ITU Approach

The end of the NWICO was not the end of the search for a global framework for international communications. In the early 1990s, the International Telecommunication Union (ITU), an intergovernmental specialized agency of the UN system, became the main forum for the continuing and evolving discussion. The ITU developed two innovations: first, it opened the door for non-governmental members. In 1994 the ITU adjusted its constitution and introduced a second category of membership. Next to governments (big M's), institutions of the private sector (small m's) could also join the ITU.[7] Secondly, the ITU introduced a new kind of international consensus document. A number of intergovernmental ITU conferences with broad participation of the private sector adopted, instead of legally binding conventions, a "Memorandum of Understanding" (MoU). The MoU's on mobile telephony, global mobile personal communications by satellites (GMPCS), and Internet Domain Names, looked like conventions but were not legally binding documents.

Two other Geneva-based UN specialized agencies, the World Intellectual Property Organization (WIPO) and the World Trade Organization (WTO), operated in a similar way. As intergovernmental organizations, they invited private industry to participate in the negotiations. They were looking for a new type of international agreement that combined the stability of traditional legal mechanisms with the flexibility needed to react to the challenges of quickly changing global markets in the field of information and communications.

While the efforts by the ITU, the WIPO, and the WTO signaled a new approach to the challenges of the global information economy, they remained sectoral efforts with natural limitations. They did not answer the fundamental political and legal questions raised by the global information society. This new political challenge was seen first by then-US Vice President Al Gore when he proposed to the ITU World Conference on Communication Development in Buenos Aires in March 1994, the creation of an integrated global policy framework for the information superhighway and the development of a "Global Information Infrastructure" (GII).[8]

## The "Parallel Approach" and the New "Trilateralism"

Some months later, in February 1995, a G7 conference in Brussels defined a number of basic principles for a global information society.[9] Both Al Gore and Martin Bangemann, the European Union Commissioner responsible for telecommunications and the information society, stressed during the meeting that a GII/GIS should not be built primarily by governments but rather the agenda should be driven by the private sector. Parallel to the G7 meeting in Brussels, a so-called "Business Roundtable" brought together business leaders from the main telecommunications, media and computer companies of the world. The Business Roundtable defined a number of basic political principles for the global information economy that mirrored the governmental declaration, but differed in scope and priorities. The "parallel approach" illustrated that governments are no longer the only players in global negotiations. It also demonstrated a new self-confidence within private industry, which was ready to play a greater independent policy role that went beyond an advisory or consultative function to national governments.

The "parallel approach" was further advanced by a landmark Ministerial Conference on "Global Information Networks," that took place in Bonn, Germany, July 6 – 8, 1997 with high level European and American representation from both the public and private sectors. The conference adopted three declarations: a "Ministerial Declaration," an "Industry Declaration," and a "Users Declaration." All three documents try to define, from a different perspective, basic principles for the global information society.[10] Conceptually the Bonn conference went beyond the G7 Brussels meeting by also bringing the users (consumers/citizens) to the negotiating table, thus broadening the "parallel approach" into a "trilateral approach." In this "new trilateralism," governments, private industry and users/consumers/citizens are inter-linked in a process of drafting regulatory frameworks and building governance institutions of the global information society. The three groups have different roles and responsibilities; and they have identical as well as conflicting interests.

While the Bonn *Ministerial Declaration* defines the future role of government as "providing the framework," "stimulating new services," "building confidence," and "empowering the users," the *Industrial Declaration* formulates key principles for issues like convergence, intellectual property rights, encryption, data protection, and taxation. In contrast to these two documents, the *Users Declaration* stresses that "sovereignty in the information society must belong to the people; their preferences should determine its uses and how the new technology will be applied." But it also recognizes that "public policy-makers and industry have already gone to great lengths in stimulating and developing the information society and global information networks. Currently the technological side is leading the process and stronger user participation is considered essential to bridge the current gap and ensure successful deployment." Security, confidentiality, data protection, media pluralism, reliability of services, consumer protection, education and training, and complaints mechanisms are issues raised by the *Users Declaration*.

This new trilateralism is undoubtedly an innovation in international communications negotiations. Never before had a ministerial conference produced three separate and often conflicting documents on the same issue.

The Bonn conference opened the door but did not really enter unknown territory. Nothing was said about the interrelationship of the three parallel documents. And no mechanism was introduced to stimulate a future, trilateral dialogue among governments, industry and users or to formalize the interaction among the three parties. Nevertheless, the innovative aspect of the Bonn conference was that, for the first time, it was demonstrated in public that not only governments and private industry but also users could constitute themselves as "global actors" in the GIS. And the conference demonstrated that these actors could no longer be grouped in traditional camps, defined by geography or ideology like North vs. South or East vs. West. Neither geography nor ideology plays a central role any more. Rather, one's status as a private organization, a government or a user, defines special roles, interests and concepts for policy and legislation.

While industry must look first at markets, business opportunities, costs, shareholder value and a return on investment, governments are more interested in public policy issues, in stability, security and taxes. In contrast, users are concerned with prices, trust, quality of services, privacy, freedoms and human rights. The new interdependence does not lead to the disappearance of conflicts among the partners. But while in the past such conflicts did lead to a zero-sum-game with winners and losers in a concrete conflict situation, the GIS produces, at least in its early stage of development, a win-win-constellation where the benefit of one side can produce positive results for the other sides.

Since the Bonn conference, the emergence of two new global institutions – the Global Business Dialogue on e-Commerce (GBDe) and the Internet Corporation for Assigned Names and Numbers (ICANN) – have given this new trilateralism a greater profile.

The GBDe was established in January 1999 by nearly 100 CEOs of private companies. The GBDe is a platform of business leaders representing the global players of the Internet, computer, telecommunications and media worlds. The Steering Committee of the GBDe is composed of 19 CEOs from companies like AOL/Time Warner, Bertelsmann, Vivendi, Fujitsu, IBM, Nokia, Daimler/Chrysler, Hewlett Packard and EDS. The GBDe promotes industry self-regulation concerning the Internet and rejects the emergence of "patchwork legislation" with dozens of different national Internet regulations. The GBDe has invited governments to co-operate in the development of global political and legal frameworks for e-commerce via global self-regulatory systems. In addition, it is looking for a dialogue with consumer and user organizations as well as with NGOs and institutions like the European Parliament.

ICANN was established in October 1998, mainly by the Department of Commerce of the US government, but with broad involvement of the global Internet community and the European Commission. ICANN, although it has a more technical mandate, is the main global policy body responsible for the core resources of the Internet. ICANN is a private, global corporation incorporated under Californian law. Its board of directors is composed of 19 representatives of the private sector and of Internet users from all over the world. Governments are not allowed to send representatives to the board but can send (non-binding) recommendations via a "Governmental Advisory Committee" (GAC).

## The Global Business Dialogue on e-Commerce (GBDe)

It is one of the ironies of policy-making that the formation of the GBDe by private industry is the result of a public initiative. In 1997, the EU Commissioner for Telecommunications Policy, Martin Bangemann, launched the idea of a "Global Communications Charter." Bangemann's proposal was driven by the recognition of the need to develop a global political and legal framework for the information economy and to harmonize relevant national approaches.

Bangemann used the ITU "Inter@ctive Conference" in Geneva in September 1997 to propose the Charter. According to Bangemann, such a Charter could summarize the main principles for the information society. During an EC-sponsored conference in Brussels in October 1997, Bangemann suggested that this Charter would not be a "binding legal convention," but a set of basic principles that would give the three different groups – governments, industries and users/citizens – common guidelines to co-ordinate their activities. While recognizing the role of the existing international organizations, Bangemann proposed that such a new Charter should not be driven by governments alone. Rather, the ITU, WIPO and other intergovernmental organizations should participate in the process as equal partners next to private industry and user/consumer groups. Bangemann hoped to adopt the "Global Communications Charter" in December 1998, 50 years after the adoption of the "Universal Declaration on Human Rights," which was also a legally non-binding instrument with a high political profile.

The discussion of Bangemann's proposal, which was backed by the EU Commission, produced a basic dilemma. While there was a broad agreement on the general objective of the initiative, namely, the development of a universal political and legal framework for the GIS, there was also uncertainty about the procedure to reach this target. Although Bangemann clarified several times that his initiative was not intended to create more governmental legislation, private industry and a number of non-governmental organizations argued that this was exactly the consequence of the initiative. Therefore, the central issue of the debate became who should take the lead in the formulation of such a framework: governments or private industry?

Ira Magaziner, the Internet adviser to then-US President Bill Clinton, supported the idea in principle, but stressed that the private sector must take the lead in creating future frameworks. Based on the recommendations of the Clinton administration for electronic commerce, Magaziner told the Brussels conference that the time was over when industry would come to Congress to lobby for special legislation; in the future, government would have to go to industry to lobby, so industry would take public interest into account while building the information highway and developing the traffic on it.[11]

To stimulate the process towards a "Global Communications Charter," EU Commissioner Bangemann invited a group of business leaders from around the world to a "Business Round Table on Global Communications" to discuss the issues in more depth. The Round Table took place in July 1998. In its final communiqué, the participants agreed that the elaboration of unified global principles would be helpful for the further development of the GIS. But they agreed also that this process should be "led by the industry and driven by the market." Governments should be "invited, if needed."[12]

## Defining the Role of the Players within GBDe

By implementing this recommendation on January 14, 1999, business leaders from leading global computer, telecommunications and media companies established the "Global Business Dialogue on eCommerce" (GBDe) in New York. The GBDe was established to discuss global solutions with regard to international electronic commerce and would give recommendations to governments and intergovernmental organizations such as the WTO, the ITU and the WIPO on how to create favourable conditions for electronic commerce around the globe. "We feel we have a role to play in the shaping of public policy," said Gerald Levin after the inaugural meeting of the GBDe. "We are capable of rising above narrow geographic issues and competitive issues to realize the majesty of the new medium."[13]

The GBDe established nine working groups and prepared a first world conference that took place in Paris in September 1999. During the Paris GBDe conference, the working groups presented their policy papers with recommendations to governments. The GBDe recommendations are not economic and/or commercial by nature but step into a public policy territory that was exclusively dominated by governments in the past. They called for the Internet as a "tax free zone," dealt with consumer rights as well as regulation of information content. The general spirit of the Paris GBDe recommendations was that governments should be very restrictive in passing national legislation with regard to the Internet. As the Position Paper on Content Regulation says: "Nations that attribute a high priority to job creation in the digital content sector must, therefore, be particularly mindful of the need to attract capital investment. Excessive national regulation of any sort, including content restrictions, could distort the global market and adversely affect competitiveness. More specifically, national content restrictions could drive away potential investment, or drive up access costs to the end-user by otherwise limiting revenue opportunities."[14] Consequently, the GBDe proposed that governments should trust "industry self-regulation" and not waste resources on laws that could be already outdated when they are adopted.

During the plenary of the Paris conference there was an interesting dialogue between Steve Case, CEO of AOL and Lionel Jospin, prime minister of France. After Jospin explained the approach of the French government to Internet legislation, Case commented that the Internet will develop faster than the law makers can react. While both sides, private industry and governments, agreed that some regulation is needed for the Internet, after the Paris conference it remained an open question as to what kind of regulation should be developed and by whom – and who should lead this process.

After the Paris conference, governments and the GBDe held a series of joint meetings that paved the way for a second world conference held in Miami in September 2000. During this process, governments recognized that in various areas, industry self-regulation should be the preferred means, while in other areas governments should take the lead. They proposed a "co-regulatory" system with clearly defined core responsibilities by keeping the ultimate public authority in the hands of governments. On the other hand, the private sector recognized that governments have and will continue to have key responsibility for a number of areas but they preferred the term "policy co-ordination" instead of "co-regulation" to define the relationship between governments and the private sector.

But the Miami conference was also attended by high-ranking governmental representatives who did not concur with a basic agreement. Although both sides agreed in principle to find quick solutions for the main pressing areas, the details remained controversial and the procedures for coming to a universal regulatory framework remained as nebulous as they had since Bangemann launched the idea of the "Global Communications Charter" in 1997.

## The Internet Corporation for Assigned Names and Numbers (ICANN)

On October 2, 1998, the Internet Corporation for Assigned Names and Numbers (ICANN) was incorporated as a not-for-profit private corporation under Californian law. ICANN is responsible for Internet domain names, address space, and Internet protocols as well as the root server system, the backbone of the networks. Until October 1, 2001, ICANN will be fully operational as a unique global institution. It represents both the public Internet community at large (probably up to 500 million users by the year 2003), as well as private industry and the business world, which expects to make more than one trillion US dollars in e-commerce over the next five years.

Although ICANN is responsible for one of the key global issues of the 21st century, its constitution, structure and membership do not fit into similar political and organizational schemes that have been established to manage global phenomena in the past. ICANN is neither an intergovernmental treaty organization (IGO) nor a classical non-governmental organization with individual or institutional members (NGO). It is also not a typical profit-oriented transnational corporation (TNC). ICANN is a new type of global organization without any precedent, representing different types of stakeholders from all over the world. It is structured uniquely with elected bodies and nominated representatives, numerous committees, councils, constituencies, and supporting organizations. ICANN creates an unusual triangle where the "business world" and the "Internet community" are equally represented in the highest decision making body, while governments take a backseat with only an "advisory" function.

Debate continues about whether ICANN is only a "technical body" responsible for the practical management of a technical resource. Many commentators feel that while the legal mandate of ICANN, described in Article 2 of its bylaws, gives the corporation only a "technical mandate," ICANN's decisions concerning the management of the Internet will have substantial political, economic, cultural, and social implications.

ICANN's bylaws describe the private corporation as a "nonprofit public benefit corporation" that "is not organized for the private gain of any person." It is organized under the "Californian Nonprofit Public Benefit Corporation Law for Charitable and Public Purposes"[15] and will be operated "exclusively for charitable, educational and scientific purposes."

Although this constitutional mandate is primarily a technical task, it will be nearly impossible for ICANN to avoid political conflicts. Conflicts will appear as inherent elements of technical decisions as well as the consequence of ICANN's responsibility for the primary assets of the Internet. This can be seen, in particular, in the following five areas:

## Public Political Issues and ICANN

### a. Recognition of Registrars

One of the driving forces behind the launching of ICANN was the need to de-monopolize the registration business of domain names. The domain name system was introduced at a time when the registration of .edu domains (used by the educational institutions that first started the Internet) outnumbered the dot-com domains and registration was free. Based on a contract with the US Department of Commerce, Network Solutions Inc. (NSI) received a de facto monopoly from the US government for the registration of domain names in the generic Top Level Domain Name space (gTLDs). When the US government stopped its financial support of the Internet via the National Science

Foundation (NSF) in 1995, the NSI started to charge for registration in the .com, .org and .net domain name space (US$35 per year).

The introduction of a fee coincided with the beginning of the dot-com boom. While in the beginning there were only a couple of thousand dot-com registrations, the dot-com registration exploded in the second half of the 1990s and reached more than six million registrations in early 2000. Registration of domain names became "big business" with hundreds of millions of US dollars at stake. Against this backdrop, the call for de-monopolization of the registration business became stronger. A first effort to introduce competition into the registration business undertaken by an "International Ad Hoc Committee" (IAHC) in 1997, failed.[16] Their approach was to establish an intergovernmental organization under the umbrella of the Geneva-based ITU and within the United Nations system. This was to be a private not-for-profit called the "Council of Registrars" (CORE), which was registered under Swiss law and composed of 28 international "recognized registrars." It was to introduce seven new gTLDs. CORE would have been under the control of a "political advisory committee" (PAC) and a "political oversight committee" (POC), in which national governments would have a final say.[17]

The approach was watered down both by the US government, which was against an Internet corporation under Swiss law, and by parts of the private sector that feared ITU involvement would lead to more governmental control over the Internet. Only three months after the gTLD-MoU was signed by nearly 100 governments, institutions, and other organizations in Geneva, the US government proposed, in the Clinton/Gore global e-commerce paper, an alternative approach.[18] The US government argued in favour of a not-for-profit, private corporation under US law without any governmental involvement. This proposal paved the way for the incorporation of ICANN in October 1998.

## b. The Root Server System

The second issue regards the domain name system that works via name servers. If somebody sends an e-mail address or goes to a Web site, the name server asks the root server for the relevant top level domain. The root server, which manages the top level domains (TLD), can be seen as the material heart of the Internet. Without the root server, Internet communications would cease. There are 13 root servers now in the world, ten of them based in the United States. Each root server mirrors the TLDs of the A root server which is based in Herndon, Virginia, managed by NSI and still under control of the US government.

The issue of the ultimate control over such a critical element of the global information infrastructure is also of concern for a number of governments. A representative of the German government asked an academic conference in February 2001 in Zurich, whether it would be possible for the US government to use its ultimate control over the A root server as a potential weapon in a trade conflict with another nation. The controller of the A root server is in a position to take TLDs out of the root.

The control over the root server constitutes a very sensitive security problem. While the management of the root server is primarily a technical task, its role for the global Internet brings ICANN into the spotlight of global security policy.

## c. Uniform Dispute Resolution Policy

A third issue facing ICANN is the need to create a system for the settlement of disputes between trademark holders and domain name holders. Registration of domain names was handled on a "first come, first served" basis and was used by the ITU in its early days for the registration of frequencies. The rather simple and liberal practice of domain name registration produced the practice of "cybersquatting." Individuals made a living from registered brand names and selling the registered domain name directly to the trademark owner (or its competitor). They also sometimes misused the brand names for their own business activities, creating consumer confusion.

While trademark owners called for an extension of the copyright and trademark system to the Internet, a wider part of the Internet community opposed such an extension. Freedom of expression and free speech, they argued, includes the right to choose freely a domain name. For example, if an individual named Jeff McDonald uses his own personal name he should not be sued by McDonald's Restaurants and punished for a trademark infringement. Furthermore, critics of McDonald's should have the right to use the branded and trademarked name in domain names for critical evaluation of the practice of the company as part of their right to freedom of expression.

The settlement of the fast growing number of domain name conflicts by courts became increasingly difficult, time consuming and expensive, in particular when the conflicting parties were in different jurisdictions. ICANN was asked to look for a solution. Based on an extensive report of the World Intellectual Property Organization (WIPO),[19] the ICANN board of directors developed a Uniform Dispute Resolution Policy (UDRP) that allows conflicting parties, regardless of jurisdiction, to settle their conflicts online as an alternative to the courts.[20] The UDRP concentrates on a "behaviour in bad faith" in the gTLD space.[21] The whole procedure is fast (not more than two months) and cheap (not more than US$2000).

Nearly 4000 cases were brought to the UDRP between December 1999 and December 2000. While each conflicting party has the right after the end of an UDRP procedure to go to an ordinary court, the majority of its first cases led to an acceptable solution. ICANN's UDRP could lead to a model for other conflict resolution mechanisms in the global Internet world, including e-commerce conflicts between businesses and consumers.

## d. Recognition of ccTLDs

When Jon Postel, the founder of the domain name system, introduced top level domain names for countries, he wanted to avoid any policy involvement. The Internet community, he said, is not in a position to define a country or recognize a territory or another geographical unit as a "country." Postel used the ISO 3166 code based on a United Nations register of 243 "recognized territories" and asked individuals or academic institutions in these countries to overtake the responsibility for the management of the ccTLD. No governments have been involved in the definition of ccTLDs and its delegation to a manager. The operations of the relevant national registries and registrars started without any legal foundations in the "territories." By following the ISO list, Postel added the two letter code to all the "recognized territories," to full member of the United Nations system like Germany (.de), China (.cn) and Mexico (.mx), to "territories" like the British "Isle of Man (.im), the Australian "Christmas Islands" (.cx) and to small Pacific Islands like Tongo (.to), Tuvalu (.tv) or Nouie (.nu).

As long as there was only a limited number of registered domain names, this system was workable. However, when the number of registered domain names grew beyond a critical mass, some governments started to investigate the practice and the legal basis for a ccTLD registrar. However, in Germany where the number of registrations in its .de domain crossed the three million line in November 2000, no reference exists in the German legal system – from the Telecommunications Law to the Multimedia Law – that specifically regulates the German ccTLD. Neither the German government nor the DENIC Corporation, responsible for the .de domain, views this as a problem. They enjoy a friendly bilateral relationship in which the government does not interfere in the registration business and DENIC respects the general laws. The situation can be different if a government is dissatisfied with the practice of the registration in a given country and wants to change the registrar. It is not unrealistic to have a situation where the government of Iraq or of Serbia or North Korea is dissatisfied with the policy of the national ccTLD registrar and wants a change. Or a prime minister of a corrupt government wants to give the right for the profitable ccTLD management to his brother-in-law. Another problem is that there is no unified practice of registration among the ccTLDs. While one group of registrars allows registration under the national code only for citizens of that country, others have a more open practice and some others have even sold the right to manage the ccTLD to private investors. Tuvalu, an island with seven computers (1998), sold the right to manage the .tv domain for US$15 million.

While ICANN, according to its technical mandate, has no special right to decide who should be the registrar in a given country, it can block the registration of a new ccTLD registrar. To clarify the legal relationship between national governments, ccTLD registrar and ICANN, an international governmental advisory committee (GAC) developed a contractual relationship between the three parties.[22] According to the proposed drafts, a change of responsibility over ccTLD registration would need both the support of the "relevant administration," the "national Internet community" and the recognition of ICANN. The GAC draft was presented during the ICANN board meeting in Cairo (March 2000) but was criticized from different corners. One group feared that the contracts will give governments too much power, others saw ICANN's role as too strong. The US based Internet Rights Coalition rejected any approach that would refer to the involvement of governments.

## e. Introduction of new gTLDs

The fact that there are only seven generic TLDs has no technical explanation. Jan Postel defined the gTLDs according to the needs of the late 1980s. While .edu (for educational institutions), .mil (for the military) and .gov (for governmental institutions) were to be used in the US only with the .int domain reserved for intergovernmental treaty organizations, only .com, .org, and .net were widely available. Later Postel advocated for the definition of up to 150 new gTLDs, according to the growing needs for new domain names. Technically, there can be any number of gTLDs.

During the negotiations of the IAHC, the group discussed creating a limited number of seven new gTLDs (with names like .shop, .arts, .sport and .rec) and then adding on to them based on the success of the first few. The proposal was blocked, mainly by trademark owners who feared a new wave of misuse of brand names. In 1998, then-US President Clinton's Internet adviser, Ira Magaziner, argued for five new gTLDs but said that ICANN should make the final decision.

When ICANN was established, its Board of Directors looked first to WIPO. In its May 1999 report on Domain Name Disputes, WIPO recommended that new gTLDs should be introduced only after the adoption of a dispute resolution policy for domain names. The adoption of the UDRP in August 1999 removed the barriers to the introduction of new gTLDs. The "Domain Name Supporting Organization" established a working group and, in April 2000, recommended starting with a limited number of new gTLDs in a phased process. At its Board meeting in Yokohama in July 2000, ICANN started the process. Four months later it selected seven new gTLDs (.info, .name, .coop, .biz, .pro, .aero, .museum) from about 200 proposals, presented by 45 companies.

## ICANN and the Legitimacy of Cyberdemocracy

The agreement that nine of the ICANN directors should be elected by Internet users, was a precondition for the recognition of ICANN by the US Department of Commerce. It was, in particular, Ira Magaziner who pushed the idea through against the will of Jon Postel. But the final agreement reached in October 1998 did not produce a solution as to how an ICANN At-Large-Membership (ALM) could be defined and constituted and the nine ALM directors, elected.

To clarify the status of an ordinary ICANN member, the ICANN Board established a Membership Advisory Committee (MAC) in January 1999. The MAC, with assistance from the Harvard Law School, presented its final recommendations to the ICANN Board in May 1999. According to the recommendations, each Internet user with an e-mail and postal address who is older then 16 years of age, should be seen as a potential ICANN member and should be invited to participate in the election of the nine directors. The recommendation passed the board in principle, with some modifications. Instead of nine only five director seats were opened for elections in a first test phase. In early 2000, the first global election of ICANN directors began. In October 2000, five directors were elected.

While ICANN expected that not more than 5,000 to 20,000 users would participate in the election, 160,000 users voted. More than 200 candidates were running for the five seats, partly nominated by an ICANN Nomination Committee and partly self-nominated with the support of a membership quorum. The elected five directors included Karl Auerbach, vice-president of Cisco Systems, Nil Quaynor, the manager of the ccTLD of Ghana, and Andy Mueller Maguhn, a famous "hacker" from the German Chaos Computer Club.

The elections were seen as a great innovation and a huge success. However, they were not free from deficiencies. Besides the technical problems that arose in the management of the 160,000 applications, some countries benefitted from the actions of local media that organized public campaigns for their own national candidates.

While ICANN membership and global online elections remains a controversial issue that needs more study and clarification, it is clear that the subject is not a technical one. ICANN is unavoidably drawn into a political debate about cyberdemocracy, legitimacy, and representation.

With global elections of some of its directors, ICANN enters a fundamental public policy area. Elections are the main source of legitimacy for a government. During the ICANN meeting in Marina del Rey in November 2000, there was an interesting dispute about legitimate representation between Michael Leibrandt, a member of the German federal government and the German representative in the GAC, and Andy Mueller Maguhn, the new elected ICANN director. While Leibrandt argued that the German Internet community, as part of the German electorate, had given him, via his election to parliament, the legitimacy to act on behalf of the German Internet users, Mueller Maguhn argued that his own legitimacy comes directly from the European Internet users, including the German users, who have elected him in direct elections. The dispute did not produce a consensus but it signalled the beginning of a new debate about legitimacy and representative democracy.

## Conclusion

The global character of the Internet calls for a global system of governance. National governments and intergovernmental organizations now understand that traditional law and policy-making cannot be simply transferred to the Internet. To avoid a "responsibility vacuum," a new mixture of governmental and non-governmental governance systems must be developed. Whether ICANN wants it or not, as the first and (at the moment) only "new global Internet corporation" it can not escape political responsibility. Whether ICANN will be only a service to other "new corporations" dealing with global Internet problems – from content regulation to cyber-crime – or whether ICANN itself will broaden its mandate to become something like the "United Nations of the Information Age," is highly speculative in these early years of the new Internet century. Regardless of what ICANN decides, very concrete political conflicts will emerge even if it restricts itself to a very narrow interpretation of its technical mandate.

While this trilateral relationship sounds good in theory, how will it be defined in detail and who will have ultimate control? Who will define the aims, norms, principles, criteria and procedures? How will the three sets of global players constitute themselves? The pressure for new, innovative answers comes from a practical reality. With increasing Internet-related governance problems, the call for a functioning system without "holes" will become louder, regardless of whether such a system is constituted by governmental or non-governmental actors.

It is obvious that we live in a transition period. The "information revolution" has led to a "social evolution" that will lead to a new quality of political life. Rules and values are changing. In his *Cluetrain Manifesto*, Christopher Locke puts it in this way: "The future will be about subtle differences, not wholesale conformity; about diversity, not homogeneity; about breaking rules, not enforcing them; about pushing the envelope, not punching the clock; about invitation, not protection; about doing it first, not doing it "right"; about making it better, not making it perfect, about telling the truth, not spinning bigger lies; about turning people on, not packaging them; and perhaps above all, about building convivial communities and knowledge ecologies, not leveraging demographic sectors." And he adds that the revolution already takes place in the streets. "But if you are looking for Molotov cocktails and tear gas, beleaguered cops and firebrand radicals, you are bound to miss what's really happening. Just because you're not seeing a revolution – or what Hollywood has told you a revolution ought to look like – doesn't mean there isn't one going on" (Locke *et. al*. 2000).

Four hundred years ago, after the beginning of the industrial revolution, the first "new industrialists" realized that the governance system at the time, based on kingdoms with an absolutist monarch at the top, did not satisfy the new needs of the industrial age. The search for a new governance system in the 17th century led to a historical and grand political compromise: the introduction of the constitutional monarchy. The constitutional monarchy was to a certain degree a co-regulatory system. While the king and the feudal institutions (the old system) still had some concrete power inherited by birth, new institutions that gained power through elections were established, like national parliaments and bourgeois governments (the new system). At this time, nobody wanted to abolish the kingdoms in general (and even today, there are still numerous kingdoms in existence with kings and queens trying to keep their role and influence). But the need for more stable rules that would function independently of an absolutist monarch, produced a new alternative system. The first constitutions of the 17th century in which rights and duties of citizens and governments were defined, did not yet create a republic but they opened the door for the emergence of a new governance system. The constitutional monarchy enabled philosophers like Montesquieu, Rousseau and others to develop a more detailed system of governance with concepts like the "division of the branches of power" and the "social contract." Only in 1789, the king was killed in a revolution, paving the way for our present system of representative democracies. A simple system became more complex.

The present system of governance in the 21st century with nearly 200 nation-states has functioned more or less satisfactorily over the last 200 years. But with globalization, the system based on the sovereign nation-state, shows some cracks when confronted with global challenges. Like in the early days of the industrial revolution, the call is not to change the system but to make it more flexible for a changing economic environment.

The call for co-regulatory systems tries to combine the positive values of stable governmental regulation within and among nation-states, with the new flexibility needed to meet the challenges of globalization in the information age. One result of this process is a new diversification of power on a global level. New actors that create new institutions are emerging and moving into the new territory, filling emerging gaps regardless of whether there is a governmental order or not. National governments will not disappear in the next century but they will become one actor among others, obliged to join into co-operative networks and consensual arrangements with other global actors and to share power with them. On the other hand, the new emerging global actors, both private industry and global civil society (still in its infancy), must not only prove their legitimacy but they must also learn that the rights and freedoms for which they are fighting are linked to duties and responsibilities.

While it is still too early to make any predictions of how a new governance system might look, it seems clear that the present complex governmental system will appear simple in comparison with a new global governance system. Its complexity is growing and conflicts will remain the driving force for development. To define which areas of life will fall under "citizenship," which will come under "netizenship," and how co-existence between different governance bodies will develop, will take more than one Montesquieu and one

Rousseau. We are only at the beginning of the emergence of the global knowledge-based information society. Nobody can predict the future, but the excitement is already here.

## Notes

1   See, among others: Cairncross (1997); Leer (2000); Castells (1996).

2   United Nations Resolution 2526 (A/RES/25/26), *Declaration on Fundamental Principles of International Law*, October 25, 1970.

3   See, for example, *Court tells Yahoo...* (2000).

4   Draft Convention on Cyber Crime. See: http://stars.coe.int/doc/doc01/EDOC9031.htm.

5   UNESCO, Resolution 4/19, adopted by the General Conference at its 21st session, Belgrade, September 23 to October 28, 1980.

6   See http://mirror-us.unesco.org/webworld/com_media/communication _democracy/windhoek.htm.

7   Recently, ITU had 188 governmental "Members" and about 450 private "members."

8   For a summary of this speech, see Gore (1994).

9   See http://europa.eu.int/ISPO/intcoop/g8/i_g8conference.html.

10  See http://europa.eu.int/ISPO/bonn/i_index.html.

11  See http://web.ansi.org/public/iisp/docs/gisconf.html.

12  See *Launching a Global Business Dialogue: Business Round Table on Global Communications*. http://e2i.e2i.at/_e2i/nummer0398/is3.htm.

13  See *Origins of the GBDe*. http://www.gbde.org/nn/archive/origins.html.

14  See the *Final Conclusions of the Global Business Dialogue on electronic Commerce (GBDe)*. Paris, September 13, 1999, in www.gbd.org; see also OECD, in www.oecd.org.

15  Articles of Incorporation of ICANN as revised November 21, 1998, Paragraph 1, in: www.icann.org/general/articles.html.

16  The IAHC was composed of the Internet Engineering Task Force (IETF), the Internet Society (ISOC) Scotland, the Internet Assigned Numbers Association (IANA), the World Intellectual Property Organization (WIPO), the International Telecommunication Union (ITU), and the International Trademark Association (INTA).

17  See Final Report of the International Ad Hoc Committee, *Recommendations for Administration and Management of gTLDs*, Geneva, February 4, 1997, *Establishment of a Memorandum of Understanding of the Generic Top Level Domain Name Space of the INTERNET Domain Name System (gTLD-MoU)*, Geneva, February 28, 1997; *80 Organizations Sign MoU to Restructure the Internet*, Press Release ITU/97-8, Geneva, May 1, 1997.

18  See William J. Clinton / Al Gore Jr. *A Framework for Global Electronic Commerce*, 21. The White House, Washington, July 1, 1997: 16, RFC on the Registration and Administration of Internet Domain Names, Washington, July 1, 1997, in: http://www.ntia.doc.gov/ntiahome/domain.

19  *Final Report of the WIPO Internet Domain Name Process*, Geneva, April 30, 1999, in: http://ecommerce.wipo.int/domains/process/eng/processhome.html.

20  Uniform Domain Name Dispute Resolution Policy, in: http://www.icann.org/udrp/udrp.htm.

21  *Evidence of Registration and Use in Bad Faith*. See: http://www.icann.org/udrp/udrp-policy-24oct99.htm.

22  *Principles for the delegation and administration of country code domains,* in: http://www.noie.gov.au/projects/international/DNS/gac/index.htm.

## References

Cairncross, F. 1997. *The Death of Distance.* Boston: Harvard Business School Press.

Castells, M. 1996. *The Rise of the Network Society.* Oxford: Blackwell Publishers.

*Court tells Yahoo to block Nazi auctions in France.* 2000. Paris: Reuters, May 22.

Gore, A. 1994. The Global Information Infrastructure: Forging a New Athenian Age of Democracy. *InterMedia* 22, 2: 4-6.

Leer, A. 2000. *Welcome to the Wired World.* London: Pearson Education.

Locke, C., R. Levine, D. Searls and D. Weinberger. 2000. *The Cluetrain Manifesto: The End of Business as Usual.* Cambridge (MA): Perseus Publishing.

Moschovitis, C., H. Poole, T. Schuyler and T.M. Senft. 1999. *History of the Internet: A Chronology from 1943 to the Present.* Santa Barbara: ABC-CLIO.

# Supranational Governance and the Shifting Paradigm in Communications Policymaking: The Case of the European Parliament

**Katharine Sarikakis**

Supranational, regional organizations, with predominantly economic agendas, have come to be major players in the field of communications policy in the last 20 years. Globalization processes in the economy have given rise to political and other formations that acquire an international character and are suitable to respond to the changing environment. The European Union is such a formation, and in many respects a unique political system with none similar in the world. Although its economic focus is a common point of reference for a variety of scholars, an oversimplified conclusion as to the nature and role of the Union and its institutions fails to recognize the multifaceted dimension of its institutional politics. The European Parliament is the most ambiguous institution within this complex polity and, although it is the only one directly elected by the 375 million citizens of the EU, it has been, until recently, the least powerful in legislative terms.

In many ways, the European Parliament can be seen as a form of future political representation in governing settings characterized by a contradiction of regional *and* supranational sovereignty. Meanwhile, media policy in Europe has intensified and rapidly expanded. A shift in the policy-making paradigm can be identified mainly in two areas: first, a change in the objective of policy formation and second, a change in the policy subject. Especially in the mechanisms of the EU polity, communications (or "media") policy has never been according to some Commission officers and MEPs (members of the European Parliament), a distinct policy area. The European Parliament brought attention to this area in 1982 with a report[1] that emphasized the cultural and political potential of the "new" media (EP 1982). Since then, a series of interrelated factors has been influential in the formation of media policies in the EU Rapid technological advancement, the globalization of economies, and the revival of neo-liberal politics are the main socio-economic conditions observed world-wide. Moreover, as regional "groupings" – political or economic – have increased, so has the pace of European integration involving not only economic but also cultural, social and even political integration. Communications policy[2] is an example of this integration process.

## Global interdependence and governance

The second half of the twentieth century has witnessed structural changes in world economies in the areas of transaction flows, international competition, trade and investment. Companies have sought to create links to market forces and form alliances in order to achieve higher volume production and improve market penetration (Dent 1997: 233). In Europe, as domestic markets became saturated, the domestic, national territory became increasingly restrictive for the maximization of profit. Nation states could no longer resolve complex realities of transborder trade and human mobility. At an international level, in an attempt to recapture a sense of control and facilitate a further expansion of the markets, several organizations with their origins in the Bretton Woods agreement were developed. Such organizations as the International Monetary Fund (IMF), the General Agreement on Tariffs and Trade (GATT) and the International Bank for Reconstruction and Development (IBRD), provided an international forum for the negotiation of multilateral agreements that would then produce a form of policy. American domination, the rise of Japanese multinationals, increases in internalization (intra-firm trading and investment) and the accelerated pace of technological development resulted in further establishment of networks, this time at a regional level and under the umbrella of inter-governmental agreements. With the internationalization of markets, the most pressing international economic problems cannot be solved by countries acting in isolation, especially in a world of continuous changes in technology and frequent market transformations (Jovanovic 1998: 179).

The current contradictory phenomena of regionalism and globalization are the expression of the necessity for abolition of trade barriers or the reduction of transaction costs together with the rationalized redefinition of administration and organization among regions and nations to correspond to prevailing changes. Economic union, as an advanced form of international/regional co-operation, is argued to have the potential to increase efficiency in the allocation of resources in relation to a common market and to secure trade flows (Jovanovic 1998: 170). The European Union, as an "internal" facilitator, that is an agency primarily conceived to mediate among and administer for its member states, as well as an international actor, is better placed to accomplish these efficiencies when responding to external factors than member states (Jovanovic 1998: 202).

Interdependence proves to be a major catalyst in modern societies but it cannot alone explain the direction of European integration (Caporaso 1998). Regional economic integration has expanded to many regions in the world such as Asia and the Americas with schemes such as the Mercado Comun del Sur (MERCOSUR) that intends to move from free trade union to common market initiatives (Jovanovic 1998: 328), and the Central American Common Market (CACM). However, it is only in Europe that integration has taken dimensions beyond economic objectives. Integration has proceeded into the political and social sphere undergoing much debate as to the degree, real or potential, of cultural integration. Institutionalized integration and political administration has matured in the last 50 years and resulted in further integration.

The European community was forced to construct a political system capable of administering the transformation of European economies into large-scale economies and reinforcing the position of European capitalism in global negotiations, in particular with Japan and the United States. Members of the European Union, such as Germany, the UK and France are some of the strongest economic powers in the world. In order to avoid wasteful duplication of resources in research and development, harmonization and co-operation is needed among economically strong, but also smaller, countries. Moreover, changes in the world markets not only affect the direction of technological development but are also affected by technological change itself especially with the outgrowth in communication technologies and biotechnologies.

Meanwhile, the particular realities and historical traditions and experiences of the European nations that contributed to the construction of such diverse societies have promoted a discourse of social integration along hegemonic cultures fostered within the common denominator, the notion of (bourgeois) "democracy" as the dominant political system. Political unification for the safeguarding of peace has always been put forward as a crucial motive behind the integration process of the Western European countries. (Middlemas 1995; Coombes 1999). Such traditions found expression in parliamentary democracy and resulted in the creation of an international European body, with only consultative powers initially, that grew into an institution with strong legislative powers, the European Parliament.

As the polity adopts common policies, they create other areas that need to be addressed as new issues of policy. The "spill over" effect in policy domains results in the increase of the number and frequency of policies that need to be dealt with at a supranational level. Similarly, increase in international transactions and the expansion of areas of transaction solicited further solutions through the supranational route. A considerable amount of policy is now negotiated not in national parliaments or within national governments but at a supranational level. Although this phenomenon does not necessarily mean that national governments have less power in their hands, it does presuppose that some of these powers have to be "shared" with representatives at a European level (Jovanovic 1998): harmonization of laws and coordination of policies are the main characteristics of European legal integration. It would be an impossible and cost ineffective situation for transnational and multinational corporations to attempt continuous adjustment to an enormous number of laws and regulations, sometimes very different from each other in such a confined space as Europe.

Harmonization of laws and the abolition of trade barriers have further facilitated the globalization of trade. This can be seen in the case of re-regulation of telecommunications: multinational corporations, as a consequence of the increasing internationalization of competition and the need for effective and low cost transnational, transborder telecommunications, have teamed up with telecommunication companies and pressed for the liberalization of the sector in Europe (Sandholtz 1998), while transborder satellite and computer mediated communication have begun to have an impact on communication structures on the continent.

## Parliamentary supranationalism: a response to market integration

Established in 1979, the European Parliament has evolved from a body of 78 members restricted to a consultative role assigned by national governments, into the only international, directly elected parliament with 626 members and a major legislative role in supranational politics. The EP has steadily acquired greater powers through a series of treaties including the 1992 Maastricht Treaty and the 1997 Amsterdam Treaty. Its increased role in supranational governance can be seen in its position in the legislative process that consists of a bilateral chamber: a Council of Ministers acting together with the Parliament. The Parliament's significance also lies with its role in representing political accountability and the power to exercise scrutiny of the Council and the executive administration.

Supranationalism implies binding laws for all members whilst detailed rule making and implementation are carried out through national institutions. The EP is a supranational institution in that its members have relative autonomy towards their national political parties and are independent from the national governments. The EP has no stable or preconceived coalition, as it does not support a government. Coalitions are built on a subject by subject basis, allowing more flexibility but also giving a particular weight to the role that ideologies and communication can play.

The significance of the European Parliament is not restricted to a consultative or generally secondary role any more. Through the years, subsequent treaties provided the Parliament with increased powers in various stages of policymaking, notwithstanding powers to initiate legislation. Procedural issues are however not the focus of this chapter. A discussion of the issues surrounding the powers of the Parliament would be the object of an exhaustive exploration of current debates not only of the policy process but also the very essence of integration. Instead, I would like to concentrate on the political significance of the European Parliament as a democratic institution in supranational governance using communications policy-making as an example. Governments have two forms of executive power: the political, which provides leadership through policy, and the administrative that is responsible for the implementation of law. In many respects, the EU appears to bear both such characteristics (Hix 1999: 21). Although the EP is not part of a government, it is part of governance. That is, it does belong to the institutions that are directly involved with the decision-making mechanisms of the Union. The future significance of the Parliament depends on the direction of European integration (i.e. political, economic etc.), the role of the EU in general, and the legislative powers assigned to the EP. Finally, a great deal depends on the particularity of each policy area such as agriculture, fisheries or audio-visual (Wallace and Wallace 2000: 61). Two aspects of particular interest and with diachronic validity include the political and social dimensions of the EP's role.

## Supranational parliamentary activism and communication policies

Up until the 1980s, communications policy in Europe was mainly focused on separating the state's authority of the media from the public's. So for example, in Greece, the press was guaranteed freedom of speech by constitutional laws while the electronic media such as television were under the direct jurisdiction of the state (Sarikakis 2000). Telecommunications jurisdiction had been grouped together with the airwaves under state ownership. The film industry has always belonged more or less to private enterprise. Different countries have experienced different traditions, so for example, Great Britain experienced a hybrid model where independent channels (ITV and Channel Four) were publicly owned but not state-controlled. In this British model, freedom of speech had not been explicitly guaranteed by constitutional law. In the 1990s, the objectives of communication policy have shifted to a considerable degree: telecommunications and the airwaves have been deregulated and privatized, while law has expanded to re-regulate and prevent interventionist law-making to the areas of new media and convergence.

This paradigm shift in media policies has been accompanied by a parallel development of political and economic changes in Europe, such as the expansion of transnational companies, intensification of economic integration, the undermining of the nation state monopoly in policy and administration, increased privatization of state or publicly owned industries, and a seemingly unstoppable advancement in technology. However the shift has not only taken place in material structural terms, but it has also been reflected in the political discourse (Kleinsteuber 1998). In Europe before the mid-1980s, media policy and communications policy in more general terms had been focused mainly on two areas: freedom of speech and patterns of ownership of the electronic media. The media had been regarded as facilitators of ethical and political objectives such as the protection of democracy, a notion that originated in the post war period and lived up to that time (ie McQuail 1998). While there had been variations in national media systems and policy provisions, some commonly shared values characterized the philosophy behind these variations. These include the preservation of national and public heritage by public service broadcasters, the preservation of information flow and freedom of speech, and an emphasis on "quality programming."

Dramatic changes in technology and the intensification of international trade have pushed for the liberalization of a range of sectors that were until then part of public or state ownership. Communications and information soon followed in the liberalization process (ie Venturelli 1998). The expression of economic imperatives in policy-making has been translated into a market-dominated discourse. The communications policy focus shifted from a primary concern for information freedom for the citizen to participate in the political system, into freedom of the consumer to make market choices. Furthermore and most importantly, it was the freedom of media content providers, who sought "non-discriminatory" policies for the expansion of private media and information industries that became central in the dominant discourse. The era of a new, electronic colonization had begun. Supranational market mechanisms and politics (eg GATT and the WTO) were mobilized to prepare the socio-legal structure for the smooth operation of globalization and expansion of capital. The development of communication technologies explored and created new markets for audiences that had been already involved in a process of economic integration in Europe. Evidence of the transformation of discourse can be found in the official documents of the European Union where the segregation of communications policy areas into industrial and technological sectors is evident. Generally, the overarching argument for economic integration and liberalization has been that of economic growth. Specifically, the deregulation of communications and the dismantling of barriers in information flow were argued to be essential for economic growth (Mansell 1993; Winseck 1998; Thussu 2000).

The apotheosis of this discourse is the 1994 Bangemann Task Force Report to the European Council in which the foundations for an ultimate stage of privatization, liberalization and deregulation are advocated[3] (Commission of the European Communities 1994). The Bangemann report argues that economic growth is inseparable from liberalization and deregulation of all sectors of European industries but singles out those industries mostly protected from the market: the sectors of telecommunications and communication. The Bangemann Report, with the objective to study and present the potential of the new technologies, focused on the strategic economic importance of a technologically advanced audio-visual industry. Because of this report, the Commission presented an action-plan that emphasised, from an economically-liberal point of view, the need for strengthening European industries' competitiveness through vocational training and the application of new technologies.

Communications and information policy is not an issue limited to the area of technology and economics however. Current communications policy provides predominantly for *negative* freedoms, such as the freedom *from* state intervention or other control directed at the activities of private enterprise. Examples taken from European law such as deregulation of telecommunications, the controversial provisions in the audio-visual sector, or the more general view of free information production and dissemination, suggest that the focus of communications policy has shifted towards the protection of private interest. Instead of positive and instructive regulation concerned with positive freedom in the interest of the public, communication policy has transgressed into the public realm as an agent of economic wealth but remains as distant from the politicized public as possible. Communication policy, most importantly, is a political question connected directly to the question of political participation and expression of citizenship rights (Venturelli 1998). The European Parliament is a unique forum for the representation of human rights and citizenship rights and a venue for such questions to be, at least partially, negotiated. Comparing it with other European institutions, the EP is by far the least dependent and most democratic institution. The role of the Council is tempered by its relation to national governments, whose work is again compromised by their eagerness to both be re-elected and to satisfy the demands of national capital or capital acting within national boundaries. The smaller the nations are, the more vulnerable they are to the demands of media conglomerates (Hoffmann-Riem 1996). Furthermore, the Commission also directly appointed by national governments with the agreement of the EP constitutes a bureaucratic executive that lacks transparency and accountability.

The political activism of the EP is an inseparable part of its role not only within EU politics but also at a national and international level. Far from being just a forum, the EP has proven itself to actively intervene and represent important aspects of the public interest. Some of these interventions have led to significant policy initiatives from the expression of concern about the commercialization of communications in early reports (EP 1984) to more recent ones including the report adopted by the EP on public service broadcasters (PSBs). Other examples include the Tongue report (named after the rapporteur MEP Carol Tongue), addressing the EP's role in the multi-media society (EP 1996) and the Television Without Frontiers Directive (TVWF) (European Communities 1997). In particular, the TVWF Directive provides the first and most comprehensive piece of legislation, (although not without weaknesses), in an attempt to set some standards and rules in an expansively deregulated media content environment. In many respects, it is doubtful that some policies would be in place today if the Parliament had not undertaken the research, conducted the relevant studies, proceeded into the resolution, and called upon the European Commission to act.[4] Expanding well beyond procedural forms, the Parliament has sought to reach the core of communication and information normative prerequisites such as freedom to exercise communication rights and means to materialize them. Christiansen et.

al. (1999) rightly argue for more study of the political discourse of the European integration. Interparliamentary debates on communication policies reveal that the discourse remains highly political even though the ideological stands are divided:[5] The EP is not a homogeneous body; it represents diverse political, ideological and national interests and standpoints. For example, the standpoint of liberal and conservative parties regarding telecommunication deregulation or the content quotas in the TVWF remains different from that of social democrats.

The Tongue Report on the role of the PSBs in the age of convergence is an example of this. The report has provided the ideological, discursive counter-argument to the dominant liberalization discourse that threatened the legitimacy of public communication services. The "Sports Rights" debate and subsequent ruling is an example of successful use of legislative powers of the EP as well as effective use of the discourse of universal free access. This legislation advocated for the right to culture and cultural diversity as an amendment of the TVWF directive.[6] The same discourse point has been supported by the EP advocating for the exception of audio-visual products and the A/V industry from all international trade negotiations (MEP interview November 1998). However, the cultural role of the EP, as can be seen in reports and resolutions promoting the protection of national and minority languages, cultural content, and the protection of works of high quality and free universal access to sports, does not limit itself to debates about the potential of a European industry versus that of Hollywood. The deeper political and social ideological convictions find expression in advocacy for the positive freedom of expression. The right to produce and consume one's own cultural goods such as films or soap operas, extends to the right to speak for oneself, the right to present oneself in film or other forms of expression, the right not to "become invisible" (European Parliament 1995a: 259). Similarly, the "political identity" of the EP in the area of media policy has been based on a minimum of standards, strongly rooted in the notions of public service broadcasting and the diversity of opinions and values as guaranteed by the freedom of expression that extend to anti-concentration policies and the protection of PSBs (European Parliament 1995b: 270).

The *political* significance of the EP is evident in its work in areas that attract little if any attention by market-oriented forces. The first initiative for a media policy at a European level was a resolution of the EP based on the Hahn Report (European Parliament 1982; Collins 1994) that viewed television and the new media as an important tool for political and cultural integration in Europe, proposing transborder broadcasting of European cultural goods about common issues through a paneuropean TV channel. Although the idea of a paneuropean channel never materialized, many of these first suggestions, such as the common (public service) European channel, are still part of the greater discourse on the role of European media and the audio-visual industry as can be seen in parliamentary debates (ie EP 1995a). Another area where the EP has proved itself in advocating for the public good has been the protection of PSBs in the process of deregulation. Corporate interests have attacked the public service for being subsidized by the state and therefore an obstacle to the functioning of free competition among companies with equal rights. Against a proposed set of guidelines on the function of the public services prepared by the Directorate General IV of Competition Policy, the Parliament defended the right of diversity in definition of culture and refused to put public service broadcasting content and funding under scrutiny as advocated by industrialist circles. The Parliament gained the support of DGX (audio-visual) and of member states (Tongue 1998; European Report 1998; FT 21.10.1998).

Public service broadcasting constitutes a special case not only in the traditions of European societies but also in constitutional provisions as laid down in the Treaty of Amsterdam.[7] According to the Treaty, the PSB system is recognized as "directly related to the democratic, social and cultural needs of each society and to the need to preserve media pluralism" (EC 1997: 109). This is the only provision made in binding laws regulating international relations and trade within a growing number of agreements between states and regions. The role of the European Parliament has been catalytic in that it reflects not only the direct concerns of national parliaments and people but also makes a political, moral statement about public ownership of the airwaves and means of communication that is indirectly acknowledged in founding laws. The EP's advocacy for access to public service broadcasting also includes new media and services as found in support for accessing public service broadcasting in wireless applications (WAP) according to the "must carry" principle (EP 1998: para: 16). In a sense, the European Parliament has not defended public interest in a reactionary or defensive way as some critics may argue (i.e. Holland 1980) but has been proactive in agenda-setting in the legislative procedure (Tsebelis 1995), inviting public hearings, and also informing the public of the need for action. The EP has not enjoyed the same success in its repeated calls for legislation that guarantees pluralism in communications services and content (i.e. EP 1990; EP 1994a; EP 1994b). The case has now been abandoned due to enormous pressures from the industry and an unwilling Commission. (Kaitatzi-Whitlock 1996; Ress and Bröhmer 1998; MEP interview November 1999; Commission officer interview, November 1999).

The *cultural* significance of the EP can be seen in two main areas: the preservation of cultural identities and cultural diversity in Europe and the creation and realization of a new European collective identity. A practical expression of that role and commitment has been the implementation of policy designed to boost the creativity of the audio-visual sector, such as the MEDIA programme.[8] The two concepts of what constitutes European identity, (diversity but also a common concern for peace and prosperity in the area), expand well beyond the members of the European Union to European countries in general. This approach is clearly in opposition to the views of the "audio-visual think tank" of the EC that stated that cultural and linguistic diversity in Europe is an obstacle to economic growth (Think Tank 1994). Still, national agents and young directors have particularly welcomed initiatives such as the

MEDIA programme which is currently well into its third stage (MEDIA Plus) proving to be a permanent institution supporting training and production especially for works in minority languages or of small countries. The protection of European works as a major responsibility of the EU and propagated by the EP, is evident in the famous case of content quotas in the TVWF directive whereby the attempt to include the clause that European works should make up half of the programme content is undermined by the addition of "where practicable." The latter leaves open the possibility for programme providers to not comply with the clause reserving half of the programme quota for European works with the justification that such a task is impossible to fulfil. The clause "where practicable" remained in the amended directive, not because it lacked EP's support but because of the voting mechanism.[9] This indicates that the EP has agreed on the common cause of protecting culture and "the right to create one's own stories" (Tongue 1997) even though this was not fully supported in the weak language of the legislation.

The work of the EP takes on social significance in its promotion of the redistribution of wealth through certain industrial policies. In the field of communication and media, an example of this is the contribution of ten per cent of program budgets or airtime by private channels and media owners to the making of independent films and to European A/V production (TVWF article 5). This might not seem to be a huge contribution but it does lay the foundation for the responsibility of private enterprises towards public interests that are not met through the free market mechanisms. The Parliament's role in the centre of discussions about the interpretation of the Treaties ensures representation of the public interest. The EP's role is significant in that it positions itself against particularistic interests that are easier addressed within the Commission or the European Court of Justice. The Parliament keeps as many aspects as possible open to debate (Héritier 1999). In many cases, the EP provides far more flexibility and freedom to act for the public interest than even national parliaments. Examples of such cases include the resolutions on representation of women in the media and protection of journalistic sources (ie EP 1987; 1993a; 1993b).

## Conclusion

The EP has not been regarded as an influential institution in either liberal or Marxist historical analyses of European integration. Holland for example, does not even refer to the Parliament when he discusses the role of the institutions in capitalist European federalism (Holland 1980: 134). Its increasingly active presence in European politics makes it an institution that cannot be dismissed as passive or insignificant any more. The EP remains an institution derived from the complex process of economic integration and acts as an agent that has shaped itself, expanding its reach to social and cultural areas. It has until now contributed to the making of an exceptional polity that puts the citizen as much as possible to the forefront of this process.

Although the legislative powers of the EP have equipped it with formal influence only in the last decade, its role has been more than legislative. Certainly, the EP has a number of faults, one being that the two largest political parties, social democrats and conservatives, dominate the debates – a situation that, in the long term, means that no radical decisions can ever be made. Also, compared to the power of national parliaments, it does appear to have much less power as it does not elect governments and it has not always been particularly popular, either with the press or with the voters as shown in the low rates of voter participation in Euro-elections. The fact remains however that the EP enjoys some of the most important characteristics for an institution of its size and its role in supranational and international politics. The political *symbolic character* of the EP lies with the role of the institution as the only directly elected international parliament in the world as well as the only democratic representative body in multilateral international organizations. Citizens of one member state not only can vote but also can be elected in another member state.

The European Parliament has contributed to developing and maintaining a discourse focused on the notions of public good and open, universal access to information and communication, predominantly in Europe but also worldwide, as it is often contacted by national governments of small, non-powerful states from around the world, to co-operate with them in this direction. Many European governments have been very happy to provide open access not to citizens but to media moguls. In the very distinct case of the role of PSBs, the EP has managed to save the institution of public service broadcasting and has contributed to assigning it with a new mission, in particular in countries where it has been seen as the state voice. Besides, precisely due to the increased independence of the EP from the restrictions of having to form or support a government, it has been able to represent various standpoints and promote legislation and discourse over issues that would be addressed only with great difficulty by small countries.

Historical determinants, increased transborder trade, and human mobility together with the fact that some member states are among the greatest economic powers of the world have created in Europe unique conditions for integration. Nowadays, non-economic aspects of the integration process occupy more ground than one would have anticipated in the discourse of what is the European Union. The EP has proved to be the major, and in many ways, the only significant forum representing citizens (rather than just consumers), advocating for the concept of public interest rather than private or particularistic interests and the one that puts back in the discussion notions of information welfare and social justice. Although not part of a state as we know it, the EP is part of a governance process that proves to work at multiple levels, taking account of a plurality of opinions. Forms of public representation such as this, no matter how weak, are desperately needed in a world of multilateral agreements, centralized administration, technological advancement, and globalized capital.

# Notes

1   Known as the Hahn Report.

2   With the term "communications policy" I am referring to a wide spectrum of communication means, processes and content that includes "new" and traditional media, telecommunications and information society, as well as content of traditional media (i.e. television.)

3   Commissioner Martin Bangemann was in charge of telecommunications DGXIII.

4   An MEP commenting on the difficulties the Parliament had faced in amending the 1989 Directive said, "we should be happy that there *is* a Directive even." MEP interview given to the author in November 1998.

5   This comment is based on a preliminary study of EP minutes and detailed plenary debates on issues involving broadcasting activities, information society, television without frontiers, pluralism, protection of minors, technological standards, and convergence of communication in the period 1982-1999, by the author.

6   The EP in conciliation with the Council of Ministers created a framework for the free access to major sports events in 1997. Rapporteurs were the Labour MEPs Carole Tongue and Philip Whitehead.

7   The Treaties are the constitutional laws of the European Union. There have been several treaties at several stages of the development of what is known today as the European Union, but up until 1957 the most important one has been the Treaty of Rome (article 2) establishing the European Economic Community (EEC), one of the Communities constituting the European Union today. Other treaties include Euratom and European Coal and Steel Community. The Treaty of Amsterdam, signed in October 1997 and coming into effect in May 1999, extended the provisions laid down by the Maastricht Treaty (the Treaty on the European Union-TEU- in 1993) that created a new organization for the EU based on the three pillars of the European Communities, a Common Foreign and Security Policy (CFSP) and Co-operation in the Fields of Justice and Home Affairs (JHA). The Amsterdam Treaty was significant for the integration process as it brought further institutional and policy "maturing," by strengthening the decision-making processes and capacity of the EU. One of the most important provisions was the expansion of the co-decision procedure to more policy spheres. For an extended discussion, see Nugent (1999).

8   Measures for the development of the audio-visual industries.

9   For a discussion of the voting system and policy-making in the E.U. see Corbett, Jacobs, and Shackleton (2000); Wallace & Wallace eds. (2000); Hix (1999); and Nugent (1999).

# References

Caporaso, J A. 1998. Integration Theory, Past and Future. In *European Integration and Supranational Governance*, edited by W. Sandholtz & A. Stone Sweet. Oxford: Oxford University Press.

Christiansen, T., K. E., Jørgensen and A. Wiener. 1999. The Social Construction of Europe. *Journal of European Public Policy* 6, 4: 528.

Collins, R. 1994. *Broadcasting and the Audio-visual Policy in the Single European Market*. London: John Libbey.

Commission of the European Communities. 1994. *Europe and the Global Information Society*. Bangemann Task Force Report to the European Council.

Commission of the European Communities. 1994. *Green Paper on Strategy Options to Strengthen the European Programme Industry in the Context of the Audio-visual Policy of the European Union*. Brussels: COM(94)96 final.

Coombes, D. 1999. *Seven Theorems in Search of the European Parliament*. London: Federal Trust Series.

Corbett, R. F., F. Jacobs and M. Shackleton. 2000. *The European Parliament*, 4th Ed. London: John Harper.

Dent, C.M. 1997. *The European Economy. The Global Context*. London: Routledge.

European Commission. 1995a. European Parliament and Council Directive amending Council Directive 89/552/EEC on the co-ordination of certain provisions laid down by law, regulation or administrative action in Member States concerning the pursuit of television broadcasting activities. COM (95)0086.

European Communities. 1997. Treaty of Amsterdam Amending the Treaty on European Union, the Treaties Establishing the European Communities and Certain Related Acts. Luxembourg: Office for Official Publications of the European Communities.

European Parliament. 1982. Resolution on Radio and Television Broadcasting in the European Community. In European Communities, *Official Journal of the European Communities* OJ No C87/109-112, 05 April.

European Parliament. 1987. Darstellung der Frauen in den Massenmedien (Dok. A2-95/87) 13.10.87 in Verhandlungen des Europäischen Parlaments Nr2-356: 65.

European Parliament. 1993a. Bericht des Ausschusses für Grundfreiheiten und innere Angelegenheiten über die Meinungsfreiheit und die Presse-oder Informationsfreiheit, A3-0282/93, PE200.619 endg.

European Parliament. 1993b. Bericht des Ausschusses für Recht und Bürgerrechte über die Geheimhaltung journalistischer Quellen und die Auskunftsbefugnis der Beamten, A3-0434/93, PE 205.642endg./TeilA.

European Parliament. 1990. Resolution on Media Takeovers and Mergers OJC 68/137-138. 15 February.

European Parliament. 1984. Resolution on Broadcast Communication in the European Community (the Threat to Diversity of Opinion Posed by the Commercialization of New Media), (30.03.1984), in OJ No C 117/198-201, 30.04.1984.

European Parliament. 1994a. *Debate on Pluralism and Concentration of Ownership*. Verbatim Reports of Session Proceedings. 19-20 January: 345- 356.

European Parliament. 1994b. *Resolution on the Commission Green Paper Pluralism and Media Concentration in the Internal Market* OJ C 44/179 14 February.

European Parliament. 1995a. MEDIA II- Fortbildung- Projektentwicklung und Vertrieb in *Verhandlungen des Europäischen Parlaments* Nr. 4-464/257: 15.6.1995.

European Parliament. 1995b. Politik im audiovisuellen Bereich in *Verhandlungen des Europäischen Parlaments* Nr. 4-464/270: 15.6.1995.

European Parliament. 1996. Public service television Resolution on the role of public service television in a multi-media society A4-0243/1996 02/07/1996 in OJ C277 23-SEP-96 004.

European Parliament. 1998. *Report on the Communication from the Commission: Green Paper on the Convergence of the Telecommunications, Media and Information Technology Sectors, and the Implications for Regulation* (COM(97)0623-C4-0664/97) A4-0328/98.

*European Report.* 1998. October 14, No 2350.

*Financial Times* 1998. 21 October.

Héritier, A. 1999. Elements of Democratic Legitimation in Europe: an alternative perspective. *Journal of European Public Policy* 6 (2):269-282.

Hix, S. 1999. *The Political System of the European Union.* London: St Martin's Press.

Hoffmann-Riem, W. 1996. *Regulating Media: The Licensing and Supervision of Broadcasting in Six Countries.* New York: The Guilford Press.

Holland, S. 1980. *Uncommon Market.* MacMillan: London.

Interviews by the author with Members of the European Parliament and European Commission officials and other E.P. and E.C. officials (total of 35) in Brussels in November, 1998 and June, 2000.

Jovanovic, M. 1998. *International Economic Integration, Limits and Prospects.* London: Routledge.

Kaitatzi-Whitlock, S. 1996. Pluralism and Media Concentration in Europe. *European Journal of Communication* 11(4):453- 483.

Kleinsteuber, H J. 1998. Media Concentration and the Public Interest. In *Media Policy: Convergence, Concentration and Commerce,* edited by D. McQuail & K. Siune. London: Sage.

Mansell, R. 1993. *The New Telecommunications: A Political Economy of Network Evolution,* London: Sage.

McQuail, D. 1998. Commercialisation and Beyond. In *Media Policy: Convergence, Concentration and Commerce,* edited by D. McQuail & K. Siune. London: Sage.

Middlemas, K. 1995. *Orchestrating Europe. The Informal Politics of European Union 1973-1995.* London: Fontana Press.

Nugent, N. 1999. *The Government and Politics of the European Union.* London: St Martin's Press.

Ress, G. and J. Bröhmer. 1998. *Europäische Gemeinschaft und Medienvielfalt.* Frankfurt am Main: Marburger Medienschriften.

Sandholtz, W. and A. Stone Sweet. 1998. *European Integration and Supranational Governance.* Oxford: Oxford University Press.

Sarikakis, K. 2000. Citizenship and Media Policy in the Semi-Periphery: the Greek Case. *The Cyprus Review* 12(2):117-133.

Think Tank. 1994. *Report by the Think-Tank on the Audio-visual Policy in the European Union*. Luxembourg: Office for Official Publications of the European Communities.

Thussu, D. 2000. *International Communication, Continuity and Change*. London: Arnold.

Tongue, C. 1998. Letter to Karel Van Miert, European Commission Proposed Guidelines on Public Service Broadcasting. September 22.

Tongue, C. 1997. Speaking notes for the adoption of the Television Without Frontiers Directive, Monday 9 June 1997, The office of Carole Tongue, Brussels Belgium.

Tsebelis, G. 1995. Conditional Agenda-Setting and Decision-Making Inside the European Parliament. In *The Journal of Legislative Studies* 1(1):65-93.

TVWF Article 5, European Communities. 1997. Directive 97/36/EC of the European Parliament and of the Council of 30 June 1997 amending Council Directive 89/552/EEC on the co-ordination of certain provisions laid down by law, regulation or administrative action in Member States concerning the pursuit of television broadcasting activities, OJ L 202, 30.07.97/ 60 - 71.

Venturelli, S. 1998. *Liberalising the European Media*. Oxford: Oxford University Press.

Wallace, H. and W. Wallace (eds.) 2000. *Policy-Making in the European Union*. Oxford: Oxford University Press.

Winseck, D. 1998. *Re-convergence*. Creskill (New Jersey): Hampton Press.

# Asserting Cultural and Social Regulatory Principles in Converging Media Systems

**Ben Goldsmith, Julian Thomas, Tom O'Regan and Stuart Cunningham**

Despite many recent and innovative developments in supranational, multilateral and indeed global levels of influence on media policy, the engine rooms of media policy development remain squarely at a national level, and this will continue into the foreseeable future. Policy analysts must therefore continue to compare and contrast the regulatory initiatives now apparent across the diverse field of national policy developments. To this end, this chapter seeks to generalize from many major national contexts some common issues and viable responses to meeting the challenges of preserving or even enhancing cultural and social objectives within converging media systems.

While the landscape of these converged media environments will vary from country to country, it is widely expected that such environments may be characterized by a range of technological and commercial developments including:

- the transition to digital encoding and transmission;
- more efficient and extensive use of spectrum;
- a more competitive and market-driven environment;
- multi-channel programming;
- interactive services;
- rapid application and content development and innovation;
- the growth of subscription and pay-per-view media, and the continuing relative decline of free- to-air broadcasting;
- new economies of scope in the provision of broadcast and telecommunications systems; and

- the erosion of distinctions between conventional systems.

None of these developments is inevitable; we can make few assumptions about when or to what extent such an environment will exist in any individual country. In addition, it is uncertain how users will respond to the new broadcasting environment. Regulatory systems will need to be responsive and flexible enough to accommodate changes to industry shape, structure and output, all influenced by the ways in which readers, listeners, and viewers take up new services.

While a wide range of cultural and social policy objectives are embedded in media regulations and legislation world-wide, recurring core elements include: educating and informing audiences; responsiveness to audience needs; developing and maintaining national/communal identities through cultural expression; encouraging access, equity and participation in culture; promoting cultural diversity through the facilitation of a range of programming and sources of information that might not otherwise be available; promoting high quality and/or innovative programming.

## The Forward Policy Environment

The transition to digital broadcasting presents a range of political, economic, and technical challenges for policy-makers, regulators and media players. However, it is a mistake to assume that the forward policy environment will *necessarily* be more difficult for achieving cultural policy outcomes such as ensuring a place for local television content. It is likely that the majority of these new services will be discretionary services, but it is also possible that licenses will be issued for new free-to-air services. While the entry of new services will result in fragmentation of audiences and revenue, they may well increase competition for local audio-visual product, and offset the historical decline in license fees. Since digitization enhances the capacity of different platforms to carry essentially similar kinds of services and content, program rights may be exploited across multiple platforms or through multiple "windows." Rights holders therefore have the potential and the incentive to maximize revenue by distributing their product across a number of delivery systems.

New opportunities may arise for the achievement of cultural policy outcomes such as the promotion and representation of cultural diversity in the new broadcasting environment. In Europe, the number and type of available television channels expanded dramatically during the 1990s. Partly in response to a backlash from viewers demanding local and regional programming, partly due to the emphasis at the European Union (EU) level on regionalism over nationalism, and partly as a result of policy developments that encouraged regional service as part of their public interest obligations, both public and private channels and networks began to rethink the emphasis they had placed in previous years on centralized operations and international entertainment programming. The broadcasters "became receptive to 'proximity programming' as a global competitive strategy."

On a local scale, more and more cities set up their own channels, whether public, private or mixed. Even large national private networks became interested in this phenomenon and began to place their bets on more regional or local windows. This is the case, for example, of the Spanish channels Antenna 3 TV and Tele Cinco, or the British channel ITV. In Denmark, the commercial channel TV2 has a network of eight regional centres that broadcast daily off-the-network programming to their respective territories.... Something similar happens with the private Swedish channel TV4, which broadcasts 15 local windows on a daily basis through the same number of associated local television stations. In Germany, the national private channels SAT1 and RTL broadcast regional disconnections, though it must be said that they do so by legal obligation more than by their own desire to do so (De Moragas Spà, Garitaonandía and López 1999: 8-9).

While the ways in which this strategy is pursued are not homogeneous (De Moragas Spà et. al. identify seven different models of regional television development in Europe), they share an imperative to respond to and represent cultural, linguistic, political, demographic and geographic diversity. Moreover, in Canada, where the television environment is highly developed, diverse and fragmented, content regulations have recently been extended rather than relaxed, as we discuss below. In the new environment, a number of new challenges to content regulation are emerging. These include:

*The end of "quid pro quo" rationales for content regulation.* These rationales are often associated with real or artificially created conditions of spectrum scarcity: privileged access to the spectrum is said to be balanced by requirements to provide particular kinds of program services. While analog terrestrial television is likely to continue for at least a decade in most developed countries, digital conversion promises to free up spectrum eventually. Digital conversion of cable networks will also significantly increase their capacity and the range of services that may be offered.

The potential declining relevance of the system of quid pro quos does not mean that content regulation will be impossible to achieve or to justify. While the increase in spectrum availability promised by digitization brings into question justifications for restrictions on market entry, it does not follow that justifications for content regulation are also compromised. Content regulation has traditionally been justified on the basis of the social influence of the medium; while new market conditions may encourage debate about the *relative* influence of discretionary and free-to-air media, the basic justification for content regulation is not necessarily undermined.

Many countries achieve local content goals without relying on a system of trade-offs. Canada is one example of a diverse multi-channel television environment in which content regulation is a core part of broadcasting policy but is not premised upon quid pro quo arrangements. New Zealand does not use content regulation, but has nonetheless evolved a series of mechanisms designed to ensure a place for local programming in a deregulated broadcasting environment.

*The future role of the public service broadcasters.* Previous estimates of the necessary marginalization of public broadcasters in the transition to a multi-channel environment (e.g. Tracey 1998) are being revised. A number of commentators now argue that regulation designed for social and cultural objectives may be most transparently and efficiently achieved by public broadcasters funded by governments for those specific purposes.[1] In Australia, the ABC is seeking to extend its regional programming and coverage, and both multi-channeling and datacasting may substantially increase levels of Australian and children's content available to its viewers.

*Access and interoperability.* New, increasingly powerful conditional access (CA) systems, navigation aids, and information management tools such as electronic program guides (EPGs) will require regulators to develop mechanisms (standards and must-carry requirements, for example) to ensure that viewers are not prevented from accessing the full range of channels and services. Cross-ownership exists between the developers of CA systems and media organizations. For example, News Corporation has a 100 per cent interest in the UK-based NDS, a leading global provider of CA and interactive television systems.

While these may be predominantly issues for competition regulators, they also have implications for content regulators. As the new multi-channel environment fragments audiences for broadcasting services, navigation aids become essential devices to enable the viewer to locate desired content. Navigation aids therefore have the potential to influence viewing patterns, and "any bias in the listing will have serious implications for content providers" and for viewers (Cowie and Marsden 1998: par. 20). The European Directive on the Use of Standards for the Transmission of Television Signals, adopted in 1995, attempts to deal with some of these issues by mandating equal access for all broadcasters to conditional access systems.[2]

*Regulatory convergence.* Telecommunications policy in the aftermath of deregulation has tended to define the regulatory function as one of serving the public interest by securing competition and assisting the smooth functioning of the market. Broadcasting policy on the other hand has traditionally been oriented around controls on market entry whereby the public interest is secured and served by the exercise of particular regulatory powers as trade-offs for those controls. In recent years, a growing body of commentary from the academic, industry and government sectors has argued that convergence creates irresistible pressures to integrate the institutions of telecommunications and media regulation both at the organizational level of regulation, and at the level of norms, or laws.[3] There are some features of telecommunications policy that bear a resemblance to broadcasting policy. In particular the principle of asymmetric regulation similarly imposes special conditions on dominant players analogous to the current differential content requirements of free-to-air and pay television broadcasters.

Yet it seems reasonable to expect that digitization will actually increase public use and dependence on screen-based media for information, entertainment, education and other public services. It therefore seems likely that there will be a continuing need for regulators with specialist skills and expertise in managing a regulatory framework that continues to serve the public interest in broadcasting, and in particular promotes and protects the interests of children. This may mean that social bases for regulation may need to be strengthened, which would both bolster and be informed by arguments for the regulation of children's programming, regional programming, and diversity in programming on social as well as cultural grounds.

*Governmental and non-governmental responses to liberalizing trade in services.* Despite the failure of the World Trade Organization's (WTO) 3rd Ministerial Conference in Seattle in November 1999 to strike an agreement on a work program for the "Millennium Round" of multilateral trade negotiations, and despite disagreement over the extent of the issues to be covered by the round, the WTO decided to begin negotiations on trade in audio-visual services in 2000. The majority of negotiating nations did not make specific commitments to liberalize trade in the audio-visual sector in the GATT round which concluded in 1993. Many took out exceptions to the "most favoured nation" rule for the purposes of cultural preservation to enable the retention of measures that support the domestic audio-visual sector, such as broadcasting quotas, subsidy mechanisms, and co-production agreements. While Canada and the EU, led by France, have continued to seek ways to make protections for cultural industries non-negotiable, other nations appear less committed. With the Australian government's primary focus on agriculture, despite their commitment to some form of cultural exemption in the past, audio-visual services and other lower priority areas could become bargaining chips to be traded away in order to achieve the desired result in agriculture.

On a positive note, Canada's response to the adverse findings of the WTO Dispute Resolution Tribunal in its periodicals dispute with the United States has been to seek to "forum shift." This option would shift discussions and the potential for multilateral or a series of bilateral deals to a new decision-making forum (Braithwaite and Drahos 2000: 28-9). These fora may include the International Network on Cultural Policy, a network of over 40 national cultural ministers that was established in 1998 following the United Nations Educational, Scientific and Cultural Organization (UNESCO) Intergovernmental Conference on Cultural Policies for Development, or the International Network for Cultural Diversity, a network of over 200 non-governmental organizations. The Canadians see these groups as important sites at which international coalitions premised on the preservation and maintenance of cultural sovereignty mechanisms (eg content regulations) may be established.

*The Changing Structure of Audio-visual Production.* Recent mergers have enabled multinational media corporations to enter new markets and consolidate their positions in old ones. After the failure to gain agreement on liberalizing audio-visual services in the Uruguay Round, big Hollywood players began investing in ventures and partnerships in Italy, Germany, the Czech Republic, Ireland, Australia, New Zealand and South Africa. These centres now compete with Canada, the UK and Mexico for the rising levels of "runaway" or "footloose" production, with governments offering a range of incentives to attract major projects. The local cultural relevance of these productions is hotly contested. They do generate employment and investment in the domestic economy, they help develop the skill base in the local production industry, and they offer heightened exposure for the work of local cast and crew. Historically Australia, like other comparable production sites, has carefully managed the interface between the domestic and international production industries by balancing industrial development policies against those protecting and promoting cultural identity and diversity. These internationalizing tendencies may require the management of this interface to be reappraised with implications for cultural policy objectives such as the preservation of a space for local content.

## An Analysis of National Policy Responses

As David A. Levy (1999) notes in *Europe's Digital Revolution: Broadcasting, the EU and the Nation State*, there has been no common response to digitization. Models developed in different countries have been driven by the particular political and market structures pertaining in those countries. Nevertheless, some developments show that national governments and parliaments retain significant advantage if there is political and community will to assert cultural and social regulatory principles.

*The European Union: Program quotas, "Must Carry" requirements, and the extended role of public service broadcasters.* The *Television Without Frontiers Directive* (89/552/EEC and 97/36/EC ) requires broadcasters to screen a majority of European programming "where practicable," and to reserve ten per cent of airtime or program budgets for productions sourced from independent companies within the EU. Additional cultural or public interest obligations on broadcasters tend to be confined to the public broadcasting sector. In the private terrestrial broadcasting sector, measures to achieve the public interest goal of media pluralism or diversity tend to take the form of ownership and control restrictions such as market share (or "share of voice") limits. This can be seen to be a legacy of the relatively recent end in many countries of the monopoly in broadcasting services enjoyed by state-owned public broadcasters. The digital television market in Europe is dominated by subscription satellite and cable services. Given that additional cultural or public interest obligations tend to be concentrated in the public broadcasting sector, most EU member states have introduced "must carry" requirements on digital cable and satellite operators to ensure that as transmission services multiply, viewers retain access to public service broadcasting.[4] In a number of countries, priority access or "gifted" capacity has been given (or is planned to be given) to incumbent terrestrial broadcasters, as in Australia. And several countries have reserved capacity for local or regional stations (This is the case in Sweden and Spain, and is being considered in France).

There are a number of problems with the EU systems, including difficulties in adequately policing airtime and in programming budget-based quota systems. There is also differential support among member states, with France well out in front in compliance zeal. One commentator even argues that the directive actually served to weaken national controls and enabled the entry of American programming because no limits were placed on imported programming, and because the definition of "European works" extended to official co-productions and programs made in Europe by non-European producers (Venturelli 1998: 202-5). The EU has been more successful in its development of pan-European production subsidy systems.

*United Kingdom: Production quotas, regionalism and the digital licence fee.* The UK ups the ante on the *Television Without Frontiers Directive* in terms of overall levels of European (read: British) content, independent production company sourcing as well as having a firm commitment to regionalism in programming. The UK government has accepted that the BBC required additional funding "to ensure that it continues to act as a benchmark of quality in the digital world" (Department of Culture, Media and Sport 2000: 1). The television licence fee will be increased by 1.5 per cent above the rate of inflation between April 2000 and 2006-07. This move is expected to earn the BBC an additional £200 million per year on average. The emphasis on regional programming both in the UK and in Canada as a means to increase local content should be explored further in countries like Australia, which has not had a worthwhile regional broadcasting policy focus since the late 1980s. The introduction of datacasting and any future extension of multi-channelling may offer the opportunity to institute some form of regional requirement upon service providers.

*United Kingdom: A sliding scale of regulation.* As part of the British government's ongoing planning for a regulatory framework appropriate for the digital broadcasting environment, it commissioned a number of "expert papers" from leading scholars, consultants and industry figures.[5]

Forgan and Tambini, in their *Content* paper, recommend the replacement of the principle of detailed regulation of all broadcasting with a formal version of the "existing de facto sliding scale of regulation according to the degree of consumer expectation of regulation and market share." At opposite ends of the scale are the heavily regulated core public channels (BBC and Channel 4) with a remit to provide a broad, universally accessible service, and lightly or unregulated channels targeted at niche audiences. Beginning from the twin premises that regulation can no longer be technology-specific, and that a distinction must be maintained between "invasive mass media where content regulation applies" and "private media where freedom of speech concerns prevail," Forgan and Tambini propose "a single graded classification of communications services irrespective of delivery method which would take account both of historic and of developing circumstances." Under this scheme, content regulation is determined partly on the basis of the "privileges" the content provider enjoys (for example, extent of spectrum access, EPG prominence, or "must carry" status), and partly on the basis of an index measuring invasiveness, pervasiveness, "publicness," and influence by two indicators: Consumer Expectations and Market Share, or CEMS.

Such a model offers the benefits of flexibility and responsiveness to changing situations: the rating of services would be determined by the addition of the two indicators, and this rating would in turn determine the "broad regulatory band" into which the service would fall. In addition, the model offers the benefit of constant testing against consumer attitudes, since "consumer expectations" could be systematically determined by an accumulation of methods: traditional research methods employed by market research companies; special surveys; complaint logs; and "citizens' juries," or community panels. And it can be adapted to apply to a range of current or future broadcasting services.[6]

But while the model offers the benefits of flexibility and adaptability, it also contains substantial "regulatory risk" in that the proposal to submit content regulation to constant testing against community attitudes may not offer sufficient certainty to investors and local content producers in planning production activity.

The White Paper (DTI/DCMS 2000) does not adopt the CEMS model in its entirety, but the new regulatory framework does appear to borrow from Forgan and Tambini's ideas. The priorities of flexibility and the sliding scale or differential regulation among broadcasters are maintained. The White Paper proposes four tiers of regulation for broadcasting. The first establishes standards across all broadcasting services for negative content, advertising and sponsorship, fairness and accuracy in news. The second empowers the new single regulator, OFCOM, to regulate quantitative and measurable obligations of 'the public service broadcasters', which the Report understands to include not only the BBC, Channel 4 and Channel 5, but also the commercial ITV network. These statutory obligations include independent and original production quotas, regional production and programming targets, and peak time news services. The third tier consists of qualitative obligations relating to program mix in the form of legislated levels of educational, children's, religious, arts, science and international affairs programming for public service broadcasters other than the BBC. The BBC must fulfil additional content requirements under the terms of its Charter and Agreement. The fourth tier, "tier zero" (White Paper: 56) governs broadcasting on the Internet and via telephony. Certain evaluative mechanisms are flagged. OFCOM will have the power to conduct surveys and citizens' juries, and to "establish bodies to reflect the public interest in the content of communications services" (: 72). In addition, an independently appointed consumer panel will ensure that consumer interests, which are described as "the heart of future regulation", are protected. The principle of the sliding scale provides an important elaboration of a differential, content regulation system involving more individuated negotiations between regulator and regulated in a multi-channel environment.

*Iceland: Advertising supported subsidy.* As in most European countries, in Iceland cultural obligations are centred on the public broadcasting sector, although both public and private broadcasters are expected to promote Icelandic culture and language. Ten per cent of broadcast advertising revenue is directed to the Broadcasting Cultural Fund (Menningarsjodur utvarpsstodva). The Fund provides finances to broadcasters and independent producers for the production of cultural and educational programming. Iceland's approach has the advantage of transparency, although the system has failed to meet its objectives of achieving 50 per cent Icelandic content on any channel (see Karlsson et. al. 2000).

*Finland: Contestable funds.* The state-owned broadcaster YLE is partly funded by "public service fees" levied on commercial broadcasters. In a report to the Organization for Economic Co-Operation and Development (OECD), the Finnish Competition Authority recommended the tendering out of YLE's public service obligations to allow all producers to compete for available funds. This suggestion is taken up by the OECD (1999b) in its report *Regulation and Competition Issues in Broadcasting in the Light of Convergence*, which recommends the introduction of "a system of contestable funds under which broadcasters compete with each other for the screening of content which meets the 'public service' criteria" (: 11). While by no means recommending the reallocation of public broadcasters' budgets to contestable funds, an alternative might be the treatment of local content provision as a universal service obligation that can be auctioned in much the same way that spectrum is auctioned.

*The United States: Pay or play?* The 1998 document *Charting the Digital Broadcasting Future* by the US Advisory Committee on Public Interest Obligations of Digital Television Broadcasters (known as the Gore Commission report) canvassed a number of approaches to promote public interest goals. These approaches are characterized by their flexibility, which is considered an essential attribute of a regulatory framework for digital broadcasting. The Commission acknowledged that questions remain as to how public interest obligations should apply to digital television broadcasters that choose to multiplex or multicast. The Report considers whether the licensee's public interest obligations apply to the signal as a whole thereby enabling the licensee to determine which of its program streams, or what mix of program streams would air the public interest programming. Alternatively, the obligations might be applied to each program stream offered by a licensee. The Report recommends that digital television broadcasters who choose to multiplex should assume *greater* public interest obligations, but be permitted the flexibility to choose between paying fees, providing a dedicated public service programming channel, or making in-kind contributions to fulfill public interest obligations.

One approach is the "pay or play" option whereby broadcasters would have the option of providing public interest programming of a specified level or quality, or paying another broadcaster to provide that programming. This model draws on the precedent of the Children's Television Act which allows licensees to meet part of their obligations by demonstrating "special efforts … to produce or support [children's educational] programming broadcast by another station in the licensee's Marketplace" (47 USC 303b(b)(2)). A variation of this approach, the "spectrum check-off" model, requires broadcasters to adhere to public interest programming obligations, or pay a fee for the use of spectrum. The revenue raised would then be devoted to the production of public interest programming. However, as the report notes, the "spectrum check-off" model is a one-off (or annual) deal, while the "pay or play" model could allow a number of trades in any given year. Both of these models are in effect forms of tradable quotas. Unsurprisingly, perhaps, these proposals met with substantial opposition from representatives of broadcasters.

*Canada: Refining quotas.* Canada provides the most sustained example of differential content regulations. As an early adopter of cable and satellite television, Canada has had a long history of operating local content regulations in a fragmented media environment. The Canadian government is seeking to mirror and refine analog requirements for content and distribution in the new digital environment. A new framework from September 2000 expands the designation of under-represented or priority programs; introduces new requirements for regionally produced programming, both news and non-news; amends the particular regulations applying to the largest multi-station ownership groups; and alters the system of time credits for Canadian drama.[7] In addition to existing transmission quotas that require Canadian programs to make up not less than 60 per cent of the broadcast year, and not less than 50 per cent of the six o'clock to midnight evening broadcast period, the new system defines three new types of priority programs: Canadian long-form documentary; Canadian regionally-produced programs (programs at least 30 minutes long in which principal photography occurred at least 150 kilometres from Montreal, Toronto or Vancouver); and Canadian entertainment magazine programs. The new schedule of programming definitions is also extended to apply to pay and specialty licensees in addition to conventional licensees.

The new rules extend the practice of differential regulation and allow the Canadian Radio-television and Telecommunications Commission (CRTC) greater flexibility in its dealings with groups holding multiple licenses by introducing a new procedure whereby the renewal of all conventional television licenses held or controlled by a group will generally be considered at the same time. This new procedure is designed to be responsive to corporate strategies, and to allow each group "to differentiate itself and brand its programming and scheduling to attract maximum audience" (CRTC 1999-97 par. 13). Smaller groups are also encouraged under the new system to "experiment with new genres of Canadian programming and new ways to meet the needs of their audiences" (CRTC 1999-97 par. 15). Differentially applied minimum expenditure requirements on Canadian programming for pay and specialty channels will be maintained. All cable broadcasters were required to carry the Aboriginal People's Television Network (formerly Television Northern Canada) as an essential national service along with the public service Canadian Broadcasting Corporation and certain commercial networks.

Canadian moves to give greater weighting to regional and infotainment programming signal a shift in priority of content regulation to include these alongside a continuing emphasis upon drama and social documentary. While the latter advance core cultural objectives such as quality, innovation and cultural expression, the former warrant greater consideration in converging media systems in terms of their contribution to diversity, representation, access and equity.

## Policy Strategies

It is a truism that there are a variety of models for, and practices of, cultural and social policy approaches to regulating media. There are not so many, however, that a great deal cannot be learned from related experience. As we have seen, new targets or approaches at a national level continue to be valuable. Apart from established media content (fictional drama, social documentary) traditionally targeted for input (subvention) or output (regulatory) support, governments may also target new types (certain forms of infotainment, under-represented sports). Regional (intra-country) representation is also on the agenda. The potential of digital broadcasting may be harnessed to advance social objectives such as access and equity and cultural objectives such as innovation (the latter through supporting new types of production as barriers to entry diminish). Some further challenges remain for maintaining cultural and social objectives during convergence, suggesting that some creative approaches may be necessary.

### Rethinking quota systems

How can quota systems cope with multi-channelling, interactive programming, and new media content?

*Multi-channelling.* Quotas for national, regional, local, or children's content relate to the national system as a whole rather than individual stations, which nevertheless have a requirement to account for a certain proportion of the total. This creates the possibility of a quota market, where quotas have a negative value and may be traded between different elements of the system, either license holders, stations, or channels within a multiplex. The purpose of such an arrangement would be to improve the efficiency of the quota system by concentrating local or children's content broadcasting among those services best placed to provide them. This would have the additional benefit of placing a clear value on the regulatory requirement.

*Interactive programming.* Time-based programming rules lose their force when content can be either streamed in real time, "trickled" down for local storage, or delivered on demand, (or nearly on demand). While the viewing duration of programs can still be stipulated, this will no longer equate to transmission time. Regulations specifying the time of day when quota material must be broadcast may also need to be reframed around specific periods of *availability* rather than *transmission.*

*New media content.* Should any quotas – transmission quotas or sub-quotas – apply to content that differs from traditional broadcast programming? Should modified quotas capture, for example, a hyperlinked form of interactive drama, or a vector graphic-based educational puzzle designed for children? Such material may well appear to meet the cultural and social objectives of broadcasting policy, and there may be other desirable outcomes to be achieved by encouraging the development of content of this sort alongside traditional screen content. Policy-makers seeking to adapt existing rules will clearly need to review generic programming categories.

## Rethinking subsidies

Subsidy models are widely used internationally. They enjoy advantages of transparency, flexibility, and adaptability for market-driven sectors. As budgeted transfers, they can be regularly evaluated. Further, the overall size of the subsidy need not be tied to the output of a specific number of channels. Nevertheless, there are significant emerging issues for subsidy policies in converging media environments.

*Broadcasting subsidy or production subsidy?* The objective of diversity of content might be assisted by a scheme that distributes funds widely. But should the subsidy be paid to content producers or to broadcasters? Clearly, the critical policy requirement is that subsidized material actually be broadcast, so payments to producers cannot be the sole strategy.

*How are broadcasters to be defined?* In converging media systems, providers of culturally or socially desirable screen content may use platforms other than traditional broadcasting vehicles. If audiences rather than technologies will measure the success of subsidies, then policy-makers should avoid platform-specific regulation wherever possible. Where such distinctions are unavoidable, more sophisticated devices such as Forgan and Tambini's CEMS index (discussed above) may be useful.

*How should the subsidy be allocated?* Should a subsidy fund be contestable, as some have suggested, or should it simply be allocated to eligible persons who fulfill necessary criteria? The answer may depend on the cultural or social purpose of the subsidy. For example, in the case of a cultural subsidy, allocation might be contestable according to cost, or quality, or both. The question of quality benchmarks for subsidized content will become more central as the quantum of content inexorably increases to fill the burgeoning digital "space." Options for allocating subsidies through market mechanisms are discussed below.

*Who should pay the subsidy?* Industry funding could be adapted for a subsidy-driven model of content regulation. Broadcasters could contribute levies into an industry fund, perhaps on the basis of a CEMS-style index if technological neutrality was desired. On the other hand, governments could provide subsidies as a budgeted program of transfers.

*Should subsidies be combined with market mechanisms?* The efficiency of subsidies may be increased by market mechanisms for allocation, and it is to these possibilities that we finally turn.

## Using market mechanisms to achieve universal coverage

Access to broadcasting services remains an issue for analog transmission today; the complexity and uncertainty of digital conversion will ensure that it remains a significant factor in future media policy.

A number of relevant market models have been developed in the field of telecommunications policy. In telecommunications, auctions of universal service obligations are claimed to provide a mechanism that enables the regulator to intervene in the operation of the market to meet social policy goals without restricting competition. Weller, Milgrom and Salant have developed a model "in which the obligation is *symmetric* (in that it can be applied to firms other than the incumbent) and *multilateral* (it involves a transaction entered into voluntarily, in which the carrier takes on the obligation in return for compensation)" (Weller 1999: 646 n. 2). Weller further notes that the model has a precedent in the US where subsidies to service "unprofitable" airline routes are competitively tendered.

Another example is the model developed by Peha (1999) for tradable universal service obligations for telecommunications providers, which is analogous to the regulation of air pollution in the US and is claimed to work best at times when an industry is in transition, for example during privatization, deregulation, or the periodic release of spectrum. In this model, providers or operators are motivated to roll out or "build out" infrastructure in underserved areas under a system where those commitments are "bundled with one or more items of value" such as "the infrastructure of the government carrier, permission to operate (a license), access to spectrum, and freedom from regulation for some fixed period" (1999: 366). To help operators achieve appropriate levels of expansion, Peha proposes a system of "universal service funds" – effectively, subsidies for commercial providers' expansion into unserved areas. He cites the example of Chile in which aspirant and established operators bid for the smallest subsidy necessary to fulfill particular milestones set by the regulator.

In a 1998 report for the European Commission Directorate-General XIII, Analysys, Squire, Sanders and Dempsey (1998) suggest that the model for universal service provision then operating in the telecommunications sector in Germany, Austria and Luxembourg might provide a model by which market forces can play a greater role in the provision of "public service missions" in the broadcasting sector.

Under that regulatory model, there exists a general presumption that universal service is being provided. Insofar as market failure suggests that universal service is not being provided, market players may tender to be able to provide such service. In the event that the provision of such service proves to be uneconomic, a mechanism has been established which foresees contributions being made by all relevant market players (: 219).

But other commentators argue that the universal service ideal, either as it is understood in public service broadcasting or in telecommunications, cannot be translated to broadband services because "it has to do with access to networks; it does not address access to services and content" (Blackman 1998).

There may then be an argument for government or industry subsidy in the form of a platform-neutral "equivalent digital coverage fund." This might take the form, for example, of government subsidizing provision of set-top digital receivers. Measures of this sort may be necessary to achieve a final analog switch-off in under-served areas where the value of the spectrum may not be sufficiently high to induce market-based spectrum clearance.

## Conclusion

Notwithstanding globalizing ideology that asserts that the nation is going out of business, national governments continue to develop models and working policy frameworks for asserting cultural and social principles in converging media systems. They do this, however, knowing that the environment for such activity is changing very rapidly and in very complex, unchartered ways. The final report of the Canadian Working Group on Cultural Policy for the 21st Century laid out the challenge for national governments when it identified three types of policy response to converging and globalizing media. The first approach assumes that "the force of technology is unstoppable and…public policy must acknowledge its impotence in the face of these changes."

In this view, we must dismantle any regulatory mechanisms, disabuse public policy of the capacity to regulate the Internet, and surrender control to the laws of the marketplace, which will dictate broadcasting policy based on commercial Darwinism (Canadian Conference of the Arts 1998: 38).

The second approach proposed that "existing measures be reoriented to results": "Public policy decides what the most desirable outcomes must be and then allows broadcasters all the latitude necessary to meet these objectives." The Working Group supported this approach arguing that it combined an orientation to results with flexibility. The third approach entailed "an unquestioning defence of the status quo in a rapidly evolving industry" which "may be the most direct route to the eventual dismantling of the whole policy and regulatory system" (: 39).

Similarly, the Australian Department of Communication, Information Technology and the Arts' (2000) *Convergence Report* agrees also with the second approach, arguing that the most appropriate response is one in which the "desired outcomes do not change, but the means of achieving them do" (: 31). This chapter has been written in this spirit.

## Notes

1  The future role of public broadcasters is further discussed in Andrew Graham et. al. (1999); Steve Vizard (2000) in which it is suggested that the national broadcaster "would need to provide exclusively Australian content programming, information and entertainment services" in order for Australian voices to be heard; Miquel de Moragas Spá, Carmelo Garitaonandía and Bernat López (eds.) (1999); the NZ On Air symposium on broadcasting policy in New Zealand (1999).

2  Directive 95/47/EC of the European Parliament and of the Council of 24 October 1995 on the use of standards for the transmission of television signals *Official Journal L* 281, 23/11/1995: 0051 – 0054.

3  Much of this debate was sparked by a report prepared for the European Commission's Information Society Directorate-General, KPMG (1996) *Public Policy Issues Arising From Telecommunications and Audio-visual Convergence*, a report prepared for DG XIII, London September 1996. The idea was taken up and promoted by Commissioner Martin Bangemann in a number of key speeches. See also Natascha Just and Michael Latzer (2000) "EU Competition Policy and Market Power Control in the Mediamatics Era" *Telecommunications Policy* vol. 24: 395-411; Richard Collins (1998) "Back to the Future: Digital Television and Convergence in the United Kingdom" *Telecommunications Policy* vol. 22: 383-96; Trine Syvertsen (2000) "From PSB to Me-TV? Television, Convergence and Media Policy: The Case of Norway" paper presented to IAMCR Conference, Singapore, July; Productivity Commission (2000) *Broadcasting* Report no. 11, Canberra: AGPS; DCITA (2000) *Convergence Report*.

4  The following EU member countries have introduced "must carry" requirements: UK, Denmark (which requires cable operators carrying eight or more channels to make one available for local television programming), Austria, Belgium, France, Germany, Finland, Ireland, the Netherlands, Portugal (which requires cable operators to distribute "video or radio signals from non-profit entities for research, educational and cultural purposes"), Spain, Sweden. OECD (1999a).

5  See (http://www.culture.gov.uk/creative/dti-dcms_comms-reform_white_paper.html.

6  The 1998 document *Charting the Digital Broadcasting Future* by the US Advisory Committee on Public Interest Obligations of Digital Television Broadcasters made a similar recommendation for ongoing public input through postal and electronic mail services whereby digital broadcasters gauge community needs and interests. (This committee is popularly known as the Gore Commission and its report is available online at www.ntia.doc.gov/pubintadvcom/pubint.htm).

7   See Public Notices CRTC 1999-97, 1999-205 and 1999-206 available online at http://www.crtc.gc.ca/Canrec/Canrec_e.htm.

# References

Analysys, Squire, Sanders and Dempsey. 1998. *Study on Adapting the EU Telecommunications Regulatory Framework to the Developing Multimedia Environment.* Study for the European Commission (Directorate-General XIII).

Blackman, C. R. 1998. Convergence Between Telecommunications And Other Media. How Should Regulation Adapt? *Telecommunications Policy* 22: 163-70.

Braithwaite, J. and P. Drahos. 2000. *Global Business Regulation.* Cambridge: Cambridge University Press.

Canadian Conference of the Arts. 1998. *Working Group on Cultural Policy for the 21st Century: Final Report*, June.

Collins, R. 1998. Back to the Future: Digital Television and Convergence in the United Kingdom. *Telecommunications Policy* 22: 383-96.

Cowie, C. and C. T. Marsden. 1998. Convergence, Competition and Regulation. *International Journal of Communications Law and Policy* 1. Available online at http://www.digital-law.net/IJCLP/1_1998/ijclp_webdoc_6_1_1998.html.

Department of Communications, Information Technology and the Arts (Australia). 2000. *Convergence Report.* Canberra: DCITA.

Department of Culture, Media and Sport (UK). 2000. *The Funding of the BBC: Government Response to the Third Report from the Culture, Media and Sport Committee, Session 1999-2000.* London: DCMS, March.

Department of Trade and Industry and Department of Culture, Media and Sport (DTI/DCMS UK). 2000. *A New Future for Communications.* Communications White Paper. http://www.communicationswhitepaper.gov.uk/.

European Commission's Information Society Directorate-General, KPMG. 1996. *Public Policy Issues Arising From Telecommunications and Audio-visual Convergence*, a report prepared for DG XIII, London.

European Parliament. *Television Without Frontiers Directive.* 89/552/EEC and 97/36/EC.

Forgan, L. and D. Tambini. *Content.* Available at http://www.culture.gov.uk/creative/dti-dcms_comms-reform_experts.html.

Graham, A. *et. al.* 1999. *Public Purposes in Broadcasting: Funding the BBC.* Luton: University of Luton Press.

Just, N. and M. Latzer. 2000. EU Competition Policy and Market Power Control in the Mediamatics Era. *Telecommunications Policy* 24: 395-411.

Karlsson, R., H. T. Bjarnason, T. Broddason and M. L. Gudmundsdottir. 2000. Performance of Public and Private Television in Iceland 1993–1999: An Assessment 1. *Nordicom Review* 1: 101- 42.

Levy, D.A. 1999. *Europe's Digital Revolution: Broadcasting, the EU and the Nation State.* London : Routledge: 1999.

de Moragas Spà, M., C. Garitaonandía and B. López. 1999. Regional and Local Television in the Digital Era: Reasons for Optimism. In *Television on Your Doorstep: Decentralisation Experiences in the European Union*, edited by Miquel de Moragas Spà *et. al.* Luton: University of Luton Press.

NZ On-Air Symposium on Broadcasting Policy in New Zealand. *Counting the Cultural Beat* August, 1999. Available on-line at http://www.nzonair.govt. nz/noa_symposium/symposium.html.

Organization for Economic Co-Operation and Development (OECD). 1999a. *Communications Outlook 1999: Broadcasting: Regulatory Issues Questionnaires.*

Organization for Economic Co-Operation and Development (OECD). 1999b. *Regulation and Competition Issues in Broadcasting in the Light of Convergence.* DAFFE/CLP(99)1.

Peha, J. M. 1999. Tradable Universal Service Obligations. *Telecommunications Policy* 23: 363-74.

Productivity Commission. 2000. *Broadcasting* Report no. 11, Canberra: AGPS.

Syvertsen, T. 2000. *From PSB to Me-TV? Television, Convergence and Media Policy: The Case of Norway.* Paper presented to IAMCR Conference, Singapore, July.

Traccy, M. 1998. *The Decline and Fall of Public Service Broadcasting.* Oxford: Oxford University Press.

Venturelli, S. 1998. *Liberalizing the European Media.* Oxford: Clarendon Press.

Vizard, S. 2000. *Seachange in Australian Content.* ABCzine 1: 22-3, 34.

Weller, D. 1999. Auctions for Universal Service Obligations. *Telecommunications Policy* 23: 645-674.

# Part Two

# Issues

# Broadcasting and the Social Contract

**Terry Flew**

One of the major contemporary challenges for communications scholars is to understand the institutional, policy and regulatory bases of stability and change in national media and cultural systems, particularly in the context of globalization. This chapter focuses upon these issues, with particular emphasis on the extent to which citizenship discourses, in both their political and national dimensions, have come to be embedded in the "deep structure" of broadcast media policy and regulatory processes. It will also consider the limits of such citizenship discourses and wider claims about the "governmentalization of culture" in modern societies (Bennett 1992; 1998) as manifested in policy debates surrounding broadcast media. In addition, it will investigate how globalization of the airwaves and issues surrounding media convergence have transformed the role of the citizen.

Campaigns to extend the principles of political citizenship into broadcast media policy have drawn upon the concept of the "public trust." In the broadcast world, this concept restricts and regulates private ownership of the broadcasting spectrum with broadcast licenses. Broadcast licenses have been a form of what Tom Streeter (1995) has termed "soft property," meaning that state agencies have the capacity to determine the legal and institutional arrangements as well as conditions attached to such property rights. This, in turn, renders broadcasters open to a requirement to be responsive to the "public interest." While such agencies appear powerful on the basis of their policy development and enforcement functions, and their ability to operate in a more open-ended and discretionary fashion than more traditional government institutions, such open-endedness has rendered them particularly vulnerable to "regulatory capture" (Horwitz 1989). Policy and decision-making cultures that stress the virtues of informal decision-making and consensus-building among participants can lead to minimal external scrutiny of operations and a policy community that is closed to "outsiders." A closed policy culture of this sort can reinforce the power that arises from oligopolistic broadcasting markets where a small number of powerful corporate interests have control over investment, employment, and programming decisions, as well as over information flows.

This discussion of citizenship discourses and the cultural dimension of media can be illustrated by, or seen through the prism of broadcast policy and regulation. Consideration of the relationship between broadcast media and citizenship also points to ambiguities within citizenship discourse itself. One difficulty with citizenship in liberal-democratic societies is the existence of a "participation gap," arising from the distance between actions taken on behalf of citizens by government agencies, and the actual involvement of citizens in decision-making processes that affect their lives. Debates about citizenship and broadcast media policy have also been strongly concerned with the question of what Philip Schlesinger (1991: 162) terms "communicative boundary maintenance," particularly in societies such as Australia, Canada and New Zealand, which are open to cultural imports from other English-speaking countries, primarily the United States and Britain.

In Australia, for example, the "deep structure" of commercial broadcasting and its regulation is based on what I have termed the *social contract* between commercial broadcasters, regulatory agencies, media activists and the wider community. This has arisen in an institutional context that is closer to the United States than to Britain or Europe, where the commercial sector, rather than a national public broadcaster, has been the principal element of the broadcasting system since its establishment. In such societies, the idea that broadcasting involves an essentially commercial relationship between broadcasters and their audiences has always been limited in practice by the requirement that the broadcaster serve the "public interest."

In Australia, the relationship between broadcasters and regulators centres on three key elements. First, there has been a strong capacity of the commercial broadcasters to influence the policy and regulatory environment. Second, it has been widely perceived that requirements on the broadcasters to meet social and cultural policy objectives (eg local content) are offered in exchange for exclusive access to the airwaves and the ability to earn monopoly profits. This has always existed, finally, around a counter-discourse that has demanded greater public participation and stronger regulatory influence over commercial broadcasters as a condition for their access to such profitable and influential means of mass communications.

Using Australia as an example, this discussion will identify three circumstances – national competition policy, international trade law, and media convergence – that put the concept of the social contract in peril.

## Broadcasting and the Social Contract in Australia: A Snapshot History

Four historical phases can be identified in the history of broadcast media policy in Australia, and its relationship to citizenship discourses.

## Phase One: "Hands Off" 1956-1972

In the first period, which runs from the introduction of television in 1956 to 1972, citizenship discourses have minimal influence upon public policy and, as a consequence, on the conduct of commercial broadcasters. Two decisions of the Menzies Liberal-Country Party government that introduced television in the early 1950s were critical: the decision to support a "dual system" of commercial and national public broadcasters for television, and the decision to allow the owners of existing media, most notably print, to own television stations (Curthoys 1991). One consequence of these decisions has been that Australia has developed a particularly powerful and virulent strain of media baron, well versed in traversing the corridors of political power. The other has been to promote a structure and philosophy of broadcasting where arguments for greater use of the medium for "pro-social" purposes or citizenship objectives have struggled for legitimacy and influence among governments, regulatory agencies and the wider community.

The Australian Broadcasting Control Board, established as the broadcasting regulator in Australia in 1948, exemplified the problems that Robert Horwitz (1989) has identified as those of a "captured" regulatory agency with a closed policy culture. Unlike the United States, this was not modified by the development of a well-funded mass communications research community focused on issues such as media violence or the possible impact of television on children (Rowland 1983). At the same time, the closed policy culture of Australian broadcasting was challenged by media reformists from the mid-1960s onwards, leading to alliances between local production industry interests, political activists and cultural nationalists. Groups and individuals in these alliances linked demands for greater public participation in broadcast media policy to demands for local content regulations, to promote the development of a distinctive national audio-visual culture.

## Phase Two: The Rise and Fall of Public Participation 1972-1982

Demands for greater public participation in broadcasting and its regulation gained considerable impetus with the election of the Whitlam Labour government in 1972. The election of a reformist and social-democratic government in Australia for the first time in over two decades coincided with a world-wide movement to enhance the scope for popular political participation, as a response to the concern that modern forms of government had become remote and unaccountable, and that a "participation gap" had emerged for citizens in modern liberal democracies. While the Whitlam government undertook many reforms of Australian media, including stronger Australian content regulations and the establishment of community broadcasting, it was criticized by activists at the time for failing to widen the scope for participation in policy-making processes (eg Edgar 1979).

The Australian Broadcasting Tribunal (ABT), established in 1977, sought to inject "the philosophy of direct public accountability" into the relationship between Australian commercial broadcasters and the public, who were now considered citizens as well as audiences (ABT 1977). Such initiatives were part of a wider attempt to overcome the "participation gap," as well as the unequal power of industry compared to citizens. In often-chaotic attempts to develop such processes, public license renewal hearings were held between 1977 and 1982. However, it became apparent by the chaos that a policy process based upon the direct involvement of "the public" was not realistic. As a result, the license renewal hearing process became increasingly closed and legalistic.

The demise of the ABT's license renewal hearings as a forum for public participation would seem to confirm Leonie Sandercock's criticism of participation as "the great populist red herring of the 1970s in Australia" (Sandercock 1982: 247). For all of its limitations, however, it was important to promoting collective organizations of media reformers, as well as developing among these groups a better understanding of the relationship between participation in public forums and influence over policy decisions.

## Phase Three: The Australian Content Inquiry and the Professionalization of Media Activism 1983-1989

The Australian Content inquiry undertaken by the ABT in 1983 took place in the context of some very significant shifts in the media reform movements as well as in the ways that regulatory agencies facilitated citizen participation. In contrast to the diffuse nature of concerns raised in the license renewal hearings, the Australian Content inquiry was focused around particular issues, such as local content and children's programming. The participatory processes that developed in the course of the inquiry also supported the ongoing involvement of organized advocacy and public interest groups, and in this way contributed to the "professionalization of the public interest" in the 1980s. This professionalization, which had its origins in the license renewal hearings, was in turn facilitated by the ABT as a regulatory agency committed to brokering outcomes based upon forms of bargained pluralism (Dunleavy and O'Leary 1987).

In the course of the 1980s, responsibility for contributing to policy formation processes had been gradually shifting from full-time activists and freelance academics to a professional cadre of research and policy professionals who could be employed on a full-time basis to monitor and contribute to policy formation on behalf of their organizations. The Communications Law Centre, established in 1988, was a leading example of the new kind of organization that could enable sustained involvement by media activists in the policy process by developing an ongoing and "bureaucratic" response to issues in the communications and media policy fields.

A further development arising from this period concerned shifts in the debate cultures of media and cultural studies as some Australian academics sought to align their activism with the activities of policy-oriented organizations (eg Cunningham 1992). The notion of academics acting as policy participants, or even policy entrepreneurs, had an uneven impact with some doubting that the gulf between academics, practitioners and bureaucrats had in fact been bridged (cg Bailey 1994). Glyn Davis has observed that the relationship of academics to the policy process remains essentially that of outsiders on the margins of actual decision-making processes, who find that "influence is a haphazard affair;" where academics "throw conceits at our targets, hoping to move them through force of argument" (Davis 1998: 36). At the same time, the establishment of centres such as the Institute for Cultural Policy Studies at Griffith University in Brisbane in 1989, the Melbourne-based Centre for International Research into Communications and Information Technologies (CIRCIT) in 1991, and the Australian Key Centre for Cultural and Media Policy in 1995, presented the possibility for academic involvement in media policy processes being less of a haphazard and serendipitous affair.

## Phase Four: Neo-Liberal Policy Discourse and the Broadcasting Services Act 1992

The late 1980s and early 1990s witnessed two shifts in the dominant discourses of Australian public policy, both towards a "neo-liberal" or "post-Fordist" approach involving the restructuring of governance to promote competition, the entry of new participants, and co-regulatory arrangements between industry, government and other relevant stakeholders. First, "mega-departments" such as the Department of Transport and Communications (DOTAC) were created. This move addressed the notion that broadcasting policy was a subset of wider policies of microeconomic reform. Second, economic analysis became increasingly significant to policy discourse in Australia. While such a shift is often attributed to a uniquely Australian contamination of the policy process by "economic rationalism" (Pusey 1991), it can in fact be seen as indicative of global trends towards "neo-liberal" or "post-Fordist" modes of governance, whereby the will to "govern without governing society" (Rose 1996: 61) achieves new forms of expression through the extension of principles of economy upon the practice of government.

A further contextual factor was the impending transformation of telecommunications in the context of communications convergence. It was becoming increasingly apparent through the 1980s that telecommunications was central to information-based economies and that the traditional model of public monopolies or highly regulated private providers offering broadly equitable access to a "plain old telephone service" , was becoming increasingly untenable (Westerway 1990). As a consequence, governments throughout the world were re-thinking the bases of telecommunications regulation as a shift towards competition, value-added services such as mobile telephony, and economy-wide expectations about the quality of communications infrastructure, took place (Collins and Murroni 1996).

The bureaucrats in DOTAC who drafted the *Broadcasting Services Act 1992* sought to implement a neo-liberal policy discourse, proposing a new regulatory regime based upon the promotion of new technologies and new services, "light touch" regulation, and "regulation by exception" (eg DOTAC 1993). The outcomes of Australian broadcasting in the 1990s reveal a far more mixed picture. One clear consequence of the change in legislation, policy discourse and institutional practices in the 1990s was that the room for public interest and media advocacy groups to be involved in policy diminished. The liberal-pluralist models of the policy process saw such involvement as providing a necessary source of countervailing power in the context of industry concentration. In contrast, the emergent neo-liberal approaches viewed this involvement as symptomatic of a sector where limits upon the full functioning of markets had led to the emergence of interest-group coalitions, and a "political market" that operated to the detriment of consumer interests. The claim that interest groups could or should "speak for" media audiences was thus being increasingly questioned by government agencies.[1]

The Australian Broadcasting Authority (ABA), established in 1993 to replace the ABT, was expected to fashion co-regulatory arrangements with peak industry bodies based on modes of governance that were less formal and legalistic, but rather based on informal negotiations, consensus building and mutual understanding between stakeholders (Jessop 1998). While critics were concerned that such an approach would leave the scope for participation by media advocacy and public interest groups largely at the discretion of the ABA (Davies and Spurgeon 1992; Chadwick *et. al.* 1995), a move toward more discretionary dealings with the commercial broadcasters was welcomed within the sector itself.

### Challenges to the Social Contract: Competition Policy, International Trade Law and New Media Technologies

It is no surprise to find that the policy settlement I have described as the *social contract* and that has prevailed in Australia from the 1960s to the 1990s, is under challenge – as it is in virtually all national broadcasting systems in the developed world. Three sets of factors seem to be common across national systems. The first is the growing influence of neo-liberal policy discourses that point to an increasingly important role for competition policy as a "generic" form of industry regulation. These policy discourses are also critical of "public interest" rationales for restricting competition that are seen, in many cases, as prone to regulatory capture. Second, international trade agreements are moving the locus of media governance from national, discretionary and industry-specific forms of regulation, towards internationalized, legally binding and generic forms of media governance. Finally, digitization and media convergence (particularly "next generation" convergence that entails the generalization of the convergence phenomenon into the entire services sector), are breaking down the historic forms of industry demarcation and entry control that have underpinned pro-social forms of content regulation in the broadcast media sector.

### Competition Policy and the Productivity Commission's Inquiry into Broadcasting

Neo-liberal or "advanced liberal" (Rose 1993; 1996) policy discourses have promoted a shift in thinking about the role of state regulation as protecting the public interest against corporate power. The state is now increasingly seen as the promoter of national and international competitiveness in the context of pervasive technological and structural change. There is a concern that, in too many cases, industry-specific regulation based on "public interest" rationales leads to regulatory capture − a policy culture that consistently favours organized policy "insiders," to the detriment of consumers and economic welfare. For all of the apparent talk of a new competition-based broadcasting regime leading up to the *Broadcasting Services Act*, the reality was a continuation of the commercial broadcasting oligopoly with less external scrutiny from public interest groups, albeit with competition from the pay TV sector that has grown over time. This sector now has 20 per cent of TV households subscribing and expects to reach 30 per cent by 2002.

Since the 1990s, competition policy has become increasingly significant to broadcast media policy world-wide (OECD 1993; OECD 1999). In Australia, the Productivity Commission, an agency within the treasury responsible for overseeing regulatory compliance with National Competition Policy legislation, undertook an inquiry into Australian broadcasting and its legislation in February 1999. The Productivity Commission's *Final Report* (Productivity Commission 2000) was highly critical of current legislation that it considered to be not only contrary to competition policy and other public policy principles, but also an inadequate base from which to respond to the challenges of digitization, technological convergence, and new media services. It focused, in particular, upon what I've termed the social contract, and what it termed the regulatory quid pro quo, arguing that such anti-competitive arrangements had not only failed to deliver satisfactory outcomes to consumers, but also to the sections of the Australian production industry that had traditionally supported such restrictions on market entry as necessary for "pro-social" policy goals (eg Australian content and children's programming):

> It is questionable whether the restrictions on entry are a necessary trade-off for imposing such obligations on the commercial broadcasters. Few industries enjoy entry restrictions to compensate for public obligations...All industries must meet the requirements of various codes, standards and regulations...It is not clear why the broadcasting industry is marked for special treatment and compensated for meeting its obligations. Higher costs do not justify restrictions on entry (Productivity Commission 2000: 319).

The Productivity Commission was most critical of attempts to extend the social contract or quid pro quo arrangements into the digital broadcasting environment. It outlined five criticisms of the current government plan for the transition to digital broadcasting that mandated high definition TV: (1) it prohibited multi-channeling by commercial broadcasters; (2) it required analog and digital simulcasting until 2008; (3) the plan set restrictions upon the development of datacasting and interactive services; (4) it extended the prohibition on new commercial broadcast licenses until 2006; and (5) it would extend the logic of "trade-offs" and protection of incumbent broadcasters into a media domain that was likely to be profoundly different. The Productivity Commission instead argued that, in an environment of pervasive technological change and uncertainty about the impact of new services, governments should take the opportunity to "design a structure to serve Australians better [based upon] greater competition, less regulation, spectrum licensing reforms, and the rapid release of spectrum" (Productivity Commission 2000: 254).

## The WTO and the Millennium Round of the GATS

The current round of the General Agreement on Trades and Services (GATS) negotiations to be conducted through the World Trade Organization (WTO) also presents a clear challenge to attempts to align restricted access to domestic markets with guaranteed levels of domestic production. The elements of the GATS Agreement that cause most concern in this respect are Article II (Most-Favoured-Nation), Article XV (Subsidies), Article XVI (Market Access) and Article XVII (National Treatment). While the Uruguay Round was based upon an "opt-in" approach to the GATS agreement, the United States is proposing in the current round that the GATS framework should be based upon an across-the-board rather than sector-specific approach to regulatory liberalization (Hoekman and Kostecki 1995; Watson et. al. 1999). This would prevent member states from exempting themselves from particular GATS disciplines in the audio-visual sector, as the European Community and most other member states were able to do in the Uruguay Round (Miller 1996; Grant 1995). By contrast, the European Community proposed a "cultural exception" to the GATS that would incorporate audio-visual services; Canada had sought a "new international instrument on cultural diversity" that would trigger exemptions to the GATS where issues of cultural sovereignty and/or the maintenance of cultural diversity arose. Such debates parallel those around the appropriate domain of competition policy as the OECD has observed in considering the growing significance of competition policy to rules governing the delivery of network-based services (OECD 1999).

Australia's overall negotiating position on the GATS and trade liberalization is a highly supportive one since Australian trade negotiators conceive of the nation as a small, open economy that benefits from multilateral trade agreements that require greater market access on the part of larger and potentially more influential nations and regions. Moreover, the experience of the tariff system in manufacturing has helped to generate a "free trade consensus" or, put differently, an anti-protectionist alliance, at the higher levels of Australian policy culture (Anderson and Garnaut 1987). At the same time, the concerns of the audio-visual sector about the potentially adverse effects of such legally-binding trade agreements are recognized by the government department in charge.

The work of Australian media and cultural studies academics has been relevant here as it has established that local content regulations and subsidy arrangements for Australian film and television were not primarily about defense of a national culture through economic protectionism. Rather, they have been primarily concerned with ensuring the existence of "a limited local presence alongside the Hollywood product" (O'Regan 1992: 91), or what Cunningham and Jacka termed a "safety net" for local content (Cunningham and Jacka 1996: 224). This safety net ensures limited local production in import-competing genres such as drama in a context where linguistic and cultural proximity to the United States made Australian television "one of the *least* protected and cosseted of international television industries" (O'Regan 1993: 76). Industry participants involved in the Uruguay Round of GATS negotiations observed that such "hard intellectual work" was important to the sector in developing an informed policy position that could present a case for exempting audio-visual services from Australia's final GATS commitments without rejecting entirely the GATT framework or presenting a case that smacked of special pleading.

## *Digitization and "Next Generation" Convergence*

The processes of digitization and convergence challenge national regulatory frameworks and the institutional foundations, such as the social contract as it has evolved in the Australian context. Convergence between information technologies, telecommunications, and broadcast and print media has already occurred at the levels of delivery networks, institutional alliances, and new industries and services (Miles 1997; Barr 2000). In the early 21st century, the move is taking place from the convergence of IT, telecommunications and media, towards *next generation convergence*, where the implications of convergence extend into the entire services sector, including financial, retail, community, health and education (CSM 1999: 5-6). In this context, technological convergence is associated with structural convergence, or the shift from traditional service industry models to convergent service industry models. The Australian Department of Communications, Information Technology and the Arts (DCITA) has noted that the traditional service industry structure in areas such as telecommunications and broadcasting was characterized by:

- distinct and vertically integrated industries;

- strong economies of scale leading to dominant infrastructure providers who regulated access to content;

- standardized and "mass appeal" content; and

- limits to international distribution that made the scope of service markets typically domestic rather than international.

In such an environment, "national regulators are able to control service providers on an industry-by-industry basis by controlling entry to domestic infrastructure markets" (DCITA 2000). Content could be regulated through limited access to scarce electromagnetic spectrum resources within the domestic market. By contrast, convergent service industry models are seen as being characterized by:

- disaggregation of infrastructure, delivery mechanisms and applications or content, as content can be re-purposed for multiple delivery platforms;

- blurring of traditional market boundaries, as digital infrastructure networks can support multiple applications;

- reduced barriers to entry for new players, and greater product and service innovation;

- user customization of applications, services and content, and the scope to develop content that is "tailored" to user preferences; and

- internationalization of service markets, especially where services are delivered electronically.

Policy-makers must grapple with how to meet cultural policy objectives (e.g. national content, children's programming, and diversity of content), when the traditional mechanisms of industry regulation and restricted market structures may be less applicable than in the period from the 1960s to the present.

There are important interconnections between competition policy, international trade law, and media convergence in terms of their impact upon domestic broadcast media policy. The Organization for Economic Co-operation and Development (OECD) envisages that "with the increasing number and variety of network-based services, competition policy…needs to play a much greater role in the regulation of audio-visual content" (OECD 1999: 12).

International trade theorists argue that the international harmonization of competition policies and the relationship between international trade policies and domestic competition policies will emerge as one of the major issues on the trade policy agenda in the years ahead (Trebilcock and Howse 1995). While the Productivity Commission chose not to refer to international trade agreements in its final report, it called for an independent public inquiry into Australian audio-visual and cultural policy to be completed by 2004. It also explicitly refers to the problems likely to arise with current Australian content regulations in the context of convergence and the emergence of new services (Productivity Commission 2000: 416-422).

## The End of the Social Contract?

This paper has drawn attention to three powerful forces – national competition policy, international trade law, and media convergence – that have the potential to render the "social contract" in a national broadcasting system, where commercial industry protection is exchanged for content regulations, untenable. An important lesson of the 1990s, however, was that claims about the imminent "death of broadcasting" were premature (Given 1998), and that commercial television networks world-wide continue to be profitable economic and powerful political entities. Moreover, for all the bright talk about media abundance and networked interactivity, questions remain unresolved concerning culture, citizenship and the role of public policy in broadcast or post-broadcast media that are not resolved by policy measures to increase the total number of distribution outlets. Three major issues remain unresolved:

- How can we secure levels and types of local programming that meet cultural development objectives as well as sustaining a viable audio-visual production industry in an era of media globalization and international trade regimes (such as GATS) that limit the capacity to use public policy to deliver competitive advantages to domestic producers?

- How can we guarantee the availability of a diverse range of program genres in formats that are widely accessible to all sections of the community, particularly in the areas of children's programming and local production?

- How can we ensure that media distributors have some degree of accountability to the public as citizens in their use of public resources for commercial purposes?

A further issue arises about the politics of media reform. It has been argued in this chapter that the "public trust" doctrine of Australian commercial broadcasters' use of the public airwaves provided the basis for ongoing activism in the policy process by media reform and advocacy groups, particularly in the 1970s and 1980s. Such capacity for intervention by organized interest groups was diluted significantly with the *Broadcasting Services Act 1992*, but it is apparent that such legislation has neither been consistent in its neo-liberal orientation towards consumer sovereignty, nor have the co-regulatory regimes it promoted sufficiently addressed public concerns about the conduct of media organizations.

There is a growing need to develop ways to promote local content across all sectors of broadcast media that are not premised upon the regulation of market entry into the commercial free-to-air broadcasting sector. The criticisms of the regulatory quid pro quo made by the Australian Productivity Commission and others point to a need for new policy approaches to the production and distribution of local content that do not hinge upon the restriction of competition or upon the restriction of development of new technologies and services. Elsewhere in this volume, Goldsmith *et. al.* (2001) have noted that, while the transition towards digital broadcasting and media convergence presents new challenges, "it would be a mistake to assume that the forward policy environment will *necessarily* be a more difficult one for achieving cultural policy outcomes such as ensuring a place for local television content" (Ibid.) They evaluate a range of new policy instruments, such as "must carry" requirements, contestable subsidy schemes, and quota trading, as ways in which local content production can be promoted in a more competitive broadcasting environment and that take advantage of the new opportunities for content creators and audience demand for local and regional programming in a multi-channel system. They also point to the need to consider the current and possible future roles of national public broadcasters in sustaining a viable local television production industry, and in providing "proximity programming" for local and regional audiences in a relatively transparent and efficient manner (cf. Graham 1998).

The question of regionalism has also become more, not less, important in an era of multilateral trade agreements. It is apparent that the hostile nature of the *Project Blue Sky* case between Australia and New Zealand stemmed not so much from the actual threat presented by New Zealand-produced programming in Australian audio-visual markets, but rather from concerns that deregulation of the New Zealand broadcasting industry and the dismantling of local content requirements could promote a "race to the bottom" in terms of trading off domestic content regulations for international capital (Crotty, Epstein and Kelly 1998).[2] It is increasingly apparent that as the overwhelmingly dominant partner in Australia-New Zealand audio-visual trade relations, Australia has little to fear from trade liberalization if it is not perceived as the "thin end of the wedge" for abandoning local content regulations.

The political economy of multilateral trade negotiations is also an issue that needs greater consideration. For their critics, multilateral organizations are understood as a kind of "Trojan horse" for the usurping of national sovereignty and the exercise of unfettered corporate power. By contrast, John Ruggie (1993) has viewed this as indicative of a tendency in international political theory to see norms and institutions as essentially "epiphenenomenal ... to the real relations of force or the relations of production" (: 5). Ruggie argues that multilateralism as an institutional form is first and foremost about the conditions under which states can adopt shared norms and generalized principles of conduct, and that such arrangements have existed for as long as states themselves.

Multilateral organizations, on the other hand, were largely a phenomenon of the 20th century based on the premise of the prior existence of shared norms and principles of conduct among nation states. Ruggie's clarification of the nature of multilateralism as an institutional form is useful since it reminds us that multilateral organizations are not simply the epiphenomenal forms of globalized corporate power or imperial hegemony, but are in fact a central and ongoing component of statecraft, and hence of domestic policy. In audio-visual trade, no less than in primary product markets, small and open countries such as Australia need multilateral trade agreements because they are, as Jock Given has described it, less vulnerable in an environment of multilaterally endorsed trading rules than "in the dog-eat-dog world of bilateral trade wars" (Given 1993: 4). Moreover, an association of multiliteralism solely with economic agreements loses sight of its significance in providing the framing discourses in domestic legislation in areas as diverse as sexual discrimination, racial discrimination, and environmental protection. Even if one adopts a critical perspective, it could be argued that the emergence of opposition movements within transnational civil society has been dialectically related to the development of global modes of governance. Perhaps paradoxically, the success of opposition movements has been related in part to their ability to influence national elites who have felt excluded from multilateral decision-making processes.

The relationship between the internationalization of media industries and media markets to the internationalization of media governance is not simply reflective of the globalization of economic activity in the cultural industries, but of the mutually reinforcing relationships between competition policy, international trade law, and media convergence. All three of these tendencies are moving media regulation away from frameworks that are national, sector-specific and discretionary, towards frameworks that are generic, compatible with international trade law, and legally binding. Such trends can be seen as pointing towards the internationalization of media governance, where domestic laws, policies and regulatory frameworks are developed with at least one eye on their compatibility with binding bilateral, pluri-lateral and multilateral trade agreements. In this respect, the significance of national broadcasting regulations to multilateral trade agreements such as the GATS may have less to do with the compatibility of existing legislation to this framework, and more to do with how the existence of the GATS framework will shape future forms of broadcasting regulation.

There is also a need to reconsider the assumption that the internationalization of governance, in the media or in other sectors, necessarily entails a "race to the bottom" outcome. In their comprehensive survey of global business regulation, John Braithwaite and Peter Drahos (2000) propose that there is no necessary tendency for lowest-cost locations and least stringent regulations to be most attractive to global business. Indeed, for Braithwaite and Drahos, the enforcement of best practice regulation, strategic trade theory, and the literature on competitive advantage and continuous improvement in corporate management, suggest that it is possible to link "progressive" corporate thinking to activist regulation and a place at the table for "public interest" and activist non-governmental organizations. Interestingly, they propose that the latter organizations will most effectively challenge business power and champion popular sovereignty by using competition policy to divide and conquer business, and by championing the use of competition law enforcement to "ratchet-up" standards and promote continuous improvement in business conduct. This is very different from the quasi-corporate logic of the social contract in broadcasting where production sector representatives and other interested parties reluctantly "fellow travel" with the existing commercial broadcasting interests, accepting policies that actively hinder the emergence of new players and new technologies in order to extract a small tithe from monopoly profits made at the cost of product innovation.

## Notes

1    Former Communications Minister and prominent Labour Party "hard man" Graham Richardson provided a particularly colourful critique of claims that the public are interested in open policy processes such as those surrounding broadcast license renewals:

> It depends on where you are coming from: should everything be done by open public hearing process? It's always been put to me, "Ah, it's in the public interest." Well, I will take you for a walk down the shopping centre of any place in the western suburbs. Go up to the first hundred people and ask what are the issues facing this country. We won't find one that tells us the ABA must have public hearings. Not one! Who's interested in it? A very small, elite clique who claim to represent the people out there but who could not give a stuff (Richardson 1992: 129).

2    The *Project Blue Sky* case involved a claim made by sections of the New Zealand audio-visual production industry that Australian content regulations contravened the Closer Economic Relations (CER) trade agreement between the two countries, as well as Section 160(d) of the *Broadcasting Services Act 1992* which stated that the Australian Broadcasting Authority which administers the Australian content standard must "perform its functions in a manner consistent with ... Australia's obligations under any convention to which Australia is a party or any agreement between Australia and a foreign country." The High Court of Australia found in favour of the Project Blue Sky interests in a 1998 judgement after five years of legal actions in the Australian courts.

## References

Anderson, K., and Garnaut, R. 1987. *Australian Protectionism: Extent, Causes and Effects.* Sydney: Allen & Unwin.

Australian Broadcasting Tribunal. 1977. *Self-Regulation for Broadcasters: A Report on the Public Inquiry into the Concept of Self-Regulation for Australian Broadcasters.* Parliamentary Paper No. 170/1977, Parliament of the Commonwealth of

Australia, Canberra: Commonwealth Government Printer.

Bailey, J-J. 1994. The Policy Process: Film Policy-Who Talks to Whom? In *Film Policy: An Australian Reader*, edited by A. Moran. Brisbane: Institute for Cultural Policy Studies: 67-73.

Barr, T. 2000. *newmedia.com.au*. Sydney: Allen & Unwin.

Bennett, T. 1992. Putting Policy into Cultural Studies. In *Cultural Studies*, edited by L. Grossberg, C.Nelson and P. Treichler. Routledge, New York: 23-37.

_____.1998. *Culture: A Reformer's Science*. Sydney: Allen & Unwin.

Braithwaite, J., and Drahos, P. 2000. *Global Business Regulation*. Cambridge: Cambridge University Press.

Chadwick, P., Ferguson, S., and McAuslan, M. 1995. Shackled: the Story of a Regulatory Slave. *Media International Australia* 77: 65-72.

Communications Strategies & Management (CSM). 1999. *The Development of Datacasting Technologies and Services*. Report prepared for Department of Communications, Information Technology and the Arts. February.

Collins, R. and Murroni, C. 1996. *New Media, New Policies: Media and Communication Strategies for the Future*. Cambridge: Polity Press.

Crotty, J., Epstein, G., and Kelly, P. 1998. Multinational Corporations in the Neo-Liberal Regime. In *Globalization and Progressive Economic Policy*, edited by D. Baker. G. Epstein and R. Pollin. Cambridge: Cambridge University Press: 117-143.

Cunningham, S. 1992. *Framing Culture: Criticism and Policy in Australia*. Allen & Unwin. Sydney.

_____, and Jacka, E. 1996. *Australian Television and International Mediascapes*. Cambridge: Cambridge University Press.

Curthoys, A. 1991. Television Before Television. *Continuum: An Australian Journal of Media and Culture*. 4, 2: 152-170.

Davies, A., and Spurgeon, C. 1992. The *Broadcasting Services Act*: A Reconciliation of Public Interest and Market Principles of Regulation? *Media Information Australia* 66: 85-92.

Davis, G. 1998. Policy from the Margins: Reshaping the Australian Broadcasting Corporation. In *Activism and the Policy Process*, edited by A. Yeatman. Allen & Unwin: Sydney: 36-55.

Department of Communications, Information Technology and the Arts (DCITA). 2000. *Convergence Review: Issues Paper*. URL: www.dcita.gov.au/text_welcome.html.

Department of Transport and Communication (DOTAC). 1993. *Broadcasting Reform: A New Approach to Regulation*. AGPS. Canberra. 29 January.

Dunleavy, P., and O'Leary, B. 1987. *Theories of the State: The Politics of Liberal Democracy*. London: Macmillan.

Edgar, P. 1979. Radio and Television. In *From Whitlam to Fraser: Reform and Reaction in Australian Politics*, edited by A. Patience and B. W. Head. Melbourne: Oxford University Press: 214-232.

Given, J. 1993. Cars, Culture and Comparative Advantage. Paper for Centre for Telecommunications Law and Policy seminar, *Australian Content: New Rules and Policies*, Melbourne: Melbourne University. 30 October.

_____ 1998. *The Death of Broadcasting? Media's Digital Future*. Sydney: UNSW Press.

Graham, A. 1998. Broadcasting Policy in the Digital Age. In *Digital Broadcasting and the Public Interest: Reports and Papers of the Aspen Institute Communications and Society Program*, edited by C. M. Firestone and A. K. Garmer. Washington: The Aspen Institute: 37-46.

Grant, J. M. 1995. Jurassic Trade Dispute: The Exclusion of the Audio-visual Sector from the GATT. *Indiana Law Journal* 70: 1333-1365.

Hoekman, B., and Kostecki, M. 1995. *The Political Economy of the World Trading System: From GATT to WTO*. Oxford: Oxford University Press.

Horwitz, R. B. 1989. *The Irony of Regulatory Reform: The Deregulation of American Telecommunications*. New York: Oxford University Press.

Jessop, B. 1998. The Rise of Governance and the Risks of Failure: The Case of Economic Development. *International Social Science Journal*. 50, 1: 17-46.

Miles, I. 1997. Cyberspace as Product Space: Interactive Learning about Interactive Media. *Futures*. 29. 9: 769-789.

Miller, T. 1996. The Crime of Monsieur Lang: GATT, the Screen, and the New International Division of Cultural Labour. In *Film Policy: International, National and Regional Perspectives*, edited by A. Moran. New York: Routledge: 72-84.

OECD. 1993. *Competition Policy and a Changing Broadcast Industry*. Paris: OECD.

OECD. 1999. Directorate for Science, Technology and Industry. Committee for Information, Computer and Communications Policy. Working Party on the Information Economy. *Policy and Regulation Issues for Network-Based Content Services*. DSTI/ICCP/IE(96)6/Final. Paris: OECD.

O'Regan, T. 1992. The International, the Regional and the Local: Hollywood's New and Declining Audience. In *Continental Shift: Globalization and Culture*, edited by E. Jacka. Sydney: Local Consumption Press: 74-98.

_____. 1993. *Australian Television Culture*. Sydney: Allen & Unwin.

Productivity Commission. 2000. *Broadcasting: Inquiry Report*. Report No. 11. Canberra: Ausinfo.

Pusey, M. 1991. *Economic Rationalism in Canberra: A Nation-Building State Changes its Mind*. Cambridge: Cambridge University Press.

Rose, N. 1993. Government, Authority and Expertise in Advanced Liberalism. *Economy and Society*. Vol. 22, No. 3: 283-299.

_____. 1996. Governing Advanced Liberal Democracies. In *Foucault and Political Reason: Liberalism, Neo-Liberalism and Rationalities of Government*, edited by Barry T. Osborne and N. Rose. London: UCL Press: 37-64.

Rowland, W. D. 1983. *The Politics of TV Violence: The Policy Uses of Communication Research*. Beverly Hills: Sage.

Ruggie, J. G. 1993. Multilateralism: The Anatomy of an Institution. In *Multilateralism Matters: The Theory and Praxis of an Institutional Form*, edited by J. G. Ruggie. New York: Columbia University Press: 3-47.

Sandercock, L. 1983. Who Gets What Out of Public Participation? In *Urban Political Economy: The Australian Case*, edited by L. Sandercock and M. Berry. Sydney: George Allen & Unwin: 78-88.

Schlesinger, P. 1991. *Media, State and Nation: Political Violence and Collective Identities*. London: Sage.

Streeter, T. 1995. *Selling the Air: A Critique of the Policy of Commercial Broadcasting in the United States*. Chicago: University of Chicago Press.

Trebilcock, M. J., and Howse, R. 1995. *The Regulation of International Trade*. New York: Routledge.

Watson, P., Flynn, J., and Conwell, C. 1999. *Completing the World Trading System: Proposals for a Millennium Round*. The Hague: Kluwer Law International.

Westerway, P. 1990. *Electronic Highways: An Introduction to Telecommunications in the 1990s*. Sydney: Allen & Unwin.

# "Illegal and Harmful" Content

## Monroe E. Price

*This chapter is adapted from a forthcoming book by the author:* Journeys in Media Space: Identity, Law and Technology in the Global Environment (*2002*).

In these days of coming to grips with the Internet, fear and loathing of content deemed "illegal and harmful" strangely influence discussions about establishing cyberspace norms and enforcing them. There are other markers of concern including gaming, terrorism, and copyright infringement, but content issues have risen to the surface of these concerns. The evolution of meaning for these words is a small part of a struggle, state by state, between those who see norms defined by law, and those who seek to embed norms in the actions of individuals. One part of this equation involves the evolution of statute and the articulation, within and across national boundaries, of standards to control illegal and harmful content on the Internet. A second part involves the process of what is called "empowerment," which can be illustrated by the emergence of the V-chip, an electronic system to screen out pre-rated television programming. Here law gives way to a redefinition of the relationship between the individual and the image. The V-chip is a transitional and political bandage, the chief consequence of which has been to increase public understanding of the potential for labelling and filtering gateways to information. In its singular format, it became limited in time and in international space. The debate over illegal and harmful content on the Internet, in contrast, is part of an ongoing, complex debate in national and international fora over the extent of power of the state, the norms that should influence speech, and the evolution of new forms of co-regulation between industry and government.

## Statutes and Standards

The words "illegal and harmful" have gained, in international debates, a secondary meaning, an association with pornography or similar material harmful to minors. But illegality and harm could include, and sometimes do by

131

law, terrorist communications, hate speech, heightened violence, computer hacking, fraudulent advertising, speech that endangers national security or promotes war, slights on leaders or friendly neighbours or even copyright violations. While all these areas and more lurk in the background of regulation debate, the discussion, here, is largely limited to the core meaning. When politicians seek headlines, there is much popular fear to exploit. In the United Kingdom, a famous pop star is convicted for downloading thousands of images of child pornography. An American college professor is indicted for images stored in his computer. Dangers lurk behind the innocent-sounding exercise of a search engine's functions. Each time there is a prosecution and ensuing coverage there are renewed calls for more statutes, harsher penalties, and more perfect enforcement. The public demand for law increases. The United States Congress and the courts have been locked in a theatre of debate over what modes of defining and implementing law on popularly reprehensible content are constitutionally permissible. In India, Malaysia, and much of the Middle East, attacks on the media, linked to programs from abroad, emphasize the capacity of media to corrupt public morals. Indeed, loss of national control over content is inevitably linked to public corruption. An entire international infrastructure of industry and other groups has developed to provide avenues for response and furnish some sense that progress toward control is being made consistent with maintaining openness on the Internet and in the media (Waltermann and Machell 2000).

It goes, almost without saying, that states have long sought to regulate, moderate, or shape the generation and transmission of images within their own boundaries. Governments do so for reasons of maintaining political power, preserving national identity, reflecting popular desires, and assuring national security. Individual politicians make claims of protection sometimes from a position of personal belief, sometimes from a desire for control, and sometimes based on political pandering. It is also clear that traditional modes – the invocation of legislative or administrative language as a mode of control then asserted against a set of actors – are declining in their effectiveness. Yet, the function of the state as a definer and enforcer of values continues. Nor can the state claim immunity from responsibility because of the source of images. The distinction between information generated within and without a state's boundaries is diminishing. Some legal systems base power on such a distinction on the grounds that the state has clearer power and jurisdiction over messages that both arise and descend within the country's borders.[1] But increasingly, practicalities, efficiencies and international agreements, not nationally imposed limitations, will keep such boundaries in place. Thus, save for bilateral or multilateral agreements from the perspective of the state, the origin of messages may have little if any jurisdictional significance. In this sense, all messages, wherever they originate, are domestic in impact and, as a result, fall under the responsibility of the state (Goldsmith 1998).

In this respect, the problem of making law to regulate behaviour could be considered one of technique, not sovereign authority, and actual capacity, not the theoretical issue of whether that capacity, if available, should be exercised. Some states may argue, in fact, that the authority, including moral authority, to control messages is greater if the source of the message is outside the state's boundaries. To take the surprising example of the United States, the First Amendment could be interpreted as permitting Congress greater rights to limit messages that come from abroad. Certainly, the Television Without Frontiers Directive is structured to recognize a difference between the broadcasting of messages that arise from outside, rather than within the European Union.[2]

This authority over domestic imagery is being reinterpreted because of new technologies and changing international standards. What constitutes "illegal and harmful" or their equivalents can demonstrate how styles of regulation develop across boundaries. A kind of dialogue among stakeholders – content providers, service providers, consumers and states – over how to treat illegal and harmful speech on the Internet and on television has come into being. The development of norms in an international debate and the consequent influence of doctrine adopted in one jurisdiction upon decisions in another, has been the result. A complex discourse about the effort to develop national solutions – in an environment where technology makes such national debates superfluous – has sprung up around the regulation of illegal and harmful content on the Internet.

Norms are imprisoned in language, though language betrays the complexity of thought that lies behind most definitions. The phrase "illegal and harmful," or some variant, is increasingly the comfortable way of describing content that should be controlled or regulated on the Internet. Forms of words that approximate this phrase in literature addressing the Internet and its future can be found in European Union documents, the laws of its member states, United States statutes, developing law in Australia, and elsewhere. These words roll off the regulatory tongue. But is there an iron distinction between "illegal" and "harmful," and do the two words encompass the universe of what states seek (within their constitutional powers) to modify, regulate, or prevent in some way? More important, does the division of the world between "illegal" and "harmful" uncover some deeper problem in establishing norms for the flow of information, especially for the Internet? The formula may be constructed because such laws cannot easily be enforced in cyberspace or because the norms applied elsewhere are not readily transferrable or transportable.

Words found in one document are then repeated elsewhere as a result of efforts at harmonization across borders or co-operation to prevent content from entering a country where it is illegal. For the Internet to be regulated effectively, most players have accepted that some co-ordination can be beneficial and should possibly be required. Language may dart, virtually unexamined, from one legal setting to another. A phrase gathers traction, exists as a precedent, and, then, is lofted from document to document. As states have tried to capture the meaning of the dichotomy and cope with political challenges in fashioning a legal response to the Internet, interpretations have differed and expansions and changes in the overall formula have occurred. Especially because of the vital speech interests that are involved, the possible approaches to content regulation take on special significance. It would not be surprising if both the formula of words and meanings and implications attributed to them differed from society to society. What is more difficult is the attempt at harmonization that accompanies globalization.

It is difficult precisely to trace the origins of this verbal pairing. They entered the Internet world formally in EU documents in October 1996. At that time, the European Commission adopted the Communication on Illegal and Harmful Content on the Internet (European Commission 1996a). The two words, "illegal" and "harmful" fairly clearly stood for two pillars of content. The clearest distinction would limit "illegal content" to material the utterance or publication of which would be subject to criminal penalties as defined by individual EU Member States. "It is a matter for Member States to define what is illegal by law and to enforce it by detecting illegal activity and punishing offenders." In contradistinction, the pillar called "harmful content" would cover a more vague but important area of discourse: material not subject to criminal sanction but that "may offend the values and feelings of other persons." As the document put it:

> What is considered to be harmful depends on cultural differences. Each country may reach its own conclusion in defining the borderline between what is permissible and not permissible. It is therefore indispensable that international initiatives take into account different ethical standards in different countries in order to explore appropriate rules to protect people against offensive material while ensuring freedom of expression.

There is an explicit argument here that "illegality" resides in things that are almost universally prohibited (child pornography), while what is "harmful" is more culturally relative. As it turns out, this proposition is problematic. Even those things that are more or less banned in almost all societies ("illegal") have differences in definition, penalty, or range of enforcement, while content that is "harmful" within the definition are prohibited in some societies or in some circumstances, while not in others. There is hardly any standard that is absolute and universal.[3]

In the European context, the meaning of the phrase "illegal and harmful" was illuminated, obliquely, by the fact that, at the same time as its Internet Communication, the Commission issued a Green Paper on the Protection of Minors and Human Dignity in Audio-visual and Information Services (European Commission 1996b). This Paper – not specifically directed at the Internet – offered a variant on the "illegal and harmful" pairing used in the Internet-related Communication. The universe of concern is not "illegal and harmful," but something else: a distinction between material banned for all by particular Member States and "certain material that might affect the physical and mental development of minors," i.e., material that might be permissible for adults but harmful for children. One might assume that the "banned" material is congruent with the idea of the "illegal," but the term was not used. The rationale for the variant was that different solutions are required for restricted access to the two media. For example, material harmful for children would and could be subject to a watershed restriction (no broadcast prior to a certain time) on television or a technical device could be required that would aid parents in blocking and filtering. The annex to the Green Paper adds one additional justification for the prevention of harm that broadens the meaning past minors, namely "the desire to protect sensitive people" from confronting offensive material. "Sensitive people" include "average" citizens who suddenly and unexpectedly see material from which they may wish to have been protected. It is worth quoting the relevant section from the Green Paper:

> The arrangements made to protect minors and human dignity may vary from country to country and from time to time. But it is important to distinguish two types of problems relating to material: Firstly, access to certain types of material may be banned for everyone, regardless of the age of the potential audience or medium used. Here it is possible, irrespective of differences in national legislation, to identify a general category of material that violates human dignity, primarily consisting of child pornography, extreme gratuitous violence and incitement to racial or other hatred, discrimination, and violence. Secondly, access to certain material that might affect the physical and mental development of minors is allowed only for adults. These measures should not be confused with other objectives of general interest, such as consumer protection, which might help to protect minors (notably in terms of advertising, where exploitation of their credulity is to be prevented). The aim is therefore limited to preventing minors from encountering, by accident or otherwise, material that might affect their physical and/or mental development. The issues are sometimes confused for one reason or another, but it is essential to maintain the distinction between these different questions: they are different objectives that raise different problems and call for different solutions. Clearly, the measures required to enforce a total ban are different from those needed to restrict access by minors or to prevent chance access by adults.

Here again, the idea of bifurcation arises: bifurcation between minors and adults, bifurcation between material that is somehow *malum prohibitum* (universally disdained) and material that is only dangerous when minors (or other sensitive people) are exposed to it. One possibility for a difference in categories lies in the technological distinctions between the Internet and television, at least as the two media were conceived in a pre-convergence era. In television, one could distinguish between material that was to be received by minors by scheduling time or otherwise dealing with a fixed group of distributors of signals. The universe for regulation is wholly different for the

Internet where time zones had no meaning and where content providers were legion. The technological imperatives of the Internet require a new mindset. When the European Parliament's Committee on Culture, Youth, Education and Media reported on the Internet Communication, it reinterpreted the distinction with an intriguing approach (European Parliament 1997). A "fundamental distinction has to be made between illegal content, which appertains to the field of law, and harmful content, which concerns minors and appertains essentially to the domain of morals, whether it is conveyed by the Internet or by other modes of communication." The Committee reasserted that "it is crucial to differentiate between illegal and harmful content, which call for 'very different legal and technological responses.'"

The Committee pointed out that the main issues regarding illegal content were traceability and detection (techniques of law enforcement) while with harmful content softer approaches like blacklisting (barring objectionable sites), "whitelisting" (putting a fence around approved sites), or the encouragement of neutral labelling were possible. The assumption was that for the category called "illegal," the consequence was foregone, while the principal difficulty was identification and finding the supplier of the material. For "harmful" material, the main issue was management. The report elaborated the distinction, demonstrating the scope of the "illegal" and the particular purpose of the category of the "harmful:"

> It is one thing to talk of child pornography, which is illegal and punishable by the criminal law, and another to refer to the fact that children may have access to pornographic material intended for adults, which, while being harmful to their development, is not necessarily illegal for adult consumers. In the first case (deviant pornography), one is dealing with illegal content which is outlawed in all areas of society, whatever the age of the potential consumers and whatever the medium used, whereas in the second case what is involved is a form of harmful content, access to which is permitted to adults only and is, therefore, forbidden to minors [...] Other types of content are considered to be illegal by the laws of most Member States. These include pedophilia, trafficking in human beings, the dissemination of documents of a racist nature, terrorism and various forms of fraud (eg credit card fraud and offences against intellectual property).

All through these discussions flows this idea of distinction: enforcing a total ban and restricting access, the yin of illegality and the yang of coping with harmful material. Within the distinction lie elaborate assumptions about the functioning of government and the industrial infrastructure that permits each side of the formula to be carefully implemented. Within the distinction could be an important administrative counterpart. What constitutes the harmful is a matter that can be left for self-regulation and what constitutes the criminal – the subject of total ban or illegality – lies of necessity with the state (both for describing the conduct and enforcing the norm).

Not every society has the desire or the capacity to specifically define what constitutes the illegal and distinguish it from the harmful in the sense embedded in the EU approach. Not every society has the commitment to due process built into the idea of prosecuting the illegal, nor the full respect for the necessities of speech freedoms to determine whether a particular speech act is an illegal infringement. Similarly, to the extent that the "harmful" is a matter for self-regulation, the validity of the concept depends on the techniques available in any society to engage in this softer form of law. The distinction is also enlisted to describe the line between government and industry. Broadcasters or the Internet industry (particularly Internet service providers) might have a duty to co-operate with law enforcement over illegal content (and there are statutes that so provide), but that line works better in societies where industry is an agent of the state, actively assisting in ferreting out particular forms of speech labeled illegal by the government.[4]

## Interpreting the Distinction

The world has not been uniformly satisfied with this distinction, namely the two pillars of content – the illegal and the harmful. Their migration from Commission Communication or Green Paper to law is useful to examine. As the 1996 Communication permeated the member states, the distinction was reinterpreted. The European approach also interacted with efforts to determine standards in the United States, Australia, and elsewhere. Further, as standards went from document to implementation, the complexities of existing bureaucracies, constitutional limitations, and other domestic idiosyncrasies meant that a clear and overarching division would be difficult to sustain.

Within the member states, the Communication led to a variety of national studies (not all of which can be covered here). In Ireland, the Department of Justice commissioned a study called "The Internet: Tackling the Downside, The First Report of the Working Group on Illegal & Harmful Use of the Internet" (Government of Ireland 1998). The authors found 10 categories which belonged to the umbrella of potential illegality: (1) national security, (2) injury to children, (3) injury to human dignity, (4) economic security, (5) information security, (6) privacy protection, (7) protection of reputation, (8) gambling, (9) information on the sale of "controlled drugs", and (10) intellectual property. Several of these categories seem to contain material subsumed in the 1996 EU vision of material that is "harmful" though not illegal. These include injury to children and injury to human dignity. Having swept this content into the definition of illegality, the subsection on "harmful uses" is relatively short. "Harmful uses are difficult to identify with any great precision since they involve an assessment of their effect on different individuals." The working group listed "material relating to sex, violence, discrimination, graphic crime reporting, drug addiction, and cult worship" as possibilities.

In the United Kingdom, there were many entities at work trying to formulate an internal standard that would be consistent with the EU Communication. As it happened, one of the interpretive documents relating to "illegal and harmful" occurred in the UK in an unusual way. The Internet Watch Foundation is the UK service provider and self-regulatory entity subject to periodic government review. Undertaking to review the formulation of a UK standard consistent with the EU Communication, the government's Department of Trade and Industry (DTI) sought to explore the British embodiment of the 1996 EU envelope of illegal and harmful content. According to the DTI review, there should be three different categories of regulatory concern. These would be "illegal," "unlawful," and "offensive"(Government of UK 1999). Illegal material is that which is subject to criminal prosecution. Unlawful material infringes on a private right, recognized by law, although not subject to criminal law. Examples given are material that infringes on a copyright or breaches a contract. Offensive material is content that is generally not unlawful but "can be considered harmful or otherwise unsuitable, inappropriate to certain audiences, or offensive to their values and feelings." In the United States, the category, (the equivalent of "offensiveness," in this British reading), is the complicated regulatory cubbyhole, for radio and television, of "indecency."

In Germany, one of the industry associations, the Electronic Commerce Forum (ECO), worked on another form of interpretation and norm development. ECO established the Internet Content Task Force (ICTF) in May 1996 to promulgate and further self-regulate controls. Its analysis divided content into three different types: content criminal in most countries (much like the banned or illegal content category of the EU), content criminal under German law, reflecting particular German needs (for example laws banning Holocaust denial), and, separately, content that is "harmful."[5]

The problems of definition and the establishment of categories were world-wide phenomena. In Singapore, the definition of illegal and harmful content aimed at preventing the public from receiving a much broader panoply of materials. At least at an early stage in regulation, all Internet Service Providers were required to be registered by the Singapore Broadcasting Authority (SBA) (Hogan 1999). While Internet content was subject to general media laws such as the Defamation Act, Sedition Act, and Maintenance of Religious Harmony Act, an additional category of "undesirable content" was also regulated (Ibid: 436). The Singapore Broadcasting Authority Act gave the SBA the power to pass Internet regulations and in 1996 the SBA issued a notification that established "regulatable" content. The restriction included contents that "threaten public order and national security, religious and social harmony, and morality." Examples of these categories are content that promotes hatred or contempt against the government; excites disaffection with the government; denigrates or satirizes any race or religious group; brings any race or religious group into hatred or resentment; promotes religious deviation; promotes immorality (as defined by Singapore's value system); are pornographic or obscene; or depict or propagate acts deemed sexually deviant (such as homosexuality and pedophilia) (Ibid: 437-439).[6]

In Australia, neither the term "harmful" nor the term "illegal" was used in its landmark 1999 Online Services Act (Australian Broadcasting Services Amendment Bill 1999.) Instead, the vocabulary included terms such as "unsuitable" and "offensive" along with "prohibited." The question of definition was resolved in a way not used elsewhere. Content regulation was tied to standards adopted by the Office of Film and Literature Classification. Thus material would be prohibited if it would be classified RC or X by the Classification Office or if it was designated R and not protected by an approved restricted access system. The Online Services Act included provisions to restrict access to content "likely to cause offense to a reasonable adult," though there is little to explain the meaning of this open term, and it has provisions to protect children from content deemed "unsuitable" for them.[7]

The Australian Broadcasting Authority (ABA) actively negotiated an industry code of conduct, an age verification procedure for access to objectionable material and material unsuitable for minors, and a labelling scheme to alert users by threatening imposing such a code on their own if there were no self-regulatory counterpart.[8] Australia is one of the few jurisdictions in which the statute distinguishes between content "hosted in" the country, and content that is "hosted outside." If the content is Australian, in this sense, the ABA may direct the content host to remove the content from their service. If the content originates abroad, Internet Service Providers have an obligation to follow procedures set out in an industry code of practice to block access to that material. If the material is "illegal" in nature (like child pornography) then law enforcement may have a role regardless of where the material had its beginnings.[9]

The Australian solution underscores the importance of "codes of conduct." These instruments are frequently becoming part of the response of the Internet industry (especially the ISPs) to the demand for content control, and, themselves reflect the complex and confusing initiatives taken by governments. Codes of conduct are a means of mediating between the ambiguity of statutes and the ambiguity of life. They sometimes are explicit markers of agreed-upon norms, modes for defining misconduct, and methods for engineering enforcement. Codes constitute relatively transparent sites for negotiation between industry and government. The documents usually arise from the regulated sector though they often reflect the mandates of the regulator. They serve two functions: to establish and protect a space where ISPs would have no or limited responsibility and, in exchange, describe the kinds of limited responsibility they might have in specific instances. They are typically designed to counter the argument about the need for law by imposing standards themselves.

The drama over definition of prohibited and regulable content over the Internet has been relatively rich in the United States, partly because of the relevance of the First Amendment to the US Constitution. The pattern of legislation was somewhat the same. The Communications Decency Act of 1996 prohibited obscene material, a category that had been held by the United States Supreme Court to be something other than "speech" and therefore unprotected by the First Amendment. As to the strange and difficult second category of harm to minors, Congress acted twice, and its definitional attempts were on both occasions rebuffed by the courts. In its first attempt, the category of harm was captured in the term "indecent," borrowed from its history of regulation of broadcasting. The Supreme Court struck down the statute penalizing entities that knowingly displayed indecent material.[10] In a seeming effort to plug the constitutional gap, the phrase "harmful to minors" was introduced in the second legislation.[11] The lower courts have held this provision unconstitutional as well.[12]

## Empowerment

There is another interplay between the domestic and the international in the regulation of indecent and obscene or pornographic material: the discussion, in the late 1990s, of the V-chip and other parental consent, content filtering, and rating systems on television and the Internet. There was something then that remains politically mesmerizing about the idea of the V-chip. It approximates a magic wafer, a combination of wires and plastic that would help salve consciences, allow public responsibility to be satisfied, resurrect parenthood, and help persuade providers of programming to be more forthcoming as to the content and impact of the material they purvey. Public debate on this question can serve as a metaphor for the many other areas where the existence of practical authority and the search for application of state power has been affected by transnational developments.

The V-chip debate (and the debate about content filters, labels, and ratings that preceded and accompanied it) is part of a painfully visible effort by states, against technological and constitutional odds, to alter the relationship between the consumer and producer of content. The debate and reception of these approaches makes an especially interesting comparative study because the process advanced from country to country, with a kind of conversation among states. One adaptation exerted influence on another, culminating in a regional and comprehensive study in the European Union.

The V-chip, or the concept of the chip, seemed to hit the marketplace of competing ideologies at a moment when elected legislators and decision makers in Canada, the United States, Australia and elsewhere had a deep political need for this device beyond the contribution it could make in the architecture of program choice and screening. The technology permitted the inference that government was acting in a way that dealt with important cultural questions in the society while actually doing quite little to disturb the market, which presented an enormous political advantage. The genesis of the device was in

Canada, but the idea soon mushroomed and spread through the United States, Australia, Japan and Europe.

In the mid-1990s, a Canadian scientist named Tim Collings wrote a short paper on a technology that, quite simply, permitted information about a program to stream down a vertical blanking interval (a technological space that existed because of the mode of transmission of analogue signals) and trigger a mechanism in the television – preset by its owner – to block unwanted programs. Originally, the "V" stood for Viewer: a chip to give the viewer a choice. The very first transformation in the ensuing international debate was over the meaning of the V: it has moved from Viewer in Canada to Violence in the United States (and, somewhat mysteriously, into Sex or Indecency). The Canadian Radio-television and Telecommunications Commission (CRTC) sought, systematically, to determine the best possible and most efficient means of classifying program content and conveying that classification to viewers. Industry and citizens together made decisions about what questions would be asked about a program, the subject matter of the information to be gathered, and the way in which that information should be conveyed (McDowell and Maitland 1998: 23–46).

In Canada, there was a period of experimentation conducted under the supervision of the regulators that led, after hearings and industry recommendations, to the adoption of a comprehensive and relatively well-thought out public policy advanced without much recrimination or dissent. In the United States (at least in the first instance under the forced hand of Congress), because of the design of the 1996 Telecommunications Act and the supposed implications of the First Amendment, it fell almost purely to the entertainment industry to fashion the implementation of the device. Only if the US industry developed an unacceptable approach would there be a government appointed commission to develop alternatives. This method, the result of political compromise and special US constitutional considerations, had a profound impact on the initial industry offering and the debate that ensued. In the end, the trails between the Canadian and American approaches seem to have converged, but that, too, is probably an indication of how narrow the possibility of fashioning an acceptable rating system might be.

In the United States there was a melodramatic "second act," a consequence of interest group politics and the competition between industry-legislator alliances and legislator-community group alliances. In Canada, industry groups worked with public agencies and community entities during the planning process. In the US, in contrast to Canada, the initial industry-originated plan, mostly hatched behind closed doors, led to well co-ordinated objections by public interest organizations. Advocacy protest against the industry system proposed in early 1997 led to changes that – depending on the critic – may or may not have significance in the end.[13] This revised system took a leaf from the Canadian proposal and increased disclosure of content information to the basic industry version of the Motion Picture Association of America classification system, which was largely age-based.

The V-chip, in its basic form, is specific to television and is an episode in the very long series of discussions about whether the accessibility to children of violence or sexually suggestive programming on television (or broadcasting generally) deserves special attention. These discussions have an under-appreciated pre-history in the labelling of comic books, rating of films, and proscription of books (each of which, in their turn, was supposed to have domineering and magical qualities of persuasion). In this V-chip embodiment, advocacy starts with the premise that radio and television have an even more particular power to affect conduct, and, in the traditional free-to-air mode of distribution, a certain invasiveness.[14]

The V-chip approach has a noteworthy, cultural horizontal spread: from the establishment of information that would allow filtering of violent and indecent television programming to far more expansive grounds for filtering for such things as advertisements concerning alcohol or tobacco or messages filterable because of political content (Steyn 1996; "Meeting the New Chip…" 1996). Labelling and rating schemes proliferate and are no longer primarily the province of broadcasting and motion pictures. The video game industry and the music industry have responded to legislative pressure within the United States to develop labelling and rating methods of their own. An Internet Watch Foundation, founded in the United Kingdom, has established an elaborate system of self-rating, partly for the benefit of Internet providers so as to protect them from hostile government intervention. One of the most important current discussions involves the development of PICS or the Platform for Internet Content Selection, a vigorous and still controversial approach to assuring a multiplicity of voluntary ratings and an architecture freer of government involvement (Martin 2000). School boards and libraries adopt policies that incorporate voluntary rating schemes into official regulation of access. Communities design criminal ordinances that use government sanctions to enforce these restless labels.

The V-chip philosophy has its gnarled roots in contested research and conflicting ideologies, where the interest groups are divided between those who oppose state intervention and those who consider it appropriate in some circumstances. More heated is the debate between those who think the almost direct connection between television programming and violence is adequately demonstrated and those who think it has not been proven sufficiently to justify government intervention. The V-chip's introduction has been an odd occasion, as well, for a discussion, sometimes forced and artificial, about the role of parents in controlling the flow of images. There seems to be hardly any research on the relationship between parent (or caretaker) and child, and child and television set (Cantor 1998). Yet speeches proliferate about the extent to which this device will enhance the parental or care-taking role. The technology's enthusiasts believe or claim to believe that the V-chip "empowers" parents, to use the term of the 1996 US Telecommunications Act, though the evidence that parents either need empowerment or, more doubtfully, that this device empowers them, is in slim supply. There is no question that the technology has its doubters, both as to its inherent contribution, its neutrality and relationship to censorship, and to the plausibility of its implementation. Among these are skeptics who believe that the V-chip merely allows legislators and policymakers to *appear* to be addressing a problem of imagery and society while, in fact, nothing is done to address that virtually intractable issue.

While the initial concept of the V-chip was simple, its flow into the public realm has raised so many extraordinary questions that the introduction and production of the chip can serve as a case study in problems of law and public policy. Here are a few of the questions that have emerged: What research basis is necessary to require a framework for labelling and rating? What relationship between government and the image-producing industries can be characterized (for constitutional and other reasons) as voluntary as opposed to coercive? If images are to be evaluated, who should do the evaluation – the producers, the distributors, or objective third parties? In a society barraged by images, how feasibly can satisfactory rating or labelling systems emerge? In television, should a rating system be scene by scene, program by program, series by series, or channel by channel? Indeed, how much information about content can be effectively redacted and communicated? There are semiotic questions about the nature of the logos, the on-screen signals used to alert viewers: What kind of label or logo informs, and what kind persuades? What kind of logo is neutral and what kind bears its own shame-bearing or moral judgment? What kind of logo has a boomerang effect and attracts, as opposed to informs and repels, audiences for which it is to serve as a warning? What relationship is enshrined in the architecture of labelling between the industry that produces the images and the government that regulates them? How centralized or how distributed should be the process of evaluation? What guarantees of integrity are there to the evaluative or rating process? What assessment is there to evaluate whether the experiment is successful? What difference does the rate of V-chip penetration into households make? It is also interesting to examine how a government introduces or furthers a technology of filtering. The different approaches in Canada and the United States towards the role of regulatory agency, industry and government reflect political traditions and may demonstrate substantial distinctions in constitutional standards. Such a study of comparative processes – how different political and industrial systems evaluate these labels and mechanisms – have been of significance to the European Commission, the United Kingdom, and other entities studying rating arrangements after the US and Canadian adoptions.

Still, what is striking about these questions is that they assume a national ground for action. The data and experience can come from other societies; but it is almost always assumed that each society can absorb and render a decision for its own citizens. One can, however, read the interaction between the development of standards and approaches in the US and in Canada quite differently. As a laboratory, Canada influenced the United States. The United States influenced the final Canadian decision by sheer dint of overwhelming neighborliness. US pressure groups obtained, through political activity, the absorption of various elements of the Canadian approach. The ultimate Canadian approach incorporated elements of the American system for reasons of pragmatic reality and the general overwhelming inclusion of US programming on the Canadian screen.

It is hard to know how to read the aggregated results of industry proposal, group advocacy and industry change in Canada and the United States. Did these plans rest on the notion that, whether self-enforced or not, the resulting techniques were ones that could be used effectively to alter the relationship between viewer and sender of messages? Or did the results indicate that in the modern world, any effort to intervene in the intimate, though industrialized, speech practices of broadcasting was hopeless. Many people, including those in the creative community in Hollywood, criticized the industry solution as compromising free speech values. In November 1996, for example, the Caucus for Producers, Writers and Directors proposed a ratings system similar to the one finally proposed by networks with the exception of NBC.[15] A year later, in November 1997, the Caucus, after inner turmoil, publicly voiced its opposition to the new television content ratings system and reversed its earlier position. Other critics claimed that the industry had too much control over the US rating system.

No matter how much debate there was over the content of the labels, the size of their display on-screen, the number of seconds they would appear, and other details of hand-to-hand combat, the suspicion lingered that the whole exercise was merely a gambit. It was the minimum concession by industry necessary to avoid a renewal of attempts at government content regulation and the appropriate level of official noise to demonstrate concern while avoiding intervention in the economic activity of major constituents. Insufferably mild an intervention for some, the American scheme, even in its indirect mode, constituted censorship and government control for others. The ratings system, and the legislation that brought it about, could, with some winks, be viewed as a good faith effort to meet a public need, or, on the other hand, as a brilliant preemption of legislation that might more effectively and dangerously intervene and impose binding moral standards.

## Conclusion

The V-chip experience is intriguing as an exercise in cross-national regulatory influence. It is interesting to think of the impact of policy making in the United States on policy making elsewhere, particularly in Canada, especially at a time when globalization, wrapped in trade considerations, leads to a leveling of regulatory approaches. In various ways, it is the reverse or mutual influence that is worth examining as well. The Canadian attitude was a more or less rational exploration of alternatives and the testing of alternatives; the United States' approach involved the search for a political consensus and its wholesale implementation. The question then became whether the US solution would (partly because of the complexities of transborder flow of entertainment programming and the dominance of the American industry) come to reshape the Canadian debate or the other way around. American advocacy groups, seeking what they perceived as a better outcome from the legislation, sought the disclosure of more information in ratings systems, an outcome that approached the Canadian system.

No matter what the solution to the debate over the V-chip, at bottom, the public outcry, intensive as it seems, generally glides over the basic concerns about modern culture, modern mores, and the impact of the influx of images. The V-chip, though it exists largely because of unease about aspects of modernity, fixates on sex and violence, neglecting the effects on children of the loss of traditional kinds of literacy and the leveling of cultures. In this sense, the V-chip is an American-type formulation of resistance to cultural change. It is a technical solution to a preoccupation with violence and indecency and a substitute for insignificantly addressed concerns about fundamental trends in the way children are acculturated. The overarching, almost religious questions that probably lie at the root of the most sincere expressions of social concern are reflected only indirectly in the many studies of violence and media. These studies cannot satisfactorily model the question of whether images on television affect behavior, or which images on television, in motion pictures, or on the Internet affect behaviour in what ways. As with much of the scholarship and research, the very point of the chip is to tweak culture at the margin, to provide a filter, not to damn modernity.

## Notes

1   For legal systems that base power on the distinction in geographical origin of information see, for example, the Australian Online Services Act of 1999, discussed later in this chapter, which establishes different content controls according to whether the content is "hosted in" or "hosted outside" Australia.

2   See *Television Without Frontiers*(1997). Chapter III of the Directive, entitled "Promotion of Distribution and Production of Television Programmes," requires Community television stations to reserve, "where practicable," a majority of their broadcasting time for "European works." The definition of "European works" has been controversial. It includes co-productions with non-Member States provided that the co-production is "actually controlled" by the Community producer and the Community producer covers the majority of costs.

3   The EU document specifically suggests that "harmful content" could include the expression of certain extreme political opinions, religious beliefs or views on racial matters if they are carved out for non-criminal treatment by member states, which must do so consistent with the right to freedom of expression provisions of the European Convention on Human Rights.

4   This co-operation could take the form of monitoring to assist in detection, ensuring an architecture of the system that aids in tracing and that minimizes anonymity so that transgressors can be more easily apprehended, and other forms as well. It is in relationship to this question of relationship to law enforcement that the device of the hotline has gained respectability as an instrument of self-regulation and co-ordination with law enforcement (EU 1999).

5   The German Federal Act Establishing the General Conditions for Information and Communication Services (Information and Communication Services Act) was passed 1 August 1997 and extended the Law on the Dissemination of Publications Morally Harmful to Youth to the Internet. A fairly interesting initiative was a section that required the appointment of "Youth Protection Ministers," when Internet services were generally available and because they would include content morally harmful to youth. See Sieber (2000).

6   See also The Singapore Broadcasting Authority Act (1997).

7   These provisions to restrict access to content "likely to cause offense to a reasonable adult" are set out in Section III of the Act. The bill has been widely criticized as interfering too extensively with the Internet and has been called the "Net Oppression Bill" by groups in Australia. See libertus.net's discussion of the act, available online (April 2001): http://libertus.net/liberty/oppress.html.

8   For age verification procedures see Internet Law & Policy Forum, Content Blocking Working Group, *Content Blocking Report, Self-Regulatory Initiatives*, Available Online (April 2001): http://www.ilpf.org/work/content/selfreg.htm. One interesting issue that presents itself based on the action taken by Australia is how the community shapes the material that is tolerated on the Internet. The industry's code of practice must be written after "appropriate community consultation" and must "contain appropriate community safeguards." Available online (April 2001): http://www.aba. gov.au/what/online/overview.htm.

9   In New Zealand, as in Australia, the focus of Internet content has been on "objectionable" material as defined by the New Zealand Films, Videos, and Publications Classification Act, 1993. The Act defines a publication as objectionable "if it describes, depicts, expresses, or otherwise deals with matters such as sex, horror, crime, cruelty, or violence in such a manner that the availability of the publication is likely to be injurious to the public good." Self-regulation has been the standard so far in New Zealand with regard to the Internet. It is supported by the Minister of Information Technology (Internet Code of Practice 1999).

10  Reno v. ACLU, 117 S. Ct. 2329 (1997).

11  See Child Online Protection Act ("COPA"), Pub. L. No. 105-277, 1401, 112 Stat. 2681 (1998). See Miller v. California, 413 U.S. 15 (1973).

12  On February 1, 1999, the US District Court for the Eastern District of Pennsylvania issued a preliminary injunction barring enforcement of COPA. See ACLU v. Reno, 31 F. Supp. 2d 473 (E.D. Pa. 1999).

13  The opposition came from public interest groups linked both to liberal and conservative causes. Andrea Sheldon, Executive Director of the Traditional Values Coalition, testifying before the Senate Commerce, Science and Transportation Committee on the initial television ratings system in February, 1997, complained that TV-PG shows had nearly as many obscenities as TV-14. "Receiving the TV-PG rating were "Wings," "Friends," "Beverly Hills 90210," and "Savannah" all featuring pre-marital sex, sex with various partners and sex with no commitment. In addition, all of this took place during the family hour. I doubt that many parents would consider these situations acceptable for a 14-year old...Obviously, we need a rating system that is content-specific. Television viewers have a right to know what is coming into their homes. And parents should know this in advance." Testimony of Andrea Sheldon, Executive Director, Traditional Values Coalition Hearing on the New Television Ratings System before the Senate Commerce, Science and Transportation Committee, February 27, 1997.

14  And, as the notion of filtering and labelling caught the imagination of the politician and all those who wished to consider new ways to alter bargaining over imagery in society, the very idea of the chip or its equivalent moved back across technologies and forms of information. In the United States, the Federal Communications Commission came to require the installation of a V-chip or its equivalent in computers that are capable of receiving broadcast transmissions, depending on screen size, with implications for Internet screening and labelling. See FCC Ruling... (1998)

15  According to Rosalyn Weinman, head of Standards and Practices at the network, NBC decided not to add content-based labels because "we do not believe that they add any level of information to parents when they want to make decisions for their children. We believe quite the contrary that the content labels add nothing other than misconceptions and confusion to a system that was working and working well." Interview with Rosalyn Weinman, ABC Nightline (11:35 pm ET), October 17, 1997.

# References

Australian Broadcasting Services Amendment (Online Services) Bill. 1999. ("Online Services Act") No. 99077.

Cantor, J. 1998. *Children and Television: Ratings for Program Content: The Role of Research Findings*, 557 Annals 54.

European Commission. 1996a. Illegal and Harmful Content on the Internet: Communication to the European Parliament, the Council, the Economic and Social Committee and the Committee of the Regions, *COM*(96) 487, Available Online (April 2001): http://158.169.50.95:10080/legal/en/internet/communic.html.

European Commission. 1996b. Green Paper on the Protection of Minors and Human Dignity in Audiovisual and Information Services, *COM*(96) 483. Available Online (April 2001): http://europa.eu.int/en/record/green/gp9610/protec.htm.

European Parliament. 1997. Committee on Culture, Youth, Education, and the Media, *Report on the Commission Communication on Illegal and Harmful Content on the Internet*, A4-0098/97, PE 219.568/DEF.

European Union. 1999. *Action Plan on Promoting Safer Use of the Internet*, Decision No 275/1999/EC of the European Parliament and of the Council, 25 January 1999: 7.

FCC Ruling Gives Go-ahead to Tri-Vision's V-Chip 1998. Financial Post. 13 March: 3.

Goldsmith, J. L. 1998. Against Cyberanarchy, 65 *U. Chi. L. Rev*: 1199, 1224.

Government of Ireland. 1998. The Working Group on Illegal & Harmful Use of the Internet, *The Internet: Tackling the Downside, The First Report of the Working Group on Illegal & Harmful Use of the Internet*. Available Online (April 2001): http://www.irlgov.ie/justice/Publications/Internet%20Submissions/subnet3.htm.

Government of UK 1999. Department of Trade & Industry and Home Office, Review of the Internet Watch Foundation. http://www.dti.gov.uk/cii/iwfreview/.

Hogan, S. B. 1999. To Net or Not to Net: Singapore's Regulation of the Internet, 51 *Fed. Comm. L.J.*: 429.

Internet Code of Practice. 1999. The Internet Society of New Zealand. June 1999.

Available Online (April 2001): http://www.isocnz.org.nz/icop/icop99the-code.html.

McDowell, S. D. and Maitland, C. 1998. Developing Television Ratings in Canada and the United States. In *The V-Chip Debate: Content Filtering From Television to the Internet*, edited by M. E. Price. Lawrence A. Erlbaum Associates: 23-46.

Meeting the New Chip on the Block: And Imagine the Joy of Watching Television Without the Dross. 1996. *The Guardian*, March 19 : 16.

Sieber, U. 2000. In *Protecting Our Children on the Internet: Towards a New Culture of Responsibility*, edited by J. Waltermann and M. Machell. Bertelsmann Foundation Publishers.

The Singapore Broadcasting Authority Act, Internet Code of Practice, at Prohibited Material, 1st November 1997. Available Online (April 2001): http://www.sba.gov.sg/work/sba/internet.nsf/pages/code.

Steyn, M. 1996. TV Cynics Zap Clinton's Cure-All: the V-Chip, the In-home Censor, Is Coming Soon to Small Screens in the US, *Sunday Telegraph*, March 3: 24.

*Television Without Frontiers*. 1997. Chapter 5, Directive 97/36/EC, OJ L 202, 30.07.97/ 60 – 71. European Union.

# The Global Restructuring of Media Ownership

**Robert W. McChesney**

Globalization, technological revolution and democratization characterize the era in which we live. In all three of these areas, media and communications play a central – perhaps even a defining – role. Of specific interest are the main developments and contours of the media industries in this era and their relationship to globalization, technological revolution and democracy. With a critical look at the political economy of the contemporary global media and communications industries, we can cut through much of the mythology and hype surrounding our era and develop a much more skeptical view of the caliber of democracy emerging in the world today. In my view, the very notion of globalization is misleading and ideologically loaded. A superior term would be neoliberalism: this refers to the set of national and international policies that call for business domination of all social affairs with minimal countervailing force. Neoliberalism not only explains the rise of the global media system, but it highlights the severe fault lines in the world media and political economy for any viable theory of participatory democracy.

Prior to the 1980s and 1990s, national media systems were typified by domestically owned radio, television and newspaper industries. There were considerable import markets for films, television shows, music and books, and these markets tended to be dominated by US-based firms. But local commercial interests, sometimes combined with a state-affiliated broadcasting service, were the dominant forces in the media system. In this environment, the key concern was to allow the press freedom to operate without government coercion or censorship. This remains a problem across the planet, with recent press-state struggles taking place in Russia, Hungary and Angola, to mention but a few (Cullison 2000; Swarns 2000; Wright 2000; Gordon 2000). A familiar theme as well, dealt with how the dominant commercial media often had a cozy and corrupt relationship with the dominant political forces (Free to be Bad 2000; Tyler 2000; Preston 2000).

All of this is changing, and changing rapidly, in present times. The nature of the traditional concerns remains, but their context has changed considerably. In the past, media systems were primarily national; but recently, a global commercial media market has emerged. To grasp media today and in the future, one must start with understanding the global system and then factor in differences at the national and local levels. "What you are seeing," says Christopher Dixon, media analyst for the investment firm PaineWebber, "is the creation of a global oligopoly. It happened to the oil and automotive industries earlier this century; now it is happening to the entertainment industry" (McChesney 2000: 78).

This global oligopoly has two distinct but related facets. First, it means the dominant companies – nearly all US-based – are moving across the planet at breakneck speed. The point is to capitalize on the potential for growth abroad—and not get outflanked by competitors – since the US market is well developed and only permits incremental expansion. As Viacom CEO Sumner Redstone has put it, "Companies are focusing on those markets promising the best return, which means overseas." Frank Biondi, former chairman of Vivendi's Universal Studios, asserts that "99 per cent of the success of these companies long-term is going to be successful execution offshore" (McChesney 2000: 87).

The dominant media firms increasingly view themselves as global entities. Bertelsmann CEO Thomas Middelhoff bristled when, in 1998, some said it was improper for a German firm to control 15 per cent of both the US book publishing and music markets. "We're not foreign. We're international," Middelhoff said. "I'm an American with a German passport." In 2000 Middelhoff proclaimed that Bertelsmann was no longer a German company. "We are really the most global media company" (Kirkpatrick 2000b). Likewise, AOL-Time Warner's Gerald Levin stated, "We do not want to be viewed as an American company. We think globally" (Schechter 2000). Second, convergence and consolidation are the order of the day. Specific media industries are becoming more and more concentrated, and the dominant players in each media industry increasingly are subsidiaries of huge global media conglomerates. For one small example, the US market for educational publishing is now controlled by four firms, whereas it had two dozen viable players as recently as 1980 (Scardino's Way 2000).

The level of mergers and acquisitions is breathtaking. In the first half of 2000, the number of merger deals in global media, Internet and telecommunications totalled US$300 billion, triple the figure for the first six months of 1999 and exp̶ ̶lly higher than the figure from ten years earlier (Mermigas 2000a). ̶iding media firms in all of this is clear: get very big very quickly, ̶wed up by someone else. This is similar to trends taking place in ̶ndustries. "There will be less than a handful of end-game ̶EO of Chase Manhattan announced in September 2000. "We ̶d-game winner" (Talk Show 2000.) But in few industries has

149

the level of concentration been as stunning as in media. In short order, the global media market has come to be dominated by nine transnational corporations: General Electric (owner of NBC), AT&T/Liberty Media, Disney, AOL-Time Warner, Sony, News Corporation, Viacom, Vivendi and Bertelsmann. None of these companies existed in its present form as recently as 15 years ago; today nearly all of them will rank among the largest 200 non-financial firms in the world for 2000 (The World's 100 Largest Public Companies 2000). Of the nine, only five are truly US firms, though all of them have core operations there. Between them, these nine companies own: the major US film studios; the US television networks; 80–85 per cent of the global music market; the majority of satellite broadcasting world-wide; all or part of a majority of cable broadcasting systems; a significant percentage of book publishing and commercial magazine publishing; all or part of most of the commercial cable TV channels in the US and world-wide; a significant portion of European terrestrial television; and on and on and on.

By nearly all accounts, the level of concentration is only going to increase in the future. "I'm a great believer that we are going to a world of vertically integrated companies where only the big survive," said Gordon Crawford, an executive of Capital Research & Management, a mutual fund that is among the largest shareholders in many of the nine firms listed above (Bianco 2000). For firms to survive, *Business Week* observes, speed is of the essence. "Time is short" (Ibid). "In a world moving to five, six, seven media companies, you don't want to be in a position where you have to count on others," Peter Chernin, the president of News Corporation states. "You need to have enough marketplace dominance that people are forced to deal with you." Chernin elaborates: "There are great arguments about whether content is king or distribution is king. At the end of the day, scale is king. If you can spread your costs over a large base, you can outbid your competitors for programming and other assets you want to buy" (Hansell 2000). By 2000, massive cross-border deals – like Pearson merging its TV operations with CLT and Bertelsmann, or Vivendi purchasing Universal – were increasing in prominence (Mermigas 2000b).

Chernin's firm, Rupert Murdoch's News Corporation, may be the most aggressive global trailblazer, although cases could be made for Sony, Bertelsmann or AOL-Time Warner. Murdoch spun off Sky Global Networks in 2000, consolidating his satellite TV services that run from Asia to Europe to Latin America (Goldsmith and Dawtrey 2000). His Star TV dominates in Asia with 30 channels in seven languages (Jacob 2000). News Corp.'s TV service for China, Phoenix TV, in which it has a 45 per cent stake, now reaches 45 million homes there and has enjoyed an 80 per cent increase in advertising revenues in the past year (Groves 2000). And this barely begins to describe News Corp.'s entire portfolio of assets: Twentieth Century Fox films, Fox TV network, HarperCollins publishers, TV stations, cable TV channels, magazines, over 130 newspapers, and professional sport teams.

Why has this taken place? The conventional explanation is technology or, in other words, radical improvements in communications technology that make global media empires feasible and lucrative in a manner unthinkable in the past. This is similar to the technological explanation for globalization writ large. However, this is only a partial explanation, at best. The real force has been a shift to neoliberalism which means the relaxation or elimination of barriers to commercial exploitation of media and concentrated media ownership. There is nothing inherent in the technology that required neoliberalism; new digital communications could have been used, for example, to simply enhance public service media had a society elected to do so. With neoliberal values, however, television, which had been a noncommercial preserve in many nations, suddenly became subject to transnational commercial development and was thrust into the centre of the emerging global media system.

Once the national deregulation of media took place in major nations like the United States and Britain, it was followed by transnational measures like the North American Free Trade Agreement (NAFTA) and the World Trade Organization (WTO), all intent on establishing regional and global marketplaces. This has laid the foundation for the creation of the global media system, dominated by the aforementioned conglomerates. Now in place, the system has its own logic. Firms must become larger and diversified to reduce risk and enhance profit-making opportunities, and they must straddle the globe so as never to be outflanked by competitors. The upside is high; this is a market that some anticipate will have trillions of dollars in annual revenues within a decade. If that is to be the case, those companies that sit atop the field will almost certainly rank among the two or three dozen largest in the world.

The development of the global media system has not been unopposed. While media conglomerates press for policies to facilitate their domination of markets throughout the world, strong traditions of protection for domestic media and cultural industries persist. Nations ranging from Norway, Denmark and Spain to Mexico, South Africa and South Korea keep their small domestic film production industries alive with government subsidies. In the summer of 1998 culture ministers from twenty nations, including Brazil, Mexico, Sweden, Italy and Ivory Coast, met in Ottawa to discuss how they could "build some ground rules" to protect their cultural fare from "the Hollywood juggernaut." Their main recommendation was to keep culture out of the control of the World Trade Organization. A similar 1998 gathering, sponsored by the United Nations Educational, Scientific and Cultural Organization (UNESCO) in Stockholm, recommended that culture be granted special exemptions in global trade deals. Nevertheless, the trend is clearly in the direction of opening markets.

Proponents of neoliberalism in every country argue that cultural trade barriers and regulations harm consumers, and that subsidies inhibit the ability of nations to develop their own competitive media firms. There are often strong commercial-media lobbies within nations that believe they have more to gain by opening up their borders than by maintaining trade barriers. In 1998, for example, when the British government proposed a voluntary levy on film and theatre revenues (mostly Hollywood films) to benefit the British commercial film industry, British broadcasters, not wishing to antagonize the firms who supply their programming, lobbied against the measure until it died. If the WTO is explicitly a pro-commercial organization, the International Telecommunication Union (ITU) has only become one after a long march from its traditional commitment to public service values in telecommunications (Molony 1999). The European Commission, the executive arm of the European Union, too, finds itself in the middle of what controversy exists concerning media policy, and it has considerably more power than the ITU. On the one hand, the EC is committed to building powerful pan-European media giants that can go toe-to-toe with the US-based giants. On the other hand, it is committed to maintaining some semblance of competitive markets, so it occasionally rejects proposed media mergers as being anti-competitive (Stern 2000c). The wave of commercialization of European media has put the EU in the position of condemning some of the traditional subsidies to public service broadcasters as "noncompetitive," which is a source of considerable controversy (Stern 2000a; 2000b). Public service broadcasting, once the media centrepiece of European social democracy, is now on the defensive and increasingly reduced to locating a semi-commercial niche in the global system (Goldsmith 2000; Larsen 2000). Yet, as a quasi-democratic institution, the EU is subject to some popular pressure that is unsympathetic to commercial interests. Indeed, when Sweden assumes the rotating chair of the EU in 2001, it may push for its domestic ban on TV advertising to children under 12 to be extended across Europe. If it does, it will be the most radical attempt yet to limit the prerogatives of the corporate media giants that dominate commercial children's television (Hatfield 2000).

Perhaps the best way to understand how closely the global commercial media system is linked to the neoliberal global capitalist economy is to consider the role of advertising. Advertising is a business expense made preponderantly by the largest firms in the economy. The commercial media system is the necessary transmission belt for business to market its wares across the world; indeed globalization as we know it could not exist without it. A whopping three-quarters of global spending on advertising ends up in the pockets of a mere 20 media companies (Star Turn 2000). Ad spending has grown by leaps and bounds in the past decade as TV has been opened to commercial exploitation and is growing at more than twice the rate of GDP growth (Tomkins 2000). Latin American ad spending, for example, is expected to increase by nearly eight per cent in both 2000 and 2001 (Ad Spend Growth 2000). Five or six super-ad agencies have emerged in the past decade to dominate this US$350 billion global industry. The consolidation in the global advertising industry is just as pronounced as that in global media, and the two are related. "Mega-agencies are in a wonderful position to handle the business of mega-clients," one ad executive notes (Elliott 2000). It is "absolutely necessary...for agencies to consolidate. Big is the mantra. So big it must be," another executive stated (Teinowitz and Linnett 2000).

The global media market is rounded out by a second tier of five or six dozen firms that are national or regional powerhouses, or that control niche markets, like business or trade publishing. Between one-third and one-half of these second-tier firms come from North America; most of the rest are from Western Europe and Japan. Many national and regional conglomerates have been established on the backs of publishing or television empires, as in the case of Denmark's Egmont. Each of these second-tier firms is a giant in its own right, often ranking among the thousand largest companies in the world and doing more than US$1 billion per year in business. The roster of second-tier media firms from North America includes Dow Jones, Gannett, Knight-Ridder, Hearst and Advance Publications, and among those from Europe are the Kirch Group, Mediaset, Prisa, Pearson, Reuters and Reed Elsevier. The Japanese companies, aside from Sony, remain almost exclusively domestic producers.

This second tier has also crystallized rather quickly; across the globe there has been a shakeout in national and regional media markets with small firms getting eaten by medium firms and medium firms being swallowed by big firms. Compared with ten or twenty years ago, a much smaller number of much larger firms now dominate the media at a national and regional level. In Britain, for example, one of the few remaining independent book publishers, Fourth Estate, was sold to Murdoch's HarperCollins in 2000 (Kirkpatrick 2000a). A wave of mergers has left German television – the second largest TV market in the world – the private realm of Bertelsmann and Kirch (Rohwedder 2000). Indeed, a wave of mergers has left all of European terrestrial television dominated by five firms, three of which rank in the global first tier (Reed 2000). The situation may be most stark in New Zealand where the newspaper industry is largely the province of the Australian-American Rupert Murdoch and the Irishman Tony O'Reilly, who also dominates New Zealand's commercial-radio broadcasting and has major stakes in magazine publishing. Murdoch also controls pay television. In short, the rulers of New Zealand's media system could squeeze into a closet.

Second-tier corporations, like those in the first-tier, need to reach beyond national borders. "The borders are gone. We have to grow," the Chairman of Canada's CanWest Global Communications states in 2000. "We don't intend to be one of the corpses lying beside the information highway" (Brooke 2000). "We have to be Columbia or Warner Brothers one day" (Cherney 2000). The CEO of Bonnier, Sweden's largest media conglomerate, says that to survive, "we want to be the leading media company in Northern Europe" (Brown-Humes 2000). Australian media moguls, following the path blazed by Murdoch, have the mantra "Expand or die." As one puts it, "You really can't continue to grow as an Australian supplier in Australia" (McChesney 2000: 89).

Mediaset, the Berlusconi-owned Italian TV power, is angling to expand into the rest of Europe and Latin America. Perhaps the most striking example of second-tier globalization is Hicks, Muse, Tate and Furst, the US radio/publishing/TV/billboard/movie theatre power that has been constructed almost overnight. Between 1998 and 2000 it spent well over US$2 billion purchasing media assets in Mexico, Argentina, Brazil and Venezuela (Sutter 2000).

Second-tier media firms are hardly "oppositional" to the global system. This is true as well in developing countries. Mexico's Televisa, Brazil's Globo, Argentina's Clarin and Venezuela's Cisneros Group, for example, are among the world's sixty or seventy largest media corporations. These firms tend to dominate their own national and regional media markets, which have been experiencing rapid consolidation as well. They have extensive ties and joint ventures with the largest media transnational corporations (TNCs) as well as with Wall Street investment banks. In Latin America, for example, the second-tier firms work closely with the US giants who are carving up the commercial media pie among themselves. Televisa or Globo can offer News Corp., for example, local domination of the politicians and the impression of local control over their joint ventures. And like second-tier media firms elsewhere, they are also establishing global operations, especially in nations that speak the same language. As a result, the second-tier media firms in the developing nations tend to have distinctly pro-business political agendas and to support expansion of the global media market, which puts them at odds with large segments of the population in their home countries.

Together, the 60 or 70 first- and second-tier giants control much of the world's media: book, magazine and newspaper publishing; music recording; TV production; TV stations and cable channels; satellite TV systems; film production; and motion picture theatres. But the system is still very much in formation. The end result of all this activity by second-tier media firms may well be the eventual creation of one or two more giants, and it almost certainly means the number of viable media players in the system will continue to plummet. Some new second-tier firms are emerging, especially in lucrative Asian markets, and there will probably be further upheaval among the ranks of the first-tier media giants. And corporations get no guarantee of success merely by going global. The point is that they have no choice in the matter. Some, perhaps many, will falter as they accrue too much debt or as they enter unprofitable ventures. However, we are likely closer to the end of the process of establishing a stable global media market than to the beginning. And as it takes shape, there is a distinct likelihood that the leading media firms in the world will find themselves in a very profitable position. That is what they are racing to secure.

The global media system is fundamentally noncompetitive in any meaningful economic sense of the term. Many of the largest media firms have some of the same major shareholders, own portions of one another, or have interlocking boards of directors. When *Variety* compiled its list of the fifty largest global media firms for 1997, it observed that "merger mania" and cross-ownership had "resulted in a complex web of interrelationships" that would "make you dizzy." The global market strongly encourages corporations to establish equity joint ventures in which the media giants all own a part of an enterprise. This way, firms reduce competition and risk and increase the chance of profitability. As the CEO of Sogecable, Spain's largest media firm and one of the twelve largest private media companies in Europe, expressed it to *Variety*, the strategy is "not to compete with international companies but to join them" (McChesney 2000: 90).

In some respects, the global media market more closely resembles a cartel than it does the competitive marketplace found in economics textbooks. This point cannot be overemphasized. In competitive markets, in theory, numerous producers work hard and are largely oblivious to each other as they sell what they produce at the market price, over which they have no control. This fairy tale, still regularly regurgitated as being an apt description of our economy, is ludicrous when applied to the global media system. The leading CEOs are all on a first name basis and they regularly converse. Even those on unfriendly terms, like Murdoch and AOL-Time Warner's Ted Turner, understand they have to work together for the "greater good." "Sometimes you have to grit your teeth and treat your enemy as your friend," the former president of Universal, Frank Biondi, concedes (Grover and Siklos 1999). The head of Venezuela's huge Cisneros group, which is locked in combat over Latin American satellite TV with News Corporation, explains about Murdoch: "We're friends. We're always talking" (Hoag 2000). Moreover, all the first and second tier media firms are connected through their reliance upon a few investment banks like Morgan Stanley and Goldman Sachs that quarterback most of the huge media mergers. Those two banks alone put together 52 media and telecom deals valued at US$450 billion in the first quarter of 2000, and 138 deals worth US$433 billion in all of 1999 (Mermigas 2000b). This conscious co-ordination does not simply affect economic behaviour; it makes the media giants particularly effective political lobbyists at the national, regional and global levels.

The global media system is not the result of "free markets" or natural law; it is the consequence of a number of important state policies. The media giants have had a heavy hand in drafting these laws and regulations, and the public tends to have little or no input. In the United States, the corporate media lobbies are notorious for their ability to get their way with politicians, especially if their adversary is not another powerful corporate sector, but that amorphous entity called the "public interest." In 2000, for example, the corporate media giants led the lobbying effort to open up trade with China, and fought against those who raised concerns about free speech and free press (Duke 2000a). Everywhere in the world it is the same, and the corporate media have the additional advantage of controlling the very news media where citizens would expect to find criticism and discussion of media policy in a free society. The track record suggests that the corporate media use their domination of the news media in a self-serving way, hence cementing their political leverage.

But what about media content? Global conglomerates can at times have a progressive impact on culture, especially when they enter nations that had been tightly controlled by corrupt, crony-controlled media systems (as in much of Latin America) or nations that had significant state censorship over media (as in parts of Asia). The global commercial media system is radical in that it will respect no tradition or custom, on balance, if it stands in the way of profits. But ultimately it is politically conservative, because the media giants are significant beneficiaries of the current social structure around the world, and any upheaval in property or social relations – particularly to the extent that it reduces the power of business – is not in their interest.

The "Hollywood juggernaut," or the spectre of US cultural imperialism, remains a central concern in many countries for obvious reasons. Exports of US films and TV shows increased by 22 per cent in 1999 (Guider 2000), and the list of the top 125 grossing films for 1999 is made up almost entirely of Hollywood fare (D'Alessandro 2000). When one goes nation by nation, even a "cultural nationalist" country like France had nine of its top 10 grossing films in 1999 produced by the Hollywood giants (Grey 2000). "Many leftist intellectuals in Paris are decrying American films, but the French people are eating them up," a Hollywood producer noted (Lyman 2000). Likewise, in Italy, the replacement of single-screen theatres by "multiplexes" has contributed to a dramatic decline in local film box office revenues (Rooney 2000). The moral of the story for many European filmmakers is that you have to work in English and employ Hollywood moviemaking conventions to succeed (Foreman 2000). In Latin America, channels controlled by media giants overwhelm local cable television and the de facto capital for the region is Miami (US Cable Channels... 2000).

But there are problems with leaving the discussion at this point. The notion that corporate media firms are merely purveyors of US culture is ever less plausible as the media system becomes increasingly concentrated, commercialized and globalized. The global media system is better understood as one that advances corporate and commercial interests and values and denigrates or ignores that which cannot be incorporated into its mission. There is no discernible difference in the firms' content, whether they are owned by shareholders in Japan or France or have corporate headquarters in New York or Sydney.

As the media conglomerates spread their tentacles, there is reason to believe they will encourage popular tastes to become more uniform in at least some forms of media. Based on conversations with Hollywood executives, *Variety* editor Peter Bart concluded, "the world film-going audience is fast becoming more homogeneous" (McChesney 2000: 105).

Whereas action movies had once been the only sure-fire global fare – with comedies considerably more difficult to export – by the late 1990s, comedies like "My Best Friend's Wedding" and "The Full Monty" were doing between US$160 million and US$200 million in non-US box-office sales.

When audiences appear to prefer locally made fare, the global media corporations, rather than flee in despair, globalize their production. Sony has been at the forefront of this, producing films with local companies in China, France, India and Mexico, to name but a few (Brodesser 2000; Duke 2000b). India's acclaimed domestic film industry – "Bollywood" – is also developing close ties to the global media giants (Growing Up 2000). This process is even more visible in the music industry. Music has always been the least capital-intensive of the electronic media and therefore the most open to experimentation and new ideas. US recording artists generated 60 per cent of their sales outside the United States in 1993; by 1998, that figure was down to 40 per cent. Rather than fold their tents, however, the four media transnationals that dominate the world's recorded-music market are busy establishing local subsidiaries in places like Brazil, where "people are totally committed to local music," in the words of a writer for a trade publication. Sony, again, has led the way in establishing distribution deals with independent music companies from around the world.

With hypercommercialism and growing corporate control comes an implicit political bias in media content. Consumerism, class inequality and individualism tend to be taken as natural and even benevolent, whereas political activity, civic values and anti-market activities are marginalized. The best journalism is pitched to the business class and suited to its needs and prejudices; with a few notable exceptions, the journalism reserved for the masses tends to be the sort of drivel provided by the media giants on their US television stations. In India, for example, influenced by the global media giants, "the revamped news media ...now focus more on fashion designers and beauty queens than on the dark realities of a poor and violent country" (Mishra 2000). This slant is often quite subtle. Indeed, the genius of the commercial-media system is the general lack of overt censorship. As George Orwell noted in his unpublished introduction to *Animal Farm*, censorship in free societies is infinitely more sophisticated and thorough than in dictatorships, because "unpopular ideas can be silenced, and inconvenient facts kept dark, without any need for an official ban."

Lacking any necessarily conspiratorial intent and acting in their own economic self-interest, media conglomerates exist simply to make money by selling light escapist entertainment. In the words of the late Emilio Azcarraga, the billionaire founder of Mexico's Televisa: "Mexico is a country of a modest, very fucked class, which will never stop being fucked. Television has the obligation to bring diversion to these people and remove them from their sad reality and difficult future." The combination of neoliberalism and corporate media culture tends to promote a deep and profound de-politicization. One need only look at the United States to see the logical endpoint (Perry 2000). But de-politicization has its limits, as it invariably runs up against the fact that we live in a social world where politics have tremendous influence over the quality of our lives.

Finally, a word should be said about the Internet, the two-tonne gorilla of global media and communications. The Internet is increasingly becoming a part of our media and telecommunications systems, and a genuine technological convergence is taking place. Accordingly, there has been a wave of mergers between traditional media and telecom firms and each of them with Internet and computer firms. Already companies like Microsoft, AOL, AT&T and Telefonica have become media powerhouses in their own right. It looks like the global media system is in the process of becoming a globally integrated, commercial communications system where six to a dozen "supercompanies" will rule the roost. The notion that the Internet would "set us free," and permit anyone to communicate effectively, hence undermining the monopoly power of the media giants, has not materialized. Although the Internet offers extraordinary promise in many regards, it alone cannot slay the power of the media giants. Indeed, no commercially viable media content site has been launched on the Internet, and it would be difficult to find an investor willing to bankroll any additional attempts. To the extent the Internet becomes part of the commercially viable media system, it looks to be under the thumb of the usual corporate suspects.

In sum, matters appear quite depressing from a democratic standpoint, and it may seem difficult to see much hope for change. As one Swedish journalist noted in 1997, "Unfortunately, the trends are very clear, moving in the wrong direction on virtually every score, and there is a desperate lack of public discussion of the long-term implications of current developments for democracy and accountability" (McChesney 2000: 118).

But there are indications that progressive political movements around the world are increasingly putting media issues on their political platforms. From Sweden to France and India to Australia, New Zealand and Canada, democratic, left-wing political parties and social movements are making structural media reform – breaking up the big companies, recharging non-profit and non-commercial broadcasting and media – central to their agenda. They are finding out that this is a successful issue with voters.

At the same time, the fate of the global media system is intricately intertwined with that of global capitalism, and despite the self-congratulatory celebration of the free market in the US media, the international system is showing signs of weakness. Asia, the so-called "tiger of twenty-first-century capitalism," fell into a depression in 1997, and its recovery is still uncertain. Even if there is no global depression, discontent is brewing in those parts of the world and among those segments of the population that have been left behind in this era of economic growth. Latin America, the other vaunted champion of market reforms since the 1980s, has seen what a World Bank official terms a "big increase in inequality." The number of people living on less than US$1 per day increased from 1.2 billion in 1987 to 1.5 billion in 2000, and looks to continue to rise for years to come (Dickson 2000). The "me first, screw you" ethos promoted by neoliberalism has contributed to widespread governmental corruption, as notions of principled public service are difficult to maintain (Stopping the Rot... 2000). While the dominance of commercial media makes resistance more difficult, widespread opposition to these trends has begun to emerge in the form of huge demonstrations across the planet. It is far too early to predict the outcome of this confrontation, but the triumph of the neoliberal economic model and the global media system it has helped create hangs in the balance.

# References

Ad Spend Growth. 2000. *Advertising Age International*. January: 1.

Bianco, A. 2000. Deal Time at Seagram. *Business Week*. 26 June: 60.

Brodesser, C. 2000. Sony's Global Gaze Pays. *Variety*. 3-9 April: 13, 62.

Brooke, J. 2000. Canadian TV Makes a Move Into Papers. *New York Times*. 1 August: C1, C25.

Brown-Humes, C. 2000. Bonnier Scotland. *Financial Times*. 20 September: 9.

Cherney, E. 2000. CanWest Tightens Its Media Grip. *Wall Street Journal*. 2 August: A17.

Cullison, A. 2000. Russia Arrests President of Big Private Media Company. *Wall Street Journal*. 14 June: A21.

D'Alessandro, A. 2000. The Top 125 Worldwide. *Variety*. 24-30 January: 22.

Dickson, M. 2000. Gap Between the Rich and the Poor is Widening. *Financial Times*. 22 September: XXIV.

Duke, P.F. 2000a. House Vote Cracks China's Great Wall. *Variety*. 29 May- 4 June: 10.

Duke, P.F. 2000b. Robinson Explores Asian Films for Sony. *Variety*. 28 August- 3 September: 7, 128.

Elliott, S. 2000. Publicis Plans to Buy Saatchi For at Least $1.5 Billion. *New York Times*. 20 June: C1, C8.

Foreman, L. 2000. Teuton Tongues Untied. *Variety*. 14-20 August: 39-40.

Free to be Bad. 2000. *The Economist*. 11 March: 44.

Goldsmith, C. 2000. BBC Forms Commercial Internet Unit; U.S. Firms to Take Stake in Subsidiary. *Wall Street Journal*. 23 August: B10.

Goldsmith, J. and Dawtrey, A. 2000. Murdoch: Sky's the Limit. *Variety*. 28 August- 3 September: 1, 130.

Gordon, M.R. 2000. A Russian Press Beholden to Many. *New York Times*. 17 March: A10.

Grey, T. 2000. Promo Effort Key in France. *Variety*. 21-27 February: 30. 106.

Grover, R. and Siklos, R. 1999. Where Old Foes Need Each Other. *Business Week*. 25 October: 114, 118.

Groves, D. 2000. Star Connects Dot-coms. *Variety*. 29 May- 4 June: 63.

Growing Up. 2000. *The Economist*. 12 August: 57-58.

Guider, E. 2000. AFMA Exports Up 22% As Global TV Booms. *Variety*. 19-25 June: 14, 75.

Hansell, S. 2000. Murdoch Sees Satellites as Way To Keep News Corp. Current. *New York Times*. 16 June: C7.

Hatfield, S. 2000. EU Turning Into Battleground Over More Curbs On Marketing. *Advertising Age*. 18 September: 60.

Hoag, C. 2000. Empire Building: The Slow Track. *Business Week*. 11 September: 126E3-126E4.

Jacob, R. 2000. Star Is Shooting Towards Interactive TV. *Financial Times*. 10-11 June: 11.

Kirkpatrick, D.D. 2000a. HarperCollins Plans to Buy A Small British Publisher. *New York Times*. 11 July: C6.

_____. 2000b. Not Quite All-American, Bertelsmann Is Big on US *New York Times*. 3 September, Section 3: 2.

Larsen, P.T. 2000. Little Time for a Commercial Break. *Financial Times*. 25 August: 15.

Lyman, R. 2000. No Trace of Anti-Hollywood Bias in French Purchase of Universal. *New York Times*. 20 June: C12.

McChesney, R W. 2000. *Rich Media, Poor Democracy: Communication Politics in Dubious Times*. New York: The New Press.

Mermigas, D. 2000a. International Plays Take Media Firms To Next Level. *Electronic Media*. 31 July: 22.

_____. 2000b. Morgan Stanley Banks on Media. *Electronic Media*. 15 May: 17, 20.

Mishra, P. 2000. Yearning to Be Great, India Loses Its Way. *New York Times*. 16 September: A27.

Molony, D. 1999. Utsumi's CEO Think-tank to Shake Up ITU. *Communications Week International*. 4 October: 1, 74.

Perry, J. 2000. Shades of 1960 Are Superficial Amid Changes in Electorate. *Wall Street Journal*. 14 September: A12.

Preston, J. 2000. Mexican TV, Unshackled by Reform, Fights for Viewers. *New York Times*. 7 June: A3.

Reed, S. 2000. A Media Star is Born. *Business Week*. 24 April: 136-137.

Rohwedder, C. 2000. Kirch Tightens Control Over German Broadcast Assets. *Wall Street Journal*. 29 June: A18, A21.

Rooney, D. 2000. Ciao Time for Italy. *Variety*. 19-25 June: 72.

Schechter, D. 2000. Long Live Chairman Levin! *Mediachannel.org*. 5 July.

Scardino's Way. 2000. *The Economist*. 5 August: 62.

Star Turn. 2000. *The Economist*. 11 March: 67-68.

Stern, A. 2000a. EU Questions Pubcaster Aid. *Variety*. 22-28 May: 67.

_____. 2000b. EU To Change Pubcaster Financial Rules. *Variety*. 10-16 January: 105.

_____. 2000c. Microsoft/Telewest Deal Faces High EC Hurdles. *Variety*. 3-9 April: 79.

Stopping The Rot In Public Life. 2000. *The Economist*. 16 September, 2000: 41-42.

Sutter, M. 2000. Hicks, Muse Invests $1 bil in Latin American Drive. *Variety*. 17-23 January: 70.

Swarns, R.L. 2000. Tightening Control on Media Worry Journalists in Angola. *New York Times*. 20 September: A8.

Talk Show. 2000. *Business Week*. 2 October: 12.

Teinowitz, I. and Linnett, R. 2000. Eye On Mergers: Media Behemoths Up Agency Ante. *Advertising Age*. 8 May: 3, 105.

The World's 100 Largest Public Companies. 2000. *Wall Street Journal*. 25 September: R24.

Tomkins, R. 2000. Zenith Spotlights Advertising Surge. *Financial Times*. 18 July: 21.

Tyler, P.E. 2000. Russian Media Magnate Reports Kremlin is Trying to Silence Him. *New York Times*. 5 September: A12.

US Cable Channels Tighten Their Grip On Latin American Cable Viewers. 2000. *TV International*. 12 June: 6.

Wright, R. 2000. Hungary Packs Broadcasters With Party Names. *Financial Times*. 2 March: 7.

# The International Community as Media Regulator in Post-conflict Societies

## David Goldberg

For several years now, a so-called "international community" (IC) has been active with respect to media restructuring in different parts of the world wracked by violent conflicts such as Bosnia and Herzegovina (BiH), Kosovo, Rwanda, Burundi and East Timor. This involvement has taken two main forms, media development and media regulation, much of which has been contested by elements of international civil society (ICS). In this context, the international community refers to, on the one hand, inter-governmental organizations such as the European Community (EC) and the United Nations Educational, Scientific and Cultural Organization (UNESCO), as well as less formal groupings of states and institutions such as the western alliance. International civil society, meanwhile, refers to non-governmental organizations and grass-roots movements, usually constructed around particular causes, in this case media and journalistic freedom.

The sheer scale of media development assistance is largely under-appreciated, not well documented and, perhaps most importantly, not well studied by international civil society. An aim of this chapter is to call for a global, international civil society effort to document and study these issues.[1]

To offer an example of the scale of the IC's involvement in post-conflict societies, the European Community provides this summary of its involvement in the media, culture, and telecommunications spheres in post-conflict Bosnia and Herzegovina:[2]

### The European Community Media and Culture Program

Prior to and during the war in former Yugoslavia, the media were forced by the government to offer one-sided broadcasting in order to incite nationalistic hatred and public paranoia. The media in Bosnia and Herzegovina have since been working to become free and fair in order to bring about pluralism, mutual trust and help the transition into a fully fledged democratic society. As media were used as a tool for political propaganda in the past, there is a certain level of public distrust. Many media outlets are confined to their ethnic region of origin and have subsequent limited circulation. While the number of radio stations has already grown, funding is still lacking for sustaining independent and alternative services. Many regional television and radio networks remain under the control of ethnic nationalist groups.

The importance of pluralist media in the development of a democratic society that respects human rights and the peace process has been emphasized by the international community since the signing of the Dayton/Paris Peace Agreement in 1995. Since 1996 the European Community (EC) has allocated over 14 million euro to its media and culture program. The program focuses on the strengthening of independent media, progress in the freedom of movement and cross-entity exchanges, the promotion of human rights, democracy and civil society, and improvement of journalistic standards.

## The European Community Telecommunications Program

The telecommunications network in Bosnia and Herzegovina was severed during the war. The Dayton/Paris Peace Agreement of 1995 made the reconnection of the inter-entity telecommunications network a basic requirement for the peace process. Before the war the PTT Company ran the core of the telecommunications network in Bosnia and Herzegovina. It was previously established as a business system consisting of a general directorate with 13 regional PTT companies and employing 11,750 staff. The state-owned enterprise has since been divided into three companies with headquarters in Sarajevo, Mostar and Pale.

A study carried out in 1996 indicated that approximately 200,000 of the 700,000 lines were out of service that year. The European Bank for Reconstruction and Development (EBRD), which leads the Telecommunications Task Force in Bosnia and Herzegovina, has developed a master plan for this sector which has been grouped into specific sub-projects. These are principally to reconstruct local and zonal networks, including local switching. With the support of the EC and the EBRD, progress has been made in the technical and regulatory rehabilitation of the sector despite early difficulties between the three ethnic authorities to agree on inter-connections and a common set of telecommunications regulations. The EC telecommunications rehabilitation program is implementing projects that assist in the rebuilding process through the reconnection of inter-entity links between the Federation and the Republika Srpska, with the provision of a range of basic telephone services for the community, businesses and state organizations across inter-entity boundary lines. The basic aim of the rehabilitation program is to unify the country, provide the people from different regions with the possibility of communication and provide an incentive for the return of refugees.

With respect to media freedom, media freedom advocacy groups have been highly critical of regulatory moves urging that media conduct should be created by media professionals, not by governments; the goal of media regulation should be self-regulation; and the norms and procedures should conform to the best standards of international human rights law.

While this involvement is of relatively recent origin, an historical perspective, stretching back fifty years, can usefully contextualize the contemporary activities of the IC. In the aftermath of World War II, the Allied military occupation of Germany was also clearly concerned with media reconstruction. Whether that bears on the issue of justification in the present case is, of course, another matter.

## "Denazification"

Frederick Watkins (in Friedrich 1948), commenting on the perceived need following World War II by the victorious Allied powers to confront and undo the "political and social consequences of the totalitarian concept of the revolutionary occupation," wrote that "to destroy the last vestiges of German and Japanese militarism, and to establish a new order concordant with the desires of the victorious nations, [had] become the publicly avowed objective of Allied occupation policy."

The objective, the main driving force of the occupation (at least for the Americans, if not for the UK, France or the USSR) was clear: "the idea of getting democracy in Germany, a rather idealistic undertaking..." Accordingly, preventing the re-emergence of fascism made it necessary for the Allies "in their respective areas of occupation to apply the whole totalitarian repertory of police coercion, official propaganda, economic controls and puppet politics." Denazification, i.e., separating the German people from Nazism, was to be pursued in three stages: first, military occupation; second, Allied Control Authority activity; and finally, the eventual assumption of responsibility for the process by denazified German authorities.

In a rather uncanny echo of that last point, Wolfgang Petritsch (The High Commissioner for Bosnia and Herzegovina) said to a recent Peace Implementation Council meeting:

> Most importantly (...), the people of BiH must take ownership and responsibility for their own country. I am convinced they have all it takes – they can do it. But if they fail to face up to this challenge,

Bosnia and Herzegovina will descend into years of economic stagnation and social and political unrest. I believe the citizens of BiH can heal their wounds, embrace tolerance and move forward into the new millennium. It is time for the Bosnians and Herzegovinians to remember: "Ko ce pomoci ako necemo jednim drugim" – "Who will help us if we don't help each other?"[3]

Joseph Dunner (in Friedrich 1948) provides an illuminating case study of "information control" in the American Zone of occupied Germany against which contemporary experiences may be compared. The main instrument was Law No. 191 (and the various regulations promulgated thereunder). This law concerned "the control of publications, radio broadcasting, news services, films, theatres and music." The reconstruction of "democratic German information services" was to "proceed under Allied supervision, but with German personnel in all functions…the program envisaged for information control in occupied Germany called for far-flung activities, since it required a complete taking over and eventual rebuilding of the media of the press, radio and entertainment…[it] would call for exceptional skill, tact and firmness on the part of foreigners seeking to control and guide it effectively for some time."

This process of "indigenizing" the personnel of the externally-imposed media regulatory structure is similar to the approach taken by the Independent Media Commission for BiH today. In the post-Nazi era, a process of finding suitable licencees and "the final licensing of responsible Germans in the information field" ensued. However, this field was construed more broadly, embracing "culture" (or entertainment), and the Information Control Division (ICD) was heavily involved in the issuing of licenses etc for theatre, music and the cinema. Dunner concludes that:

> Aware of the tight controls of the information services under the Nazi system, American policymakers should have formulated a program tending towards the loosening of controls and the liberalization of the creative spirit…the effect of the Nazi policy on the various information media was a continuous stream of propaganda and the resulting obedience to authority. The effect of the ICD's failure to cut loose from this totalitarian policy was the substitution of American for Nazi authority and the widespread belief that "everything is now American propaganda." The idea of a purified atmosphere in which people may read and see only what the group in power wants them to see and read is a totalitarian and not a democratic concept…

> However, Dunner absolves the ICD itself from blame and considers that the shortcomings were in basic policy and personnel (many of whom were Communists), coupled with a refusal to allow adequate flowering of the creativity of those who had not accepted Nazism or totalitarian methods. The result was the imposition of a benevolent totalitarianism, with an emphasis on "dull neutrality."

In a contemporary echo of this last point, James Ottaway of the World Press Freedom Council wrote, in July 1999, that "Kosovo's print and broadcast news media suffered assault, restrictions and reprisals under the dictatorship of Slobodan Milosevic. They should now enjoy the freedom, the independence and diversity for which Kosovo's citizens and NATO allies fought so hard...Let it not be said that the democratic victory in Kosovo simply led to more censorship, under a different guise."[4]

## Types of IC Post-conflict Interventions

In the contemporary era, the international community, acting through various intergovernmental organizations, has been active in assisting with media development, particularly in post-conflict societies.[5] Here are some examples:

1. The Council of Europe

The Council of Europe provides direct support to media in former Yugoslavia through its Demosthenes program. The program was launched in 1989 as part of a strategy to promote free and independent media in Central and Eastern Europe.[6]

2. The European Commission

In 1993, the European Commission (EC) allocated 1.4 million ecu (European Currency Units) to the media in former Yugoslavia as part of a package of humanitarian aid. A further 10 million ecu were allocated in 1996. This process has been criticized, notably on the grounds that:

> Virtually all support arrives with serious delays...and bureaucratic demands cause serious problems for smaller media. Moreover, the decision-making process is unclear, and the distribution of means leaves much to be desired as well. Much funding was squandered on ambitious but hastily established projects that made insufficient use of local expertise. In Bosnia-Herzegovina, for example, the Open Broadcasting Network (OBN TV, originally also known as Bildt TV after its initiator Carl Bildt – High Commissioner in Sarajevo) incurred excessive costs because of strategic mistakes and failed to achieve its objectives.[7]

Another criticism is that "In some cases decisions seemed based on improper political arguments and the pursuit of even handedness." However, it is acknowledged that "the EC is providing a major contribution to the establishment of the independent media in the countries of former Yugoslavia, if only through the sheer magnitude of its support."[8]

3. UNESCO[9]

In December 1993, in accordance with its constitutional mandate "to promote the free flow of ideas by word and image," UNESCO launched a pilot program to assist independent media in conflict areas. Special emphasis was given to former Yugoslavia. After the signing of the Dayton Peace Accords in December 1995, UNESCO renewed its support to independent media so as to pave the way towards the democracy and peace process. Over the last four years, UNESCO has supplied several tons of equipment to electronic media, newsprint to the independent printed media, office equipment to independent news agencies and training for journalists in most of the republics and territories of former Yugoslavia.

Other territories have also been the focus of UNESCO activities:

> After a first experience in former Yugoslavia, the program extended its activities in 1995 to Rwanda and Burundi. Since that time, UNESCO has continued to support the independent media in several areas of conflict, so as to pave the way towards democracy and advance the peace process. UNESCO has placed special emphasis on establishing the conditions necessary to give the public access to non-partisan information in the Great Lakes region, where rumors and hatred propaganda replaced information during the time of the genocide and crisis. In addition, a primary goal is the promotion of a new corps of journalists to make up for the tragic losses within the community of Rwandan and Burundian journalists.

UNESCO is also active in East Timor. At the end of 1999, a conference was held in Bangkok to adopt:

> a series of measures to help restore East Timor's print and audiovisual media infrastructure – devastated during violence last autumn. The two-day conference – which included the participation of the United Nations Transitional Administration in East Timor (UNTAET) – adopted decisions concerning different aspects of journalistic activity. These include immediate assistance to reinforce radio networks, the publication of the first newspaper in independent East Timor, the establishment of a legal framework for media, as well as the provision of training for journalists. Donor pledges worth over US$1 million were made during the conference to help build East Timor's media. Implementation of these decisions was planned for January 2001. Most of the funds raised so far have been pledged by the United States Agency for International Development's Office of Transitional Initiatives (USAID-OTI) and the Konrad Adenauer Foundation of Germany.[10]

> Also, working with the World Association of Newspapers (WAN), UNESCO is attempting to rebuild the newspaper industry in East Timor.

4. The Stability Pact for South Eastern Europe

Under the auspices of the Stability Pact for South Eastern Europe, a substantial assistance package for media has been set up. By the end of 2000, the Quick

Start Package Projects had committed some 20.1 million euro in support from a wide range of donors to a total of 33 media projects. Of this total, money, equipment and services amounting in value to over 8.4 million euro had been disbursed to the project implementers before January 1, 2001.[11]

## Critics of The IC's Role In Bosnia and Herzegovina

The first shot across the IC's bow was fired on April 24, 1998, in a *New York Times* article entitled "Allies create a Press Control Agency in Bosnia." It argued that the proposal to create such a body "highlights the awkward situation in which the United States finds itself, as both an international defender of free speech and as a military power trying to enforce a peacekeeping agreement among fractious groups."

The International Press Institute expressed its concern during May 1998 to the US Secretary of Defence "over plans by the United States and its allies to create a press control agency in Bosnia-Herzogovina:"

> While IPI understands that the Western allies are concerned that inflammatory propaganda could threaten the safety of their peacekeeping forces, we are deeply concerned about any attempt by an alliance of democratic nations to impose restraints on the media in another country. The proposed agency runs the risk of suppressing legitimate news and opinion and would set a dangerous precedent for authoritarian governments desiring to curb news media.[12]

IPI said, in language reminiscent of the *New York Times* article, that it was "disturbed that the United States should be involved in the establishment of what amounts to a censorship panel."

## The Genesis of the Independent Media Commission

The "censorship panel" referred to was originally called the Intermediate Standards and Licensing Commission (ISLC). It is now known as the Independent Media Commission (IMC).[13]

Unsurprisingly, there was considerable irritation within the organization at the suggestion that the ISLC/IMC might be a censoring body. On the contrary, the organization argued that it was created as a response to the proposal of all the countries that had sponsored the Dayton Peace Agreement that ended the conflict. Also, those countries at the Bonn conference preceding Dayton had called for the establishment of a legal framework for the media – in particular for the electronic media. ISLC/IMC supporters point out that such a legal framework was lacking at the time in the territory.

The ISLC/IMC was premised on being an amalgamation of a European human rights standards body and an American regulatory agency like the Federal

Communications Commission (FCC), issuing licences. Moreover, the premise was that it would evolve into an indigenous authority (paralleling, as has been noted, the approach taken in post World War II Germany). In any case, local "national communities" were said to be overwhelmingly positive about the project, seeing it as a very welcome and long-overdue initiative.

However, at least two other prominent international civil society organizations voiced their concerns regarding the ISLC/IMC, both in general and specific terms.

First, on February 25, 1999, the International Federation of Journalists (IFJ) criticized the draft Press Code proposed by the IMC. It argued that the code was too prescriptive, full of vague and ambiguous terms, and that it failed to offer an adequate basis for resolving ethical problems. For example, the draft code told journalists "not to offend" broad sections of the community. Further, a restricted view of the public interest was adopted: excluding the right to publish information that does not disclose illegality, even if it is considered vital for an informed citizenry.[14]

Secondly, the World Press Freedom Council's (WPFC) July 1999 newsletter urged (in the context of Kosovo) "leaders to refrain from establishing bodies like those used as censorship tools by Western authorities in post-war Bosnia. Bosnia's Independent Media Commission, for example, imposed a Broadcasting Code of Practice on Bosnian broadcast media, and shut down stations deemed in violation" (WPFC 1999).

The WPFC's European representative expressed the following view at a June 1999 meeting of European press councils organized by the UK's Press Complaint Commission:

> The Independent Media Commission in Bosnia, which is an emanation of the international community, created by the High Representative, has very detailed regulations for broadcasting. It regulates broadcasting. It takes stations off the air, it fines them, and it authorizes to come back on the air. And it has a set of regulations on coverage by all media – not just broadcasters – of all elections. In that context, backed up by troops, I find it very hard to believe that the journalists' associations feel that there is no pressure on them to adopt particular kinds of codes. In fact, the first draft of their code designated the Independent Media Commission (IMC), led by foreign officials, as an appeals body for the journalists' press council. The IMC, we're assured, is about to go out of business and the journalists will take over their own policing. But what bothers me is the precedent for a neighboring situation – Kosovo. (...) The temptation to propose something similar in Kosovo is, I think, overwhelming. This won't be the last time that a local conflict will need to be moderated by the international community. These are precedents that are being set, and I would submit that they are very dangerous ones(...)[15]

The IMC itself argues that its task has been "dedicated to building and promoting a free media environment," to promoting a "just, tolerant and democratic society in Bosnia and Herzegovina through independent media committed to the highest standards of professional ethics." Thus, the IMC views its role as both creating and fostering a free media and fostering democracy through the creation of an independent media. It identifies itself as a model institution,"staffed by a contingent of local, national experts who are working as independent civil servants, free of the parochial nationalist party interests. In providing this example, the IMC in fact stands as more than a regulatory agency, and indeed as a model for a civil service agency. Precisely in that capacity, as civil servants, IMC staff members may make their greatest contribution yet to BiH's transition to institution building and stable democracy."[16]

At an even higher level of generality, the IMC is tied to the notion of state supremacy over ethnically-divided entity arrangements. This was articulated by Office of the High Representative (OHR) Legal Opinion 1999/3, entitled "On the competence of Bosnia and Herzegovina to regulate the use of the electromagnetic spectrum for telecommunication and broadcasting," which held that the state had authority to establish the Independent Media Commission:

> As among the State and the entities, the State's predominance as the competent regulatory authority must be underscored. (...) The supremacy of the State in this field is also consistent with practical considerations in a country as small as BiH, where it would be technically chaotic to permit multiple entity authorities, operating independently, to distribute frequencies and otherwise regulate broadcasters. (...)

> The international obligations of the State form a framework within which the State's domestic regulatory arrangements must fit. Without attempting a specific analysis of all such obligations, it suffices to note as examples that telecommunication related to air traffic control is largely governed by international agreements, and that ITU [International Telecommunication Union] regulations establish basic parameters which circumscribe the domestic allocation of frequencies for broadcasting and other telecommunication purposes. The international obligations associated with such agreements and regulations are those of the State, and it is the responsibility of the State to ensure that its domestic regulatory system fulfils and is in conformity with those obligations.

> The interconnectivity of network industries with international systems is regulated at the international level through a range of European and international agreements, arrangements and institutions. The state has the authority to become a party to any agreement and a member of any organization, in pursuit of the goal of

ensuring that Bosnian public utilities comply with international standards, and that Bosnian citizens, companies, goods and services enjoy access to international markets. Under the constitution, this gives the state the authority to establish regulatory structures (OHR Legal Opinion 1999).

For this reason, OHR has concluded that the state is:

> ...fully competent to regulate this sector, in a manner consistent with its constitutional responsibilities and international obligations, and in so doing to establish, as the State sees fit, appropriate regulatory bodies. The state may exercise this competence completely and directly, or it may allow the entities to enter and partially occupy the field in a way regulated by it... The electromagnetic spectrum can be viewed as a strategic resource of Bosnia and Herzegovina which must be available to the state for such use that it deems appropriate for such purposes as national security or border control (OHR Legal Opinion 1999).

The "state," however, is not simply a neutral vessel. As the IMC points out, "As Bosnia and Herzegovina moves ever so gradually towards (...) the point in its economic and political development where liberal values and a free market system become the natural and self sustaining means for national growth, a free and independent media scene will be a natural part of the polity."[17]

## Critics of The IC's Role in Kosovo

As noted, the structure and operations of the IC's involvement in BiH have been criticized by, among others, the International Federation of Journalists (IFJ) and the WPFC. The tone of the criticisms became shriller as the BiH experience was replicated in Kosovo.

The International Press Institute (IPI), for example, states that:

> The conflict in Kosovo was widely predicted by journalists and NGOs in recent years. The Albanians' complete exclusion from the Dayton peace talks invited the violence level to escalate. The fact that the international community finally decided to sit up and take action in an attempt to bring an end to the tragedy is worth celebrating. How they set about solving the problem is, however, questionable. In Kosovo itself, the international community now has a mandate under the United Nation Mission in Kosovo (UNMIK). The media comes under the auspices of the OSCE, which created the Media Affairs Department, which will operate with a staff of fifty. The new department will allocate frequencies and broadcast licences but will also carry many other powers such as monitoring compliance with their press code and ensuring "responsible behaviour" by journalists. This follows the controversial Bosnian experience where the international community has set itself up as advocate, judge and jury, with military

backing, and decrees that media content is permissible and which is not. Considering the thin divide between media development and media interference, this initiative is vulnerable to influence from national political agendas. What is in essence an instrument of censorship run by Western governments also sets an unhealthy example to leaders in the region and beyond who may harbour desires to curtail the media with internationally tolerated methods.[18]

More criticisms followed the publication of two media-related regulations by the UN Mission in Kosovo in 2000.

The first, "On the Licensing and Regulation of the Broadcast Media in Kosovo,"[19]

- establishes a temporary licensing and regulatory regime for broadcast media;

- establishes a Temporary Media Commissioner, with authority to establish the criteria and the procedures for issuing broadcast licences;

- sets out that in applying for and receiving licences, broadcasters agree to abide by a Broadcast Code of Conduct, which is to include the requirement of providing factual reporting; avoiding sensationalism; and providing balanced coverage; and

- says that the Temporary Media Commissioner will be empowered under the Code to execute a range of sanctions in the event of the Code being breached.

The second regulation, "On the Conduct of the Print Media in Kosovo,"[20] was developed "to deal with the special circumstances which exist in Kosovo" including, in particular, the perceived danger of papers publishing the names etc, of individuals, which could seriously prejudice their security. The Regulation states that:

- the Temporary Media Commissioner will issue a Code of Conduct, in consultation with the Special Representative of the Secretary-General (UN) and those involved with the media;

- the Code is to be "a temporary measure until there is effective self-regulation of the media;"

- the Code will demand that Kosovo's journalists behave responsibly and act in a way consistent with the Universal Declaration of Human Rights and the European Convention on Human Rights;

- the Temporary Media Commissioner is empowered to execute a range of sanctions if the Code is breached. Sanctions range from demanding an apology or correction be published to imposing a fine, to closing down the publication; and

- the media can appeal to an independent board set up to hear appeals against decisions made by the Temporary Media Commissioner. The Media Appeals Board is to consist of two international members and one national member. Its decisions are final.[21]

The International Federation of Journalists has condemned the United Nations Mission in Kosovo, saying that a regulation forbidding "the publication of personal details – even naming persons – if such details are considered to pose a threat to life" and "the appointment of a (Temporary) Media Commissioner with a range of powers to fine, close or suspend publications" is a "dangerous and disturbing precedent for international media controls in post-conflict regions...[and] a confused and dangerous response...[it] is heavy-handed and substitutes dictatorship for the rule of law – the worst message to send in a region that is striving to adopt democratic principles of pluralism and professionalism in the face of conflict and division."[22]

The IFJ identified a number of problems with the regulations. It says the regulations do not ensure an independent appeals procedure, they introduce the notion of legally enforceable codes of conduct for journalists, and they are in contradiction to the principles recently adopted in the Stability Pact for South Eastern Europe's Charter for Media Freedom.[23] The IFJ has called on the UNMIK to withdraw the regulations and to engage in renewed dialogue with journalists and the media: "Press freedom and democracy cannot be created on the back of dictatorship and arbitrary exercise of power. The priority must be to establish the rule of law and to place control over media content in the hands of journalists and media professionals where it rightly belongs."[24]

The World Press Freedom Committee also issued a highly critical reaction to the promulgation of the two regulations. It said that it was:

> ...highly distressed to learn that the United Nations administration in Kosovo has unilaterally issued regulations "On the Conduct of the Print Media" and "On the Licensing and Regulation of the Broadcast Media." The texts giving broad powers of censorship and of life and death over news media outlets to a "Temporary Media Commissioner" constitute a very dangerous and disturbing precedent for future media controls by official organs of the international community in post-conflict zones. They also set major negative examples that can be exploited by authoritarian regimes in the Balkans and elsewhere to similarly justify structured arrangements of their own.[25]

An important thrust of the WPFC's objection is that "issuing 'temporary Codes of Conduct' for the press, as provided by the new Regulations, undercuts the effects of the Kosovor news media to establish their own self-regulatory body with its own code of conduct. The efforts of the local news media are not being given the time to make that work."

Finally, on June 30, 2000, the non-governmental organization "Article 19"[26] expressed its concerns that the new regime "sets a dangerous precedent and is a gift to any government seeking examples to use when reining in the media."

## Conclusion

The issue which divides elements of international civil society and the international community boils down to this: (1) is there any *prima facie* legitimacy in the actions of the international community at all, or, specifically, in the media field; and (2) how important is it to think of the conditions facing the international community under which it "must" create a media strategy.

Recently, Laurent Pech has argued that, with regard to BiH, the international community was confronted by a ruling-party-controlled media on nationalistic/ethnic lines, whereby divergent or oppositional viewpoints were suppressed. He argues that.

> media reform...is part of a more general problem that the international community faces. The international administration of a "sovereign" country, in order to facilitate the transition in a post-conflict society is a difficult exercise...[I]nternational intervention was considered necessary to break the link between media and nationalist parties. However, the difficulties in imposing democracy from outside were underestimated. There is no doubt that the international community is forcing a western-based system of media regulation on unwilling elected political authorities in BiH, but not necessarily on an unwilling media community...[A] common paradox is the one of compelling any action that is meant to promote democracy...[The international community seems to favor now a "protectorate style model", which holds that the long-term peace-building efforts outweigh short-term deprivation of political rights to nationalist actors in BiH...] (Pech 2000)

Indeed, it might be necessary, argues Pech, to accommodate mechanisms such as the Office of the High Representative, with all its powers, as a kind of "dictatorship of virtue," on the understanding that it is a short-term solution, motivated by the fact that in post-conflict societies the media either have done, or still do, play a "pernicious role." There is, therefore, an arguable need for a powerful tool "in the earliest efforts to move from conflict-filled societies to stable, democratic societies', particularly in conditions such as the Balkans [which] are not like those found in advanced democratic societies, where basic freedoms, protections and responsibilities are inculcated fully and effectively throughout society" (Ibid.).

Monroe Price, too, offers several conclusions to this thorny problem in a background paper to the May 2000 UNESCO seminar on "Restructuring the Media in Post-Conflict Societies:"

- there is no single overarching strategy, with respect to the media that can be prescribed for the international community in post-conflict societies;

- context is paramount;

- intergovernmental organizations (IGOs) should be careful not to exaggerate the role media play, independent of other forces that promote hatred, conflict etc;

- IGO aid flows should be transparent;

- IGOs must balance short-term objectives with long-term ones;

- IGOs themselves must act in a manner consistent with the rule of law; throughout all planning and implementation, IGOs (and NGOS) should adhere to international principles of human rights and the freedom to receive and impart information;

- there must be an intensive dialogue between IGOs, NGOs and press freedom groups to ensure that IGOs respect the standards defined by such organizations; and

- co-ordination between IGOs inter se, and between IGOs and NGOs must be improved (Price 2000).

The broader question is whether international community intervention in the media space is justifiable in principle.

The approach thus far adopted – which assumes or argues for the legitimacy of the international community and its actions – treats each occurrence as unique. The approach is akin to that adopted with respect to alleged war criminals. In that situation, a unique tribunal has been created for each area (Former Republic of Yugoslavia, Rwanda, Cambodia and Sierra Leone).

Using the analogy of the recent efforts to establish a permanent, international criminal court with universal jurisdiction, one might propose the creation of a standing, permanent international media commission/administration, ready to intervene in appropriate circumstances.

This could draw on the best practices of models ranging from the post-World War II Allied Control Authority to the Temporary Media Commissioner in Kosovo. Its structure, procedures, methods of working and staffing would have been decided by the international community prior to the existence of any specific situation emerging for which it was deemed relevant.

Something of the sort was suggested a number of years ago by Jamie Metzl, a former UN human rights officer. Metzl (1997a) writes that the United Nations should establish an independent information unit "monitoring, peace broadcasting and, in extreme cases, jamming [hate] radio and television broadcasts." The unit would not act on a case-by-case basis but would have a standing authority to carry out its function with the Security Council maintaining veto power over its actions. Furthermore, argues Metzl, "it would go a long way towards securing human rights short of costly, large-scale military investments." Metzl recalls that the UN commander in Rwanda in 1994, General Romeo Dallaire, said afterwards "that simply jamming Hutu broadcasts and replacing them with messages of peace and reconciliation would have had a significant impact on the course of events in Rwanda." The approach advocated by Metzl would certainly present a number of advantages, in particular the speed of execution so important to media intervention.[27]

Most generally, though, the issue is, assuming the legitimacy of international community action at all, *in what fora, and measured against what standards, can the actions of the international community itself be made accountable?* Courts are usually reserved for actions between private individuals or between individuals and public bodies; international courts are usually reserved for hearing actions by states suing other states. What should be the institutional means, and by what criteria, can the decisions and actions of the international community – even when acting as a "dictatorship of virtue" – be assessed and made the subject of something akin to a judicial review, specifically in the fields of media (re)construction and regulation?

## Notes

1  The present author has, as a preliminary step, registered the domain name, www.mediaidwatch.org. Also note that this account only refers to events that occurred up until the Fall of 2000.

2  Some cited passages in this chapter have been edited slightly for clarity. The following passages were taken from http://www.seerecon.org/Bosnia/Bosnia-DonorPrograms/Bosnia-Donors-EC/Sectors/Media/1.htm and http://www.seerecon.org/Bosnia/Bosnia-DonorPrograms/Bosnia-Donors-EC/Sectors/Telecom/1.htm.

3  Address of the High Representative for Bosnia and Herzegovina, Wolfgang Petritsch, to the Peace Implementation Council Brussels, 23 May 2000. http://www.ohr.int/speeches/s20000523a.htm.

4  From www.wpfc.org (link broken).

5  Press Now's *Free Press in South-Eastern Europe* provides a useful overview. See http://www.dds.nl/~pressnow/dossier/donors.html).

6  Taken from <http://www.dhdihr.coe.fr/Intro/eng/GENERAL/demosth.htm.

7  Taken from: http://www.dds.nl/~pressnow/dossier/donors.html.

8  Taken from: <http://www.dds.nl/~pressnow/dossier/donors.html.

9  This text was taken from UNESCO's website at: http://www.unesco.org/webworld/com_media/peace_ong_projects.html.

10  See article at: http://www.unesco.org/webworld/news/000128_timor.shtml.

11  See http://www.stabilitypact.org/stabilitypactcgi/other/qsp.cgi.

12  From www.freemedia.at (link broken).

13  See www.imcbih.org.

14  The IFJ's press releases are contained on their Website at www.ifj.org. However, the releases from 1999 are no longer posted. Contact the IFJ for archives: ifj@pophost.eunet.be.

15  Taken from www.wpfc.org.

16  The Independent Media Commission's version of the first two years of its existence can be gleaned from its "Report 1998-2000" and the more recent White Paper, "Media and Democratization in Bosnia and Herzegovina." See www.imcbih.org.

17  Ibid: 52.

18  Taken from http://www.freemedia.at/publicat.html.

19  United Nations Mission in Kosovo (UNMIK) Regulation 2000/36, "On the Licensing and Regulation of the Broadcast Media in Kosovo" See http://www.osce.org/kosovo/indbodies/unmikreg.php3?ik=1.

20  Temporary Code of Conduct For The Print Media In Kosovo_(Pursuant to Section 1 of UNMIK Regulation No. 2000/37) See http://www.osce.org/kosovo/indbodies/pcoc.php3?lg=e.

21  The Code of Conduct for Broadcast Media in Kosovo was published on September 8, 2000. See http://www.osce.org/kosovo/indbodies/bcoc.php3?lg=e. It was drawn up in consultation with the Kosovo Media Policy Advisory Board. The Association of the Media of Kosovo, the IFJ, Article 19 and others also contributed suggestions. The Temporary Print Code of Conduct was published on September 18, 2000. It was to remain in force until January 1, 2001 and may be renewed at 90-day intervals, pending the establishment of an effective self-regulatory system.

22  *IFJ Accuses United Nations of "Dangerous Precedent" in Move to Control Press in Kosovo* from http://www.ifj.org/publications/press/pr/144.html.

23  See www.wpfc.org.

24  The Charter for Media Freedom is a good example of the IC promulgating standards that could well be applied to its own activities. The text is reproduced in Appendix II to this book.

25  See www.wpfc.org/Aug%201,2000%Onewsletter.html for a description in the newsletter of the WPFC's objections.

26  This is a non-governmental organization named after Article 19 of the Universal Declaration of Human Rights. They "monitor, research, publish, lobby, campaign and litigate on behalf of freedom of expression wherever it is threatened." They also "develop standards to advance media freedom, assist individuals to speak out and campaign for the free flow of information." See www.article19.org.

27  See also Metzl (1997b). From http://www.rnw.nl/realradio/dossiers /html /conclusion.html.

# References

Allies Create a Press Control Agency in Bosnia. 1998. *The New York Times.* 24 April.

Charter for Media Freedom. 2001. Special Co-ordinator of the Stability Pact for South Eastern Europe. March 2001.

Friedrich, Carl. 1948. *American Experiences in Military Government in World War 2.* New York: Rinehart.

Goff, P. (ed). 1999. *The Kosovo News and Propaganda War.* (In association with ANEM, the Alliance of Kosovo Journalists, the Albanian Media Institute and the Balkan Media Association) Vienna: International Press Institute.

Metzl, J. 1997a. Information Intervention. *Foreign Affairs,* November/December.

————. 1997b. Rwandan genocide and the international law of radio jamming. *American Journal of International Law* 91, 4, October: 628. http://www.asil.org/radio.htm.

OHR Legal Opinion. 1999/3.

Pech, L. 2000. Is Dayton Falling: Reforming Media in Bosnia and Herzegovina. *International Journal of Communications Law and Policy* Web-Doc 3-4-2000.

Price, M. 2000. *Restructuring the Media in Post Conflict Societies: Four Perspectives.* UNESCO Seminar, May.

Report and White Paper. 1998-2000. *Media and Democratization in Bosnia and Herzegovina.* The Independent Media Commission.

WPFC Warns Against Restrictions on Kosovo Press. 1999. *Newsletter of the World Press Freedom Committee for its Affiliates and Contributors and Other Media Leaders.* 1 July. http://www.wpfc.org/July%252099.html.

# Cities as the Physical Site of the Global Entertainment Economy

**John Hannigan**

As we proceed into the new millennium, the impact of economic globalization on cities has become a topic of increasing importance. It is generally acknowledged that this situation is somewhat paradoxical. On the one hand, economic globalization has been accompanied by a shift in traditional manufacturing activities from domestic to offshore locations, leaving many older cities to deal with abandoned, sometimes polluted industrial sites (Wolfson and Frisken 2000: 363). At the same time, some metropolitan nodes have emerged as "global cities," urban centres of power, influence and strategic control, both in traditional sectors of the economy such as trade and banking and in contemporary sectors such as transportation, communications and tourism (Chang 2000: 819). Of particular note here are the latter two areas, communications and tourism, at whose junction we find one important manifestation of the "global entertainment economy."

In times past, the media of mass communications tended to function nationally, relegating most activities that were local in nature to the margins. American television networks, for example, treated their affiliate stations as little more than conduits for programming produced in studios in Hollywood and New York, granting them blocks of time for hometown programming exclusively in off-hour time slots such as late at night, Sunday morning, and around the dinner hour. More recently, however, communications executives have rediscovered the lure of the local. As Andy Thornley has observed:

> The media industry has been showing increasing interest in urban development as epitomized by the redevelopment of New York's Times Square, and it has been suggested that cities are being treated as theme parks as the global entertainment business turns its attention to the potential of existing cities (2000: 690-91).

181

Broadly speaking, this renewal has unfolded within the context of a rapidly proliferating postmodern "economy of signs and space" (Lash and Urry 1993). Success in this new economy is contingent upon creating a strong "brand identity" whose value depends on attaching symbolic meanings to material products such as sneakers and sweaters and colas, and to experiential products such as NBA basketball and a trip to the museum. In both cases, "it is the product name and the symbolic associations it carries that attract new consumers and establish its value as a commodity sign" (Whitson 1998: 68).

Accordingly, the more signifiers resonate through the intended audiences in this new sign economy, the more economically successful the corporation will be (Goldman and Papson 1999). One way of achieving this is to command a recognizable presence in everyday urban landscapes and cultures. Tagliabue (1996 C1, C3 cited in Greenberg 2000: 260) quotes one prominent Disney executive who identifies that firm's corporate strategy as "think global, act local" by monopolizing global markets while packaging products in culturally specific dress and by gaining influence over regulatory bodies in specific locales. As Kipfer (1999/2000: 14) notes, "the exercise of global corporate control depends on the capacity to control and transform neighbourhoods and people in particular places such as global cities."

More specifically, cities are increasingly attractive to those who dominate the global entertainment economy for several reasons.

To begin with, cities are viewed as portals through which new products and services may enter the lives of the urban middle class. One increasingly significant channel is the "urban lifestyle magazine." Established by local entrepreneurs in the 1960s and 1970s to advance a new middle-class vision of the city, these publications are currently being taken over by major transnational corporate players such as Disney Corporation and Rupert Murdoch's News Corp. These companies are seeking to merge an urban with a corporate "imaginary" (i.e. a coherent ensemble of representations, many of which derive from the mass media). The upscale images found in their pages increasingly represent one of the most effective means of experiencing, as in a "*branded city-in-miniature*," the "increasingly commodified and inhuman landscapes" of the postmodern city. This also plays a role in shaping such trends as the "reclamation of downtowns by shopping centres and entertainment zones, the gentrification of older manufacturing districts, and the predominance of urban tourism as engines of economic growth" (Greenberg 2000: 256).

Media corporations are also attracted to cities because they constitute a rich resource in an industry that is increasingly long on delivery systems and short on content. Particular interest has been expressed in professional team sports. Unlike other sources of material, sports events occur in real time and contain outcomes that are unpredictable, and frequently both dramatic and serendipitous. Despite employing players who hail from other cities (and increasingly other nations) and who return there in the off-season, sports teams nevertheless continue to engender strong feelings of inter-city competition and local pride. Large cable company operators have become owners of professional sports franchises in order to obtain exclusive broadcast rights to their games. For example, Rupert Murdoch is said to have purchased the Los Angeles Dodgers for this reason, as did Canadian cable czar Ted Rogers who purchased the Toronto Blue Jays baseball team. In addition, "global" teams such as the Dallas Cowboys (football) and Manchester United (soccer) can generate generous profits from international sale of their branded merchandise.

Transnational entertainment companies have also discovered that cities can be branded commodities in their own right, conjuring up "a whole series of images and emotions and with them an impression of value" (Greenberg 2000: 230). Note, for example, the strategic selling of "cappuccino culture" in the motion picture "Sleepless in Seattle" and the framing of the "Notting Hill" region in the Julia Roberts movie by the same name as an increasingly trendy neighbourhood in London, England. And the popular American network television comedy "The Drew Carey Show" begins with the musical anthem "Cleveland Rocks" which celebrates that city's ethnic tavern culture.

In short, media/entertainment companies have adopted the strategy of "being everywhere for everyone in the same irreducible way" (Zukin 1999), linking their leisure and consumption products to the geographic spaces where they are produced and consumed.

For their part, cities themselves have welcomed these emissaries from the global entertainment economy on the grounds that they bring with them the means to engineer the revitalization of central urban areas. Starting in the 1980s, arts and entertainment have increasingly been deployed by urban developers to counter negative urban images of crime, de-industrialization and economic woes (Chang 2000: 820), assuring middle-class publics that cities are oases of excitement where it is possible to enjoy fantasy experiences within a safe, reassuring, and predictable environment (Hannigan 1998: 71). Increasingly, cultural expression is regarded less as a social practice and more, in its commoditized form as entertainment, as a motor of the urban economy.

This chapter profiles this rapidly developing leisure, culture and entertainment infrastructure in contemporary cities; suggests how this emerging "fantasy" or "entertainment" city is transforming both physical and cultural space; and finally, raises some concerns relating to democratic expression and public control.

## Developing Cities for Fun and Profit

As Eisinger (2000: 319) has noted, the development of large entertainment projects in American (and Canadian) cities is not entirely new. In particular, the so-called "golden age" of urban entertainment that flourished between the 1880s and 1930s was in some ways parallel to what is occurring today (Hannigan 1998; Nasaw 1993). Nevertheless, the current pattern differs from that previously encountered in four major ways.

First of all, the pace and variety of construction have markedly increased, as cities in all regions have opted to make entertainment projects the keystone of their urban economic development strategies. These projects include major-league sports facilities, convention centres and exhibition halls, festival malls, riverfront walks, and urban entertainment districts containing megaplex movie theatres, bars and cafés, performing arts centres, museums, virtual reality arcades, and "theme" retailing through branded outlets such as the Disney and Nike stores.

Second, the demographic and economic context is different. In the "golden age" the building of amusement parks, movie palaces and baseball stadiums occurred in a period of rapid urban population and economic growth. Today, many local governments in the United States have been making large public investments in entertainment facilities at the same time as the municipal tax base is declining and social welfare needs are rising.

Third, the intended patron base has shifted from the city's residents to visitors from suburbia and out-of-town. Whereas past urban recreational facilities, notably those that flourished in the latter part of the nineteenth century, were designed for use by a broader urban populace, today's entertainment facilities are deliberately designed and marketed to bring middle-class suburbanites back into the cities as day or weekend tourists.

Finally, the scale of entertainment construction is significantly greater. It is not uncommon, for example, for movie megaplexes to have 30 or more screens, while there has been a relentless ballooning in the minimum size required for convention centres to attract large trade shows. The MGM Grand Hotel and Casino in Las Vegas is so large that it operates its own hospital and parking garage exclusively for the use of its employees.

While urban entertainment development seems to have appeared out of nowhere, most of the principals in these projects are long-existing and experienced corporations. Some are *established* firms that have continued to pursue their core activities, albeit in a new context. Most of the large real estate development firms that are active in entertainment development (Forest City Ratner, Tishman Development Corporation, Simon Properties, Trizec Hahn) have extensive backgrounds in building retail complexes, notably shopping centres. Then there are *expanding* firms that have added new entertainment products and services to their core media and entertainment businesses. For example, Disney has long been involved in operating theme parks in ex-urban settings but not until very recently in the urban downtown core. One Disney strategy has been to downsize their attractions so that they will fit the constraints of smaller retail sites. "Disney Quest," a high technology arcade devised by the Disney "imagineers" (designers) for downtown sites, is a good illustration of this.

Next, there are *extending* firms, established non-media or development companies that have begun to move squarely into the urban entertainment business. Perhaps the leading example of this is Sony, a corporate electronics giant that has recently built entertainment destinations in Berlin (Sony Centre) and San Francisco (Metreon) in order to showcase and promote its brand. On a smaller scale, this also describes the strategic decision of Magna International, a major auto-parts manufacturer headquartered in the Toronto area, to spin off a subsidiary in order to buy up horseracing tracks across North America and build urban theme parks. Finally, there are *emerging* firms whose growth has been exclusively and intimately related to urban entertainment businesses. Most of these are technology-driven and are involved in producing hardware and software related to simulated leisure experiences.

The development of urban entertainment destinations is essentially a three-way partnership of a media/entertainment firm, a real estate developer and a public partner. While media companies are aggressive and savvy when it comes to marketing branded merchandise and experiences, most have limited backgrounds in navigating the complexities of zoning, planning permissions, traffic codes and other key aspects of the land development process. Consequently, they must turn to established commercial real estate firms with track records in building megaprojects. Conversely, developers need the powerful consumer brands possessed by the media firms in order to attract retail tenants, and to be taken seriously by large institutional lenders who tend to be characteristically risk-averse and still rather suspicious of proposals that don't seem to follow a conventional shopping centre formula. Disney's participation, in particular, can make the difference between a project that comes together successfully or not. Thus, in the case of the Times Square redevelopment in New York City, it was only when the Walt Disney Corporation agreed to renovate the landmark New Amsterdam Theater on Forty-Second Street that both high profile tenants (Tussaud's Group, AMC [American Multiplex Cinemas Entertainment]) agreed to make a commitment to participate in an entertainment complex.

Public partners include municipalities, business improvement districts, state and provincial agencies, and special purpose bodies. Sometimes, the initiative for a project rests with the public partner and the media and development partners are approached either directly or through a formal RFP (Request for Proposals). Their contribution is normally both financial (subsidies, tax breaks) and in the form of promising infrastructure improvements (extending sewage and water lines, new highway exits, constructing a parking garage).

One of the most extensive partnerships of this type in recent times is the US$2 billion public works and private development project that was undertaken by the City of Anaheim (California) and the Walt Disney Company to transform 1,100 acres around Disneyland into the Anaheim Resort District. For its contribution, the city rebuilt roadways, upgraded or replaced sewers, moved overhead utilities underground, planted hundreds of thousands of trees, shrubs and flowers and replaced pole-mounted signs with distinctive sidewalk-level signage, as well as completing a major renovation and expansion of the

Anaheim Convention Center. Disney, in turn, spent US$1.4 billion to upgrade and expand Disneyland and construct three new adjacent attractions: the Grand-Californian Hotel, a new theme park, Disney's California Adventure Park, and Downtown Disney, a 20-acre esplanade lined with shops, restaurants and entertainment venues. In order to help fund the Anaheim Resort District, Disney agreed to back a US$545 million municipal bond issue which allowed all the improvements to be packaged together, including the convention centre (Lockwood 2000).

Not all public-private partnerships, however, fit together as smoothly as this one appears to have. All too often, the public partner ends up accepting a bad deal that costs taxpayers more than the expected benefits. Municipalities are prone to enter into arrangements that are skewed in favour of the media corporation and/or real estate developer where they perceive the community's economic plight as desperate. In such situations, politicians and planners sometimes blunder by offering subsidies, tax holidays and infrastructure improvements that are worth more than revenues that come back in the form of parking fees, sales tax, or surcharges on the cost of lodging and transportation.

## Transforming Urban Space through Theming, Branding and Experience-making

It has long been the case that the urban landscape has reflected prevailing patterns of commerce and control. In the corporate city of the 1960s and 1970s, for example, the shift from an industrial economy to one based on financial services was reflected in the colonization of North American downtowns by soaring glass and steel bank and insurance towers—"contemporary cathedrals" that radiate a sense of power and legitimacy. At the same time, the relentless growth of the "fast food nation" according to the formula devised by the McDonald's restaurant chain resulted in the appearance everywhere of suburban restaurant strips characterized by their sense of "placelessness" (Relph 1976).

In the same way, today's entertainment-centred economy is creating a new genre of location-based projects and influencing the look and feel of many commercial and culture-building developments." Beck (2000: 48) describes this as "a new design marketplace driven by a fusion of environmental design, media technology, and narrative." This emerging genre of entertainment design, he claims, is inspired by world's fairs, theatrical environments and leisure attractions and is preoccupied with communication and emotion rather than by architectural form or style. The "fantasy cities" (Hannigan 1998) that result from this are the products of three strategic processes: theming, branding and experiential storytelling.

Taking their cue from Disney and Las Vegas, retail emporia, restaurants, sports and gaming facilities, museums and other cultural attractions, and even Main Street itself, are heavily themed around an exotic geographic locale (Bourbon

Street, a tropical rainforest, a Moorish bazaar), a distinctive historical period (pioneer days, medieval times, the roaring 20s), a sports and entertainment celebrity (Wayne Gretsky, Dolly Parton, Bob Marley) or a popular motion picture/television show (Star Trek, Coronation Street, The Flintstones). Theming represents an important way of unifying and marketing leisure sites and experiences by integrating a host of individual landscaping and architectural details such as signage, fountains and shop facades (McNair 1999: 94). Thus, the Forum Shops at Caesar's Palace Hotel and Casino in Las Vegas, the world's highest grossing (per square foot) shopping centre, surrounds its high-end shops and restaurants with convincing reproductions of ancient Roman buildings, fountains and animatronic (robotic) statues, all situated under a computer-controlled artificial sky that changes hue according to the time of day. While scarcely a novel design strategy, theming has become pervasive, perhaps as Ritzer (1999) suggests, because it is a means of "re-enchanting a world which has become excessively dull and practical." As such, it represents an "intermediary between the real and the fantasy" (Pearson 2000: 140).

Increasingly, themed landscapes are simultaneously "branded." For example, the World Wrestling Federation (WWF) plans to build a wrestling-themed casino/resort in Las Vegas, as well as a chain of WWF-themed restaurants; Volkswagen operates "Autostadt (Auto City)," a 62-acre "infotainment" theme park in Germany that is designed to celebrate different VW brands of cars (Audi, Bentley, Lamborghini); and Tetley Tea has opened a chain of suitably decorated cafés in British towns and cities. Branding here has three related dimensions (Hannigan 2000). First, it requires instant recognition; hence the "synergies" with the sports and entertainment industries with their rosters of high-octane celebrities. Second, successfully branded leisure spaces play on our desire for both comfort and certainty, key attributes of Disney-style theme parks. Finally, branded environments provide a point of identification for consumers in an increasingly crowded marketplace.

In addition to being themed and branded, urban entertainment culture is increasingly constructed around the creation of guest-centred experiences. Writing in a recent issue of the *Architectural Record*, Clifford Pearson (2000: 140), observes that the business bestseller, *The Experience Economy* (Pine et. al. 1999), is the book "that every entertainment architect seems to be quoting from right now." Beck (2000: 48) claims that "we are now fully engaged in an 'experience economy' where environments, products and services are judged by their quality of personal interaction," and where television and publishing conglomerates race to produce "brand experiences" in corporate attractions all across town. He cites as an example of this "American Girl Place" in Chicago, winner of a retail design award from the Themed Entertainment Association. American Girl Place includes a 145-seat, Broadway-quality theatre complete with a live orchestra in an attempt to combine retail and educational functions through the use of narrative experience. Along the same lines, the NASDAQ (the high-tech stock market) has located its virtual stock exchange together with a paid guest attraction at the junction of Forty-Second and Broadway in Manhattan. At Autostadt, Volkswagen customers can watch as a computer-controlled system moves the car they have purchased from the factory through underground tunnels to the 20-story "AutoTurme" (Auto Tower) from whence it descends to the KunderCenter (Customer Centre) where they await delivery. This experiential process "transforms a once-mundane activity into a high-tech event" (Weber-Hof 2000).

One consequence of all this has been "an environmental blurring that makes museums and airports look like shopping malls and restaurants like theme parks" (Pearson 2000: 139). Furthermore, different types of retail and leisure activities are becoming intertwined. Thus, in Las Vegas, the high-end Bellagio Hotel and Casino houses a world-class collection of Impressionist paintings, while patrons of the new Venetian Casino Resort will soon be able to visit a branch of the Guggenheim Museum situated right within the casino complex itself. Bob Rogers, founder of BRC Imagination Arts, a California-based company that designs and produces projects for world's fairs, amusement parks, museums and service centres, has observed that major museums such as the Smithsonian in Washington, D.C., can no longer assume a certain level of prior knowledge on the part of its visitors who "speak a new, graphic, experiential language emblematic of the multi-media age." As a result, these cultural institutions are finding it necessary to borrow narrative techniques from Disney-style theme parks in order to "motivate and inspire museum guests and achieve their educational missions" (Interview with Bob Rogers 2000). This results in a further blurring of urban settings and activities.

## The Entertainment City, Democratic Access, and Local Control

As Raboy (1999: 1) has argued, access to the institutions and practices associated with the mass media, cultural industries and information/communications technologies, both in the role of a sender and as a receiver of information, is "critical to any individual or social group's capacity to participate fully and meaningfully in public life." While Raboy is referring mainly to new communications and information technologies such as the Internet, his observation applies equally to the policy implications associated with the growth of the entertainment city.

Evans (2001) points to a "crisis in local governance" where communities are neither the originators of plans for cultural venues nor the producers of the cultural products at the centre of the thrust of globalization. The themed "brandscapes" that dominate the fantasy city substitute a transnational culture based on sports heroes, Hollywood celebrities and cartoon characters for an indigenous urban culture based on "place" and "tradition," which Scanlon (2000) describes as the anchoring soil in past conceptualizations of community. Similarly, Zukin (1991) draws a contrast between "places" and "markets" and maintains that the latter has increasingly come to replace the former. There is a danger here of romanticizing the industrial landscapes of the past in contrast to the present forms that are more associated with the service and leisure industries. Nevertheless, it is difficult to see how these new developments can in any way meaningfully enhance local identities when they are primarily designed to build commercial equity and identity for a handful of megacorporations which have come to dominate the global entertainment economy.

Accordingly, the case against the present wave of urban entertainment development rests on several arguments.

First, critics charge that it smacks of hubris to claim that you can redefine urban places by parachuting in entertainment megaprojects that have no organic linkage to the community itself. Molotch et. al. (2000) have pointed out that efforts to alter the texture and trajectory of places by "plopping in" a new museum, science park or stadium "all carry the risk of artificiality." In particular, it is wrong to think that places are fundamentally interchangeable, and therefore, that the entertainment infrastructure that is so successful in Las Vegas or Orlando will work equally well in Pittsburgh or Montreal. When places try to imitate other locales, the context is different and the advantage of being the first has been lost (2000: 817-18). This is not to say that the character of an urban community is completely frozen, unable to evolve or be transformed. Rather, it is the case that urban traditions arise "through interactive layering and active enrolments over time, something that is difficult to produce all at once" (Ibid.). The distinctiveness of an urban place is thus both a reflection of its "character" and of how this character travels through time to constitute a local "tradition."

Second, urban entertainment development raises the hackles of its critics because it is viewed as being fundamentally top-down and undemocratic. Despite operating under the auspices of "public-private partnerships," the new cultural/entertainment economy at best only superficially solicits local neighbourhood and community input.

In Britain, this has meant that municipal councils have all but been excluded by partnerships formed among private interests, the national government and key cultural organizations. In the case of the star-crossed "Millennium Dome," for example, the local Greenwich Council was only brought in at a late stage after the Blair government had already attracted competitive bids (Thornley 2000). In the London borough of Southwark, along the south bank of the Thames River, the Council felt tremendous pressure from private sponsors and from the approval of National Lottery funding to approve the establishment of a "cultural" quarter featuring the new Tate Gallery and Globe Theatre. Feeling it fruitless to attempt any further efforts at community development, the Council reduced its main activities to that of "image-making" (Newman and Smith 2000).

Urban regeneration strategies that revolve around entertainment, tourism and the arts have also been challenged on the basis that they exclude small-scale cultural producers: artists, musicians, dancers, actors and playwrights. While contemporary media/entertainment moguls occasionally hire creative trailblazers (for example Disney's choice of Julie Taynor to direct the theatrical version of The Lion King), mostly they opt for artistic content that is derivative and non-controversial. In similar fashion, the theme-park formula (slavishly used in organizing and building these urban entertainment developments) relies on ethnic and national stereotypes that leave little room for cutting-edge experiments in such things as pan-ethnic expression or fusing traditional and modern identities. Furthermore, urban entertainment districts and destinations may negatively affect local cultural producers by forcing them out of low-rent residential districts. This phenomenon has been well documented in relation to the gentrification of artists' lofts (see Zukin 1982) and has recently re-appeared.

Finally, the emergence of "entertainment-based retail place-making" (Levine *et. al.* 1997: 24) as a standard formula for use in revitalizing urban centres, has led to a greater degree of social exclusion, especially with reference to disadvantaged groups. As Evans (2000) has noted, city regeneration that relies on an external formula "will inevitably presage a winners' and losers' game in which a few 'prestige' projects located in the downtown core and along the urban waterfront are surrounded by mile after mile of continued decay and despair wherein it is difficult to discern any visible benefits for the local residents."

Perhaps the most extensive case study of this is Marc Levine's examination of the effects of the "festival marketplace" development in Baltimore, Maryland, from the mid-1970s up to the present time. With the successful opening in 1980 of Harborplace (developed by the Rouse Corporation), Baltimore immediately gained a national reputation as a "renaissance city" that had found the magic formula for attracting middle-class suburbanites back into the central city. Levine severely doubts whether the creation of a renaissance city at the Inner Harbor has made much of a dent in Baltimore's mounting social and economic success, or whether the "carnival city" strategy is generating socially sustainable development (2000: 134). He especially questions the widely touted maxim that states that "a rising tide lifts all ships." After nearly two decades, the prosperity generated by spending more than US$1 billion on publicly financed sports stadiums, tourist attractions and an expanded convention centre has failed to "spill over" to the rest of the inner city, remaining primarily at the waterfront. Just a few blocks inland, blight and decline continue. The traditional retail district on the western edge of downtown remains moribund, with vacant storefronts, dilapidated buildings and seedy street life. One reason for this is that Baltimoreans are afraid to wander much beyond the waterfront "tourist bubble" lest they be mugged or murdered by inner city residents. When Levine first began his research in Baltimore in the 1970s, most of the new jobs at Harborplace and other tourist businesses around the Inner Harbor went to white suburbanites, but during the 1980s downtown growth began providing significant employment opportunities for the city's black community. However, the majority of workers in Baltimore's tourist and entertainment business—waitresses, housekeepers and kitchen workers—earn less than US$15,000 per year. Levine describes the quality of these jobs as "dubious;" they are not unionized, contain few fringe benefits or career ladders, are typically part-time and pay about 60 per cent of the average wage (Levine 2000: 135).

One frequently expressed criticism of urban entertainment projects is that they siphon off money that could otherwise be spent on social and community services such as education and low-income housing. Torjman (1999) has termed this the "Phantom Menace," noting that local governments are under increasing pressure to be "smokestack (or perhaps microchip) chasers" who end up diverting funds from other projects such as transportation and social housing. For example, in Detroit, Michigan, the Downtown Development Agency has diverted money previously devoted to small commercial and housing projects to land acquisition, site clearance and infrastructure improvements associated with building two downtown sports stadiums and three gambling casinos (Eisinger 2000: 330). When he first looked at the Baltimore case in the 1970s, Levine observed something of the same phenomenon, noting that the Inner Harbor development failed to generate surplus revenue the city could use for neighbourhood development projects. In his most recent report, he notes that after three decades of "fantasy city" redevelopment strategies and much heralded community development initiatives, none of the city's core difficulties had been successfully attacked and "it may well be that Baltimore is past the point of no return" (2000: 151).

For their part, proponents of fantasy city developments attempt to counter such criticism by asserting that such projects increase rather than decrease public access and democratize culture and the arts. Pearson (2000: 140) compares what is happening here with the Internet which "is blurring distinctions on a global scale. Just as a mass-market economy has been pulling down the walls that once separated the fine arts from their popular cousins," projects such as the "Cybercenter" in Hong Kong "will make the business of information fun and accessible to the public" (Ibid.). In similar fashion, Beck (2000: 48) calls the growth of entertainment design and the experience economy "a populist uprising" which is reshaping our attitudes about the character of everyday places. Hype aside, they are mostly referring to "postmodern" architectural styles that are characterized by a heavy referencing of commercial popular culture. Beck's claim that the present generation of entertainment destinations incorporate architectural techniques for environmental storytelling that "engage large groups of people with compelling ideas" (Ibid.) is somewhat fanciful, given the kind of evidence of inequality reported by Levine and others.

## Conclusion

Commenting on the view that politics is irrelevant in a world where popular culture and its market have been universalized, Street (1997: 75-6) identifies two elements as being central to this claim:

The first is that there are no effective political controls or institutions at the global level, only the corporations with their purely commercial interests. The second is that at the level at which political controls do exist, at the national or sub-national level, the responsible organizations are powerless, attempts to resist the intrusion of transnational corporations in the name of local culture or economic autonomy inevitably fail.

In the case of the urban entertainment economy, the source of this powerlessness is the new orthodoxy among city politicians and planners which prescribes a central role for cities as public partners in megaproject development. To a considerable extent, this is an extension of the "urban growth machine" model that views metropolitan elites as united in their beliefs that development is the proper path for cities and that this precludes any alternative vision of the purpose of local government or the meaning of community (Logan and Molotch 1987: 51). For such elites, the tourism-entertainment nexus is important because it can lead to "a reimaging of the city, a reorientation of local priorities, consolidation of power by elites" and, as Mommass and Van der Poel (1989) have argued, it also leads to a new "social and spatial segregation and new private and public cultures" (Holcomb 1999: 68). In his study of the 42nd Street Development Project in New York City, one of the largest urban entertainment destinations to emerge over the last decade, Alexander Reichl (1999: 119) identifies a core triad of interests at the heart of the pro-growth alliance. In addition to the business community and public officials, the traditional mainstays of the urban growth machine as described by Molotch and Logan, a third group consisting of a collection of civic, professional and business organizations concerned with historic preservation, the arts and urban design, was emerging as a primary participant in urban growth politics. As Kipfer (1999-2000: 15) observes, it is not entirely new for municipalities such as Toronto to equate economic development with strategies to promote a city's "competitiveness as a centre of finance, corporate headquarters, entertainment and tourism." However, what does seem to be happening is a new centralized process of policy making in which transit buses, community centres, social housing, and health clinics are displaced as priorities in favour of "spectacles, condominiums, entertainment complexes and megaprojects such as the Olympics [and], the Opera House…"

In the face of this, stricter regulation and public control over the local leisure culture and entertainment infrastructure is very difficult. Municipal governments are increasingly being downloaded with increased responsibilities for social issues but have reduced funds and very few levers for monitoring and enforcement. Local agencies whose role it is to deal with arts and culture are usually part of the growth machine and are thus more concerned with promotion than with regulation. Zoning and building code restrictions can be enforced but these are not meant to explicitly address issues of cultural content. As a result, the global entertainment economy can be expected to slip under the radar of both national and transnational mechanisms and policies that seek to ensure that global commerce operates in the public interest.

## References

Beck, G. 2000. Entertainment and Culture Now. *Entertainment Design* 34 (11): 48-9.

Chang, T.C. 2000. Renaissance Revisited: Singapore as a Global City For The Arts. *International Journal of Urban and Regional Research* 24: 818-31.

Eisinger, P. 2000. The Politics Of Bread And Circuses: Building The City For The Visitor Class. *Urban Affairs Review* 35: 316-33.

Evans, G. 2001. *Cultural Planning: An Urban Renaissance? An International Perspective on Planning for the Arts and Culture*. London: Routledge.

Goldman, R. and Papson, S. 1999. *Nike Culture: The Sign of the Swoosh*. Thousand Oaks, CA: Sage.

Greenberg, M. 2000. Rebranding Cities: A Social History Of The Urban Lifestyle Magazine. *Urban Affairs Review* 36: 228-63.

Hannigan, J. 1998. *Fantasy City: Pleasure and Profit in the Postmodern City*. London & New York: Routledge.

_____. 2000. Branding Urban Space: Corporatization, Privatization And The Global Entertainment Economy. Paper presented to the Conference on Cultural Change and Urban Contexts, Manchester Metropolitan University, September 8-10.

Holcomb, B. 1999. Marketing Cities for Tourism. In *The Tourist City*, edited by D. Judd and S. Fainstein. New Haven & London: Yale University Press.

Interview with Bob Rogers. 2000. *Entertainment Design* 34 (11): 38.

Kipfer, S. 1999/2000. Whose City Is It? Global Politics in the Mega-City. *CityScope*. Winter: 13-17.

Lash, S. and Urry, J. 1993. *Economies of Signs and Space*. London: Sage.

Levine, J., Lockwood, C, and Warpole, K. 1997. Rethinking Regeneration. *Special Report on Urban Regeneration*. London: World Architecture 58, July/August.

Levine, M. 2000. A Third World City in the First World: Social Exclusion, Racial Inequality and Sustainable Development in Baltimore. In *The Social Sustainability of Cities: Diversity and the Management of Change*, edited by M. Polese and R. Stein. Toronto: University of Toronto Press.

Lockwood, C. 2000. Anaheim's Excellent Adventure. *Planning* 66 (12): 4-9.

Logan, J.R. and Molotch, H. 1987. *Urban Fortunes: The Political Economy of Place*. Berkeley: University of California Press.

McNair, J. 1999. Retail Entertainment. *Urban Land*. February: 34-7; 94-5.

Molotch, H., Freudenburg, W. and Paulsan, K.E. 2000. History Repeats Itself, But How? City Character, Urban Tradition and the Accomplishment of Place. *American Sociological Review* 65: 791-823.

Mommass, H. and Van der Poel, H. 1989. Changes in Economy, Politics and Lifestyles: An Essay on the Restructuring of Urban Leisure. In *Leisure and Urban Processes: Critical Studies of Leisure Policy in West European Cities*, edited by P. Bramham, I. Henry, H. Mommass and H. van der Poel. London: Routledge.

Nasaw, D. 1993. *Going Out: The Rise and Fall of Public Amusements*. New York: HarperCollins.

Newman, P. and Smith, I. 2000. Cultural Production, Place and Politics on the South Bank of the Thames. *International Journal of Urban and Regional Research* 24: 9-24.

Pearson, C.A. 2000. Theme Sprawl. *Architectural Record*. November: 139-41.

Pine, J. and Gilmore, J.H. 1999. *The Experience Economy: Work is Theatre & Every Business a Stage*. Boston: Harvard Business School Press.

Raboy, M. 1999. *Communication and Globalization - A Challenge for Public Policy*. Contribution to the "Projet on Trends", Ottawa: Policy Research Secretariat.

Reichl, A.J. 1999. *Reconstructing Times Square: Politics and Culture in Urban Development*. Lawrence, KS: University Press of Kansas.

Relph, E. 1976. *Places and Placelessness*. London: Pion Ltd.

Ritzer, G. 1999. *Enchanting a Disenchanted World: Revolutionizing the Means of Consumption*. Thousand Oaks, CA: Pine Forge Press.

Scanlon, C. 2000. The Network of Moral Sentiment. *Arena Journal* 15: 57-79.

Street, J. 1997. Across the Universe: The Limits Of Global Popular Culture. In *The Limits of Globalization: Cases and Arguments*, edited by A. Scott. London & New York: Routledge.

Tagliabue, J. 1996. Local Flavour Rules European TV. *New York Times*. 14 October.

Thornley, A. 2000. Dome Alone: London's Millennium Project And The Strategic Planning Deficit. *International Journal of Urban and Regional Research* 24: 689-99.

Torjman, S. 1999. Comments on J. Hannigan, *Branding Canada*. National Policy Conference, Ottawa, November.

Weber-Hof, C. 2000. Autostadt, Wolfsburg, Germany. *Architectural Record*. November: 148-53.

Whitson, D. 1998. Circuits of Promotion: Media Marketing and the Globalization of Sport. In *MediaSport*, edited by L.A. Wenner. London and New York: Routledge.

Wolfson, J. and Frisken, F. 2000. Local Response to the Global Challenge: Comparing Local Economic Development Policies in a Regional Context. *Journal of Urban Affairs* 22: 361-84.

Zukin, S. 1982. *Loft Living: Culture and Capital in Urban Change*. Baltimore: Johns Hopkins University Press.

_____. 1991. *Landscapes of Power: From Detroit to Disney World*. Berkeley and Los Angeles: University of California Press.

_____. 1999. The Disney Hydra: Imagineering the Urban Imaginary. Keynote Address, 30th Annual Conference, Environmental Design Research Association, Orlando, Florida, June.

# Part Three

# Practices

# Gender and Transversal Cultural Policies

**Alison Beale**

L ike other contributions to this volume, this chapter concerns a policy environment for communications and culture that no longer emphasizes national modernization, but instead is preoccupied with national relationships to globalized trade and technology. The feminist research already negotiating this national-transnational link can contribute to inclusive approaches to setting policy agendas and to governing the institutions that will affect culture and communications in the future. To neglect this work will perpetuate some of the existing theoretical and political limitations of policy research. This chapter, therefore, explores aspects of the policy context that have been the object of feminist concern. It will also demonstrate that in transversal cultural and communications policy, gender is a key analytical concept.

The recent interest in transversal policy-making among academics reflects a coming-to-terms with the patchwork of trade, technological, intellectual property and human rights conventions that now govern the communications and cultural sectors. To borrow the language of privatization, this interest reflects the need to "be flexible" and to "create partnerships" in the face of economic and political authorities whose forms and capacities have changed significantly. In the politics and scholarship of the women's movement and other social movements, the opportunities and limitations of this situation have been apparent for some time.

Feminist scholarship has shown that by neglecting gender, significant gaps have been created in political economy and policy studies. Yet, the pertinence of gender-conscious research in these fields has not been accepted (Beale 1999a: 487-494). Additionally, there is much unfinished business in gender equity and intersecting aspects of social equality in the communications and cultural sectors, especially when considered from a world-wide perspective (Gallagher 1995; Cliche *et. al.* 1998; Danner *et. al.* 1999). While the feminist movement, feminist theory and feminist research agendas have been altered by a recognition of the movement's diverse international history and the intersection of class, race, ethnic and sexual identities in women, the "old" problems have not been solved even as new ones have come to the fore.

Two final prefatory notes: arguably, the most profound and disruptive contribution of feminist theory and research has been methodological and epistemological. Feminist work has questioned and even shifted the bases on which knowledge is legitimated. Changes in the way policy is conceptualized and carried out relate closely to these theoretical and methodological interventions. These shifts include questioning the social subject in cultural policy (eg the "universal" citizen, the consumer); assessments of the relative power of formal and informal political and economic institutions at the local, national and international levels; the meanings of "culture" and "society" especially in including and excluding groups of citizens and their cultural practices; and finally challenging the hegemony in policy-making and policy study of the governmental and academic discourses of economics and political science. Both the legitimacy and the stability of many of these components of "policy" have been under the scrutiny of the political movements and academic critiques of women and minorities.

The second note concerns the nation-state and the world markets as central cultural and political formations. These have been examined by feminists in ways that correlate to questions now arising in relation to transversal cultural and communications policy. Debates about the nation-state include questions about the welfare state as the provider or distributor of public goods, the gendered nature of national modernization, gender and national identity, gender and racial/ethnic minority identity, and gendered citizenship. Regarding the world market, feminists are also among those looking behind the masquerade of post-national consumer identities. The post-national identity currently marketed to us (think of advertisements for laptop computers featuring users on planes, in the Australian desert, at the beach) carries with it legends about the new personalities and abilities it confers that obscure differences and inequalities among workers, citizens and consumers on the basis of gender and other factors. As part of the myth of technologically enabled self-sufficiency, social solidarities have no place in this brave new world. But feminist politics and research have identified and reinforced such solidarities while fighting the gender-based inequalities in international production and trade.

This chapter considers the significance to transversal policy of feminist arguments that national cultures and world market culture, as well as the means by which they are regulated and researched, are gendered. This analysis also looks at the hierarchy of communications and cultural policies as well as the relationship of this hierarchy to gender. Next, the discussion reviews the shift in which the "stakeholders" in cultural policy are no longer citizens but consumers. How is gendered consumption understood in markets and in policy?

How does the focus on diversity through consumption mask the materialities of labour, access to education and services, and the ability to determine the public interest in ways that continue to affect women and men differently?

## The gendered nation

At the same time as communications, cultural studies and cultural policy critics began to query the versions of "national" cultures that are the object of cultural policy (O'Regan 1994; Gilroy 1993; Ng 1993; Morris 1992), feminist researchers began to point out ways in which male and female gender roles and gendered national symbols had been naturalized in the modern nation-state narrative (Felski 1995). These parallel critical movements – the beginnings of a critical cultural policy field[1] – were affected by disenchantment with state-centric solutions to democratic deficits in communications and cultural expression because of the financial inadequacy of the solutions and, especially, because of their failure to encompass cultural diversity. Beyond these issues, a more profound questioning of the relationship of government to culture was also going on. Major theoretical influences were as diverse as Foucault's critique of governmentality (Foucault 1991), feminist analysis of the "patriarchal state" (MacKinnon 1989), Claus Offe's concept of the regulatory state (Offe 1984) and the Frankfurt School critique (Horkheimer 1972) continued in Jürgen Habermas' work on the relation of instrumental reason to the state (Habermas 1975).

In the 1980s, complementary social movements included the brief flowering of civil-society experiments (notably in publishing) in late and post-Soviet Eastern Europe. There was also greater emphasis on community-based, rather than centralized economic development in development projects that also enhanced the participation of women. In cultural production, artists responded to inadequate financing and the slow adaptation of cultural bureaucracies to cultural change with non-profit, co-operative movements and networks of arts workers using the new Internet and other communications technologies (although it would be wrong to mythologize the democratizing power of these media which made it easier for artists to continue networking as they had done for decades). Many artists also embraced self-marketing and crossover projects with advertising, fashion and promotion in a way that blurred the separation of art from market and further broke down the distinctions between government, markets, patrons and producers (Rosler 1994). In this period, the initiative was seized from more than one political direction.

These critiques and experiments in the (re)organization of culture were significant because historians of cultural policy tend to view cultural policies as having been at the core of modern nation-states (Pick 1988; Bennett 1998). In the second half of the twentieth century, their stability and continuity in the capitalist democracies and the "welfare states", in particular, gave an impression of permanence to a certain kind of relation between culture and state. Historically, however, such policies were anything but oriented to the status quo: they had been responsible for major social transformations. In the long view, they are as associated with cultural destruction as they are with preservation. They were devised to accomplish the goal of national religious, cultural and ethnic unification (often synonymous with the hegemony of a dominant group or sub-nationality), and transfer of political allegiance away from tribe, village, or city toward the nation, to be encoded in national citizenship. Linguistic, educational, heritage and, later, broadcasting policies were some of the policy instruments contributing to the cultural and political changes sought in the modern nation-state. When ideologies of religious and cultural freedom of expression, individualism and collective cultural rights came along, they were considered to be compatible with cultures whose boundaries by then were those of the nation-state. Similarly, international bodies such as the United Nations Educational, Scientific and Cultural Organization (UNESCO), promoting modernization in "less-developed" countries, have followed the path of the development of *national* cultures. It is only recently, in response to many factors (from the loss of elements of traditional culture, to technological and political challenges, to the cultural sovereignty of nation-states) that policy-makers have begun to join their critics by placing a premium on the cultural differences that have survived the drive to form national cultures (World Commission on Culture and Development 1995).

While the current emphasis is on cultural difference as both a positive, intrinsically valuable continuity with the past and new emblem of respect for ways of life previously barely tolerated, real differences in status and citizenship rights can also be understood as having been systematically ignored within the liberal ideology of the national culture. Pointing out the inferior status that national modernities rendered invisible has been a major part of the agenda of critical cultural policy studies (Beale and Van Den Bosch 1998; Tator *et. al.* 1998).

The situation of women is a central example. Studies of culture and modernity suggest that a shift in the roles and rights of women is an essential marker of any society that has desired to call itself modern. But as critics of modern citizenship have pointed out, formal rights often conceal informal inequalities that inhibit a person's capacity to exercise citizenship (Fraser 1990; McLaughlin 1993). The invisibility of the private domestic scene behind the public, masculine persona it facilitates, perpetuates the double domestic/public workday of the woman. Furthermore, in terms of class and ethnic/race relations, a hierarchy of the exploitation of women enables the activity of dominant-group men (and more recently, women) in their roles as political persons. This hierarchy has become part of the structure of economic globalization.[2]

A further critique of modernity argues that modern "culture" itself has been defined and promoted in gendered terms. The organization of work in the arts and education, the attribution of economic and symbolic values to cultural occupations and types of production, as well as cultural management and policy spheres, are all inflected by gendered thinking in which the work of women is less valued. Less valued activities, whether carried out by women or men, are conceived of as feminine, non-essential and non-productive. The cultural sector, in contrast to technological development or finance, is an obvious example. These rankings are carried over into the policy sphere where cultural administration and many cultural policy jobs are occupied by women.[3]

National cultures, both those that are "modern" and those undergoing "modernization," discriminate on the basis of gender not in isolation but in combination with race, ethnicity or nationality. Avtar Brah argues that:

> It is crucial to make it explicit that racism is always a gendered phenomenon. While many analysts treat racism as a gender-neutral concept, it must be borne in mind that racism constructs the female gender differently from the male gender...Not only are men and women from one racialized group differentiated from their counterparts in another racialized group, but the male from a subordinated group may be racialized through the attribution of "feminine qualities," or the female may be represented as embodying "male" qualities (Brah 1993: 12).

Ethnicity and nationality are similarly gendered. Some of the more familiar ways in which this is manifest include the fact that women's dress, sexuality and public behaviour are often seen—from inside and outside—as the marker of the "ethnic" group's identity or integrity (this is particularly the case where the ethnic group is not a longstanding national minority but an immigrant group). Nationalism (especially in wartime), is bound with an ideology, associating women with the homeland ("motherland") in a manner that links the female (mother's) body to the land. In each case, the female is traditionally emotional, unintellectual and essentially corporeal. And, just as weaker or less-desirable characteristics are often characterized as feminine, so can religious and cultural differences be "racialized." In this way, both gender and race can be seen as "floating signifiers," or labels used to mark difference and rationalize discrimination in the context of national cultures.

Gender, race and ethno-cultural identities have been the subject of many human rights and cultural initiatives since the end of World War II. The civil rights movement, the women's movement and gay activism have worked against cultural and legal barriers to participation in society. These movements have been inspired, acquired their legal tools (such as the Universal Declaration on Human Rights of 1948), and even organized at international or global-regional levels. Their histories, however, demonstrate that national politics and institutions create very different national frameworks for achieving gender and race equity (Ashworth 1999). Moreover, with respect to cultural policies, the incorporation of gender and diversity considerations varies according to the scope of cultural policy in each country. In some countries, such as Canada, cultural policies are quite comprehensive; there are links between, for example, official language policies, multicultural policies, and human rights legislation and the performance requirements of cultural bodies receiving public funds.[4] In other countries, cultural policy has referred more or less strictly to the arts and heritage, and sometimes also to the media (Pick 1988; Mulcahy 1997). In addition, while these are some of the formal national frameworks of cultural policy, it is important to point out that where the overlaps between gender and diversity are concerned, a broader perspective is necessary. In addition to understanding cultural policy within a national government, other levels of government, cultural and civil associations, and the private and charitable sectors must be considered.[5]

In the 1970s, women's organizations around the world pressed for employment equity and improved representation of women in the media, and for the inclusion of women in peer review and administrative positions in the arts. While the women's movement was international in terms of important informal networks and the development of women's human rights, and emphatically localized in important areas of its philosophy and social methodology, it was within *national* institutions and through *national* laws that such changes were sought and, to an extent, achieved. National broadcasting policy and regulation has been the focus of policy initiatives regarding gender and race, principally with respect to representations (images of women and minorities) and employment opportunity. It is important to note that while critical of the state, feminists rightly identified privatized media and cultural industries as less likely to hire women and minorities, and more likely to offer the part-time and contract employment dominated by women (Beale 1999a: 444-445).

There was, and is, a strong attachment to a significant role for the state in culture on the part of feminists around the world, who more often than not are also nationalists, if critical ones. For this reason, despite evidence of limited progress in the achievement of equity and growing evidence of the state's catering to private interests in the "cultural economy," feminists (and not only "liberal" feminists) have preferred to work through the state as a means of achieving job equity and better opportunities of cultural expression. The evidence remains that state cultural agencies, state-run media and state regulated cultural industries have met gender equity targets and controls on content to a far greater degree than the private sector (Beale 1999a).

Feminist critiques of public sector-centred national cultural policies and their demands became more complex in Europe, Australia and New Zealand, and Canada and the US in the 1980s. Feminists addressed the inadequacy of levels of financial support for the arts and cultural industries, the hegemony of elite European cultural values and the racism and classism associated with them, and the centralization of cultural administration. Dominant-group women were identified as the primary beneficiaries of employment and pay-equity legislation. Some of the strongest critiques of the state have originated in movements that combine anti-racist with feminist politics. But even these protests continue to address the state, to expect a response, and to show that they feel entitled to it (Gunew and Yeatman 1993).

For researchers of cultural and communications policies, the nation-state persists as a problematic nexus of the politics, political economy and, indeed, the culture of cultural policy. Some recent studies in journalism evaluating both job opportunity and professional ideologies show how the national context cannot be taken for granted but must be treated as a potentially problematic issue in itself. They use the concept of gender to get at the mix of cultural, ideological and epistemological issues that stand in the way of various desired outcomes as gender is institutionalized and culturally deployed in the national setting.

G. J. Robinson's summary of her research (with Armande St-Jean) on women in Canadian journalism talks about a "gendered journalism" whose facets include not only the composition of the workforce, the wages of women compared to men, rates of change and obstacles to change, but also the relationship between feminist values and journalism as an "interpretive community" as well as persistent attitudinal differences between male and female journalists (Robinson forthcoming). The institutional framework and the culture in which values and attitudes are embedded are national ones and the outcomes of national employment equity and education programs are also national. Sonia Bathla argues, in the conclusion of her study of women's work and news about women in the Indian press, that specifically Indian forms of patriarchy require cultural transformations that to date have been only slightly affected by the curricula of journalism schools and by equity legislation (Bathla 1998). A collection of essays on journalism in several European countries and the United States seeks to account for the apparent paradox (very relevant to cultural policy) in which high female participation in media work and consumption co-exists with gender stereotyping, sexualization of women news subjects, gendered norms of rationality and expertise, and trivialization of "women's concerns" (Carter *et. al.* 1999; Beale 2000). Each chapter reveals the importance to these issues of national media cultures and national regulation. There is, after all, no international media regulation that applies to advertisers, employers and professional codes of conduct. As Bathla, in particular, shows (but see also McLaughlin 1999), "local," that is, national factors continue to have tremendous importance in agenda-setting, and in making news out of events. She demonstrates that national ideologies of gender and race are among the most influential factors in "making news."

By this I don't mean to suggest that national cultures have a separate, continuous life that is unaffected by policy directed at, for example, gender equity. Rather, we can see that for every national institution devoted to certain kinds of "social outcomes" there are others that work against those outcomes because they are not in their interests. And as is often the more complex case with cultural and media policy, the political economy of communications and culture is not only structured in gendered terms but also researched and regulated using tools of analysis that are gendered. Eileen Meehan has shown how in the United States, the ratings monopolists (currently the Nielsen company) have historically built up a profile of the television audience which, regardless of (or because of) its methodological shortcomings, upheld the economic interests of ratings organization, advertisers and networks alike. It ignored, that is, did not count, audiences that did not possess desired economic characteristics. It was so inflected with gender-prejudice about the economic behaviour of women, that the rising workforce participation and discretionary income of American women since the 1930s have remained underestimated. The culturally-determined demand for the approval of the white, male, 25-34 year old audience was such that this audience became, and remains, as Meehan says, not just "'where the boys were' but where the audience was" (Meehan 2001:11).[6] The flawed ratings were awarded the status of science by regulators, advertisers, networks and the public. Women, children, African-Americans and Hispanic-Americans continue to be treated as "niche" markets, under-counted and therefore under-served. Meehan does not go out of her way to describe this set of practices and the issue they raise in the political economy of American television as "American," yet clearly that is what they are.

## International markets and transversal policy

Murky waters at the national level do not become clearer in the international context. Media ratings are notoriously subject to distortion and even manipulation from interested parties, but they are confined to national markets and have an international impact only indirectly. However problems related to cultural statistics, and to the monitoring of "cultural indicators" (such as access in education, ownership of radios and television sets, prices of cultural goods such as books relative to average wages), are compounded as we move from national to international levels. The general problem of gathering useful data about women on an international scale begins with the inconsistency and incomparability of statistics gathered by national governments. But according to one review, the greatest challenges, the causes of these deficiencies as reflected in available data, are conceptual: women are undervalued and undercounted; their role in biological reproduction takes precedence over other contributions to social reproduction; and Western economic concepts are universalized (for example, women's economic contribution is only counted if part of a formal economy) and fail to take into account ethnic, geographic and class differences (Danner *et. al.* 1999). Since 1995 the United Nations Platform for Action for Equality, Development and Peace has had on its agenda "specific actions to generate and disseminate gender-disaggregated data and information for planning and evaluation" (Ibid: 249). The primary intended use for this information is in economic development and political enfranchisement of girls and women. But there are overlapping concerns related to the statistical treatment of women in the international cultural economy and in terms of their cultural and human rights (Cliche *et. al.* 1998:18-20).

It is no surprise then that methodological and statistical concerns preoccupy organizations and projects focused on a range of cultural issues affecting women and girls internationally. These issues include media-monitoring (Cliche *et. al.* 1998: 23) and such human rights as access to education, freedom of expression and freedom from ethnic and racial discrimination. They are pursued by governmental, non-governmental (NGO) and community-based organizations in collaboration with the UN, the Council of Europe and other international bodies that are also concerned with monitoring cultural indicators for which a common framework is still in progress. Problems in gaining accurate information will impact on the monitoring of programs promoting cultural diversity, including gender equity.

Feminist researchers have studied the relationship of nations to international governance and to the international economy (Grant and Newland 1991; Peterson 1992). Feminist scholars also mounted significant critiques in the fields of international relations and political economy as free trade began to dominate international agendas in the 1980s (Bakker 1994; 1996). The most significant impact of this work includes questioning the "realist" approach to international relations in which rational motives can supposedly be discerned behind national policy positions. Instead these scholars insisted on looking at the processes of governance and policy formation in terms of what interests and forms of knowledge are admitted to the table. In the economic sphere, they demanded that a holistic approach to the economic cycle and economic actors replace one in which markets and national economies remain abstractions.

This critical legacy enables us to relate national cultural strategies to cultural markets and to world-wide cultural and human rights initiatives in a way that brings the role of national governments into question. The late 1980s and early 1990s represented rather a complex policy juncture. In moves that demonstrate the relative independence of national cultural bureaucracies from their public constituencies (rather than from their private clients in the major cultural industries), countries like Canada, New Zealand and the United Kingdom moved to decrease direct public investment in culture while concurrently promoting cultural industries. At the same time as pressure from below in the form of anti-racism demands for recognition of non-European and cross-disciplinary artistic work, the "fragmentation" of the former national broadcast television audience was drawing some positive response from national cultural bureaucracies. Meanwhile, many national governments were also transferring responsibility and funding to lower levels of government.

Ultimately, this revolution in cultural policies in the capitalist welfare states came about for ideological reasons untouched by the critiques of feminists or anyone else. The relationship with industry emphasized the government's role as promoter of exports and the developer of marketing strategies. While publicly rationalized as the means of creating jobs and strengthening nationally-based industries (their self-proclaimed role in preserving diversity came more recently), the governments also spared those same "major players" the accountability for employment equity and the regulation of content. In Canada, for example, the creation of the new department of Canadian Heritage in 1993 left initiative for the "information highway" in the hands of another government department, Industry Canada. Accountability for cultural diversity and equity remained in institutions such as the Canada Council for the Arts while new communications technologies were developed (with government aid) in near absence of such scrutiny.

In the European Union, a parallel "disconnect" in terms of accountability occurred with the development of a European broadcasting policy (Beale 1999b; Pauwels 1999). There was no attempt to represent the public interest in the proceedings of the policy-setting European Commission. The only public interest to which the Commission alluded was one of strengthening Europe's ability to withstand American competition. Countries competed as the representatives of domestically-based cultural and communications industries, often those in a monopoly position and already beneficiaries of public funding or favourable tax and regulatory regimes. Where consumer options were enhanced, and where cross-national audiences were served (and there are very few successful examples of the latter due to linguistic barriers), they were by-products of a strategy primarily concerned with the development of industries and the power-politics of European integration. The representation of women's interests, notably through such bodies as the Council of Europe (as workers, creators, consumers, or members of under-served minority groups or regions), carried on as though in a parallel universe, unable to affect the Commission's proceedings. I have argued that this parallel policy process and others like it in the context of developing globalized trade, not only eliminates public interests and "special" interests (as women's interests are often known) from key fora, but also relegates significant portions of culture and communications to a second class status (Beale 1999b). This second class status is contrasted with the first class status of the information technology, telecommunications and major media industries in their institutionalized relationships with key government departments such as finance and trade. Unlike the cultural sector "writ large," elite white men dominate management occupations, investment and ownership in the first class group.

The usual response to critiques such as this is that women have gained attention as consumers and are the sought-after object of cultural marketers everywhere. Indeed, women are the principal audiences for everything but jazz, professional sport and prime-time television. But it is also a fact that women contribute the largest proportion of unpaid and underpaid labour to cultural activities, and that they create a disproportionate number of the small cultural enterprises and thus assume a greater financial risk (For what it is worth, one Australian study also confirms what many would guess, namely that a higher percentage of women than men claim to regard "culture" as intrinsically and socially valuable (Swanson and Wise 1998)). Do these views and activity translate into authority and political influence? Even if one subscribes to the view that the invisible hand translates consumption into demands identified and met, there is evidence, such as Meehan's examination of the US television ratings system, that the organized resistance of the regulated media gets in the way of the market doing its work.

From my perspective (after Meehan 2001), these gendered obstacles remain a blind spot among critical political economists of communication. Michael Curtin (1999), for example, has argued that "the current reorganization of the culture industries provides fluid and ephemeral spaces in which to imagine new gender roles, political affinities and sexual orientations," giving as his example the music video of a young woman performer in India, distributed on popular, new and unregulated satellite services. Curtin links the creation of a new genre (Indo-Pop) to satellite television and its need for programming, and reads into the narrative and visuals of the music video in question "an inversion of dominant (Bollywood) expressions of desire" (Ibid: 67). In his analysis of the video, one naked male torso becomes an opportunity for young Indian women to "fantasize about their futures outside the patriarchal representational norms of traditional religion, Bollywood film and government television" (Ibid: 67). Certainly, the ability to create change begins with the opportunity to fantasize about it. But this analysis depends too much on inferred interpretations without substantial consideration of the processes of production of the video, the marketing strategy of music producers, characteristics of the audience doing the interpreting, or indeed the political process that led to the appearance of satellite television in India. Gender discrimination is involved in each of these processes.[7]

## Conclusion

Feminists interested in policy have used the concept of gender to analyze the politics and economics of international and transversal cultural policy development and to critique and improve on the limitations of the disciplines (communication studies, political economy, international relations and others) that have been applied to this policy field.

In addition to the influence of critical understandings of gender in the different academic disciplines, these developments in feminist policy work are the outcome of struggles that are themselves both national and transversal in focus and strategy. As I noted earlier, the national/global context remains a point of considerable tension and constant re-negotiation. Currently, UNESCO and the Council of Europe along with the more than 20 national governments that make up the International Network on Cultural Policy are promoting a policy theme of cultural diversity. This is a project concerned with measures to recognize and plan for cultural diversity within nation-states and to meet the needs of cultural diaspora in their multiple locales. It promotes the development of cultural policies at the local level, using a cultural planning model that, it is argued, can treat "culture" more holistically than the prevalent consumer or national citizenship models (Baeker 2000: 50-52). At the same time, it is a classic example of top-down policy development, stemming as it does from UNESCO's World Decade for Cultural Development. This policy era was concerned with developing cultural rights as human rights, and with cultural "sustainability" in the face of globalization (Beale 1999a: 453-454). Most significantly, it is also compromised by the international trade strategies of countries seeking to carve out cultural trade (and protect their national cultural sector champions) from the ongoing merger of the world's economies (Beale 2001).

Like the communications policies with which they overlap, cultural policies become transversal when such an approach is of strategic and political value to someone. Well before the apparent forfeit of the public interest in communications by national governments had caused some of our peers to seek ways for the public interest to assert itself (working across national borders instead of through national governments), feminists included transversal strategies in their political and cultural work (Byerly 1995). The further integration of national economies with world markets and a shift from the national to the local in cultural planning (if this becomes a serious force) are the current polarities in cultural policy that are not likely to change the networking of women within and across national boundaries, or their decisions to exploit whatever resources are available at any level, whether it is international law, local planning, the development of policy networks, or business opportunity.

The discussion of transversal communications policy-making has required that the re-thinking of the public interest be carried out in the real-world context of the political, technological and economic structures of communication. It may be that the renewed public interest(s) identified in transversal communications strategies will borrow from significant characteristics of feminist politics and research from the last twenty years. There will be no singular "public," as there is no single set of "women's interests." The question of the true independence of transversal initiatives that depend on state funding will have to be addressed. The basis upon which experience and knowledge are admitted to academic, legal and political debates may shift. The gender bias that keeps the majority of women in an inferior position around the world with regard to education, media access and representation, opportunities for cultural expression and employment, may finally be acknowledged as one of the major impediments to an emancipated realm of culture and communications.

## Notes

1   Compare McGuigan (1996) and Bennett (1998). See also Tator *et. al.* (1998) and the Web site of the Privatization of Culture Project, www.nyu.edu/projects/privculture/about.htm and Denise Meredyth and Jeffrey Minson (1998).

2   "A song by the *a capella* group Sweet Honey on the Rocks [sic] outlines the complicated set of processes whereby a cotton-polyester blouse is produced, taking the listener *inter alia* to the women cotton-pickers of Ecuador, the oilfields of Venezuela, the sweatshops in Haiti and finally to the sales rack of a Sears department store, whereupon the song quizzically asks 'are our hands clean?'" (Sreberny 2001: 63).

3   Gender stereotypes prevail to a surprising degree even among jobs within the cultural sector. In 1997 over 80 per cent of camera operators in Canada were men, over 90 per cent of dancers were women (Fig. 2.1.2a in Statistics Canada 2000: 40). Consider also the disproportionate numbers of ministers of culture who are women.

4   Despite the comprehensiveness of Canadian cultural policies and the monitoring of diversity in hiring for government positions, recent reports suggest that there is poor compliance with diversity goals (Baeker 2000: 33-37; 79).

5    The complexity of a cultural policy setting such as that of the United States should not lead to the conclusion that there is no cultural policy, or that civil institutions, philanthropic foundations, and social and artistic movements are ineffective in dealing with the issues important to US.citizens.

6    Meehan's study is also a rebuke to the field of critical political economy of communications, which has failed to go the additional step in revealing the "blind spots" in studies in the economics of communication. See my comments on Curtin (1999).

7    A perceived correspondence between the display of sexual freedom and political emancipation has also led some Western feminists to attribute to sex workers a control over their bodies and lives that gives them an outlaw status allowing them to escape the limits of traditional society. A rebuke to this interpretation has come from Delia Aguilar (2000), who argues that such an argument represents wishful thinking at best and a disguised racism at worst. The sexual availability of women in the tourism linked sex trade and the sexually submissive demeanor required in many jobs in the tourism and hospitality industry are the reality for many women who are on the front lines of globalization. The international cultural encounter is a (hetero)sexualized one, and women, especially women of colour, its labour force (Enloe 1989).

# References

Aguilar, D.D. 2000. Questionable Claims: Colonialism Redux, Feminist Style. *Race and Class.* 41(3): 1-12.

Ashworth, G. 1999. The Silencing of Women. In *Human Rights in Global Politics*, edited by T. Dunne and N.J. Wheeler. Cambridge: Cambridge University Press: 259-276.

Bakker, I. (ed.). 1994. *The Strategic Silence: Gender and Economic Policy.* London. Zed Books.

_____(ed.) 1996. *Rethinking Restructuring.* Toronto: University of Toronto Press.

Baeker, G. 2000. *Cultural Policy and Cultural Diversity in Canada: Prepared for the Council of Europe Study on Cultural Policy and Cultural Diversity.* Ottawa: Department of Canadian Heritage (Strategic Planning and Policy Coordination).

Bathla, S. 1998. *Women, Democracy and the Media: Cultural and Political Representations in the Indian Press.* New Delhi and London: Sage.

Beale, A. and A. Van Den Bosch (eds.) 1998. *Ghosts in the Machine: Women and Cultural Policy in Canada and Australia.* Toronto: Garamond.

Beale, A. 1999a. From "Sophie's Choice" to Consumer Choice: Framing Gender in Cultural Policy. *Media, Culture and Society.* 21: 435-458.

_____ 1999b. Development and 'Destatisation' in European Cultural Policy. *MIA/Culture and Policy.* 90: 91-105.

_____ 2000. Review of *News, Gender Power*, edited by C. Carter et. al. *Media, Culture and Society.* 22: 522-524.

_____2001. Communications Policy, Cultural Policy and Globalization: Identifying a policy hierarchy. In *Comparing Cultural Policies: Globalization,*

*Nations and Global Cities*, edited by D. Crane and N. Kawashima. London: Routledge.

Bennett, T. 1998. *Culture: A Reformer's Science*. London: Sage.

Brah, A. 1993. Toward a Multicultural Europe? En-gendered Racisms, Ethnicities and Nationalism in Contemporary Western Europe. *Feminist Review*. 45: 9-29.

Byerly, C. M. 1995. News, Consciousness and Social Participation: The Role of Women's Feature Service in World News. In *Feminism, Multiculturalism and the Media: Global Diversities*, edited by A.Valdivia. London: Sage: 105-123.

Carter, C., G. Branston and S. Allan (eds.). 1999. *News, Gender and Power*. London: Routledge.

Curtin, M. 1999. Feminine Desire in the Age of Satellite Television. *Journal of Communication* 49(2): 55-70.

Cliche, D. *et. al.* 1998. *Women and Cultural Policies*. Bonn: European Research Institute for Comparative Cultural Policy and the Arts. http:/www.unesco-sweden.org/Conference/Papers/Paper11.htm.

Danner, M., L. Fort and G. Young. 1999. International Data on Women and Gender: Resources, Issues, Critical Use. *Women's Studies International Forum*. 22(2): 249-259.

Enloe, C. 1989. *Bananas, Beaches and Bases: Making Sense of International Politics*. London: Pandora.

Felski, R. 1995. *The Gender of Modernity*. Cambridge MA: Harvard University Press.

Foucault, M. 1991. Governmentality. In *The Foucault Effect: Studies in Governmentality*, edited by G. Burchell *et.al*. Chicago: University of Chicago Press.

Fraser, N. 1990. Rethinking the Public Sphere: A Contribution to the Critique of Actually Existing Democracy. *Social Text*. 25/26: 56-80.

Gallagher, M. 1995. A Feminist Paradigm for Communication Research. In *Rethinking Communication, vol.2, Paradigm Exemplars*, edited by B. Dervin *et. al.* London: Sage: 75-87.

Gilroy, P. 1993. *The Black Atlantic: Modernity and Double Consciousness*. Cambridge MA: Harvard University Press.

Grant, R. and K. Newland. (eds.) 1991. *Gender and International        Relations*. Bloomington: Indiana University Press.

Gunew, S. and A. Yeatman (eds). 1993. *Feminism and the Politics of Difference*. Sydney: Allen and Unwin.

Horkheimer, M. 1972. *Critical Theory: Selected Essays*. New York: Continuum.

Habermas, J. 1975. *Legitimation Crisis*. Boston: Beacon.

MacKinnon, C. 1989. *Towards A Feminist Theory of the State*. Cambridge MA: Harvard University Press.

McGuigan, J. 1996. *Culture and The Public Sphere*. London: Routledge

McLaughlin, L. 1993. Feminism, the Public Sphere, Media and Democracy, Review Essay. *Media, Culture and Society* 15:599-620 .

_____. 1999. Gender, Privacy and Publicity in "Media Event Space." In *News, Gender and Power*, edited by C. Carter et.al. London: Routledge.

Meehan, E. 2001. *On Not Being a Hot Commodity: The Dallas Smythe Memorial Lecture 2000*. Institute for Communication, University of Illinois at Champaign-Urbana: Occasional paper.

Meredyth, D. and J. Minson (eds.) 1998. *Citizenship and Cultural Policy*. London: Sage.

Morris, M. 1992. *Ecstasy and Economics: American Essays for John Forbes*. Sydney: Empress Publishing.

Mulcahy, K. 1997. *Public Support for the Arts in the United States, Western Europe and Canada: Polities, Policies, Politics*. Unpublished Paper.

Ng, R. 1993. Sexism, Racism and Canadian Nationalism. In *Feminism and the Politics of Difference*, edited by S. Gunew and A. Yeatman. Sydney: Allen and Unwin: 197-211.

Offe, C. 1984. *Contradictions of the Welfare State*. London: Hutchinson.

O'Regan, T. 1994. Introducing Critical Multiculturalism. *Continuum: The Australian Journal of Media and Culture* 8(2): 7-19.

Pauwels, C. 1999. From Citizenship to Consumer Sovereignty: The Paradigm Shift in European Audiovisual Policy. In *Communication, Citizenship and Social Policy: Rethinking the Limits of the Welfare State*, edited by A. Calabrese and J-C Burgelman. Lanham MD: Rowman and Littlefield: 65-76.

Peterson, S. (ed.) 1992. *Gendered States: Feminist (Re)Visions of International Relations Theory*. Boulder CO: Lynne Rienner Publishers.

Pick, J. 1988. *The Arts in a State: A Study of Government Arts Policies from Ancient Greece to the Present*. Bristol: Bristol Classical Press.

Robinson, G. J. Forthcoming. Theorizing the Impact of Gender in Canadian Journalism. In *Gender, Culture and Journalism: A Study of Industrialized Nations*, edited by R. Froehlich and S. Lafky. Edwin Mellin Press.

Rosler, M. 1994. Place, Position, Power, Politics. In *The Subversive Imagination: Artists, Society and Social Responsibility*, edited by C. Becker. New York: Routledge: 55-75.

Sreberny, A. 2001. Gender, Globalization and Communications: Women and the Transnational. *Feminist Media Studies* 1(1): 61-65

Statistics Canada. 2000. *Canadian Culture in Perspective: A Statistical Overview.* Ottawa: Minister of Industry.

Swanson, R. and P. Wise. 1998. *Going for Broke: Women's Participation in the Arts and Cultural Industries.* Nathan, Queensland: Australian Key Centre for Cultural and Media Policy, Griffith University.

Tator, C., F. Henry and W. Mattis. (eds.) 1998. *Challenging Racism in the Arts in Canada: Case Studies in Controversy and Conflict.* Toronto: University of Toronto Press.

World Commission on Culture and Development. 1995. *Our Creative Diversity.* Paris: UNESCO.

# Independent Media Centres: A Multi-local, Multi-media Challenge to Global Neo-liberalism

## John D.H. Downing

The confrontation that raged in Seattle on November 30, 1999 and the days following between law enforcement officers and activists of many stripes contesting the World Trade Organization's power, policies and secretive dealings, was a pivotal transition in the growing international movement opposed to global neo-liberalism (O'Brien et. al. 2000; Cohen and Rai 2000). Just as Daniel Bell wrote *The End Of Ideology* (1960), his memorial to what he saw as a bygone era of political activism shortly before the dawn of the tumultuous sixties, so Francis Fukuyama (1992) published his epitaph on anti-capitalist alternatives, *The End Of History And The Last Man*. In that seminal work he argued that the collapse of the Soviet system marked the end of an era. Many agree that it did, but as opposed to Fukuyama's gloss, it was an era in which, absurdly, Sovietism had been billed by its advocates *and* its pro-capitalist foes as the only alternative human beings could conceivably devise to capitalism. However, "the only game in town" argument began to look distinctly chilling, indeed heartlessly arrogant, as the full harshness of International Monetary Fund (IMF) and World Bank structural adjustment policies as well as the South's financial indebtedness to transnational banks laid down yet another global crisis for the enlightened capitalist economic order.

In the confrontation in Seattle, the roles of radical media of many kinds were of the highest importance. They served to prepare the ground for the demonstrations months beforehand, to enable on-the-ground communication among the demonstrators at the time, to bypass corporate media in order to inform the global public of what had transpired in the confrontation and afterwards, and to facilitate international discussion of the issues thereafter. At

215

the media heart of this political activity during the demonstrations and over the year following, was Seattle's "Independent Media Centre" (IMC).[1] In later confrontations during the World Bank meeting in Washington D.C. in April 2000, the Organization of American States meeting in Windsor, Ontario, in June 2000, the US Republican and Democratic Parties' nomination conventions later that year, the IMF and World Bank meeting in Prague in November 2000, the Summit of the Americas meeting in Quebec City in April 2001, and in still other places where the powerful gathered to forge their policy priorities, Independent Media Centres have emerged as a dynamic, original, and politico-mediatic constellation.

This chapter will address the experience of the IMCs over the first year of their lives, through the beginning of 2001. While it is too early to predict their future trajectories, they represent a major new phenomenon that bears both careful study and considered support.

## Radical media and the build-up to Seattle, November 1999

"Radical media" (Downing 1984; 2000) refers to those small-scale media of many technical and genre formats that have no allegiance to corporate, religious or governmental authority, but rather set out to suborn the status quo and propose defenses and alternatives to it.[2] Typically they operate as an alternative public sphere in close relationship to political and social movements. Currently, there is a strongly renewed interest in their operation (cf. Linder 1999; Couldry 2000; Hamilton 2000; Atton 2001; Gumucio Dagron 2001; Fairchild 2001; Halleck 2001), even though commentators to the right or the left who are obsessed with "bigness" tend to note these as pathetic pinpricks if they register them at all. In fact, their historical and contemporary roles within all kinds of social movements have been far greater than our static notions of mainstream media and their quantifiable "audiences" would suggest. Furthermore, within the framework of communications policy debate, discussion of policies for radical media is just as significant as the more conventional focus on the big players.

In the build-up to the Seattle confrontations, radical media were tremendously important. For mainstream media, it often appeared as though the opposition movements had materialized out of nowhere. But as reporter Geov Parrish (1999a), who covered the events intensively for *The Seattle Weekly*, noted in a feature dated September 11, 2000, the preparations had begun long before with a plethora of groups, from US steelworkers who had booked 1000 rooms in metro area hotels to 700 international groups that had signed on to the umbrella group, Citizens' Trade Campaign, to farming, church, environmental and peace organizations.[3]

Indeed it is arguable that the real turning point had emerged over two years previously when April 1998 demonstrations in Canada, fed by active public debate for over a year beforehand in *Maclean's*, *Canadian Forum* and other media (e.g. Schofield 1997; Clarke 1998), tipped the scales and forced the Multilateral

Agreement on Investment (MAI) into cold storage (Sinking of the MAI 1998; Haedeman 1998). The MAI planning documents were a prime example of global neo-liberal policy (Davis 1998) that many Canadians as well as others around the world saw as subverting national autonomy in vital economic, cultural and political matters. Some defined MAI as "NAFTA on steroids."

This episode simultaneously revealed the bombastic arrogance of global neo-liberal policy-making and the possibility of dealing it a sharp blow with a collective challenge aided by the Internet. The lesson was not lost in the run-up to Seattle, and indeed was underscored by 1999 riots in Geneva during World Trade Organization (WTO) consultations as well as demonstrations in dozens of cities around the world to coincide with the June 1999 meetings of the G8 in Köln. The London "Reclaim The Streets" confrontation in June 1999 received especially strong global publicity as a result of extensive property damage to the city's financial district occurring toward the close of the demonstration.[4]

The Internet was particularly deployed for debating and organizational purposes, including preparing citizens' media coverage of the confrontation and alternative news coverage of its progress. Some of the leading radical media projects included the long-established Paper Tiger Television, Deep Dish Television, and Radio For Peace International as well as the somewhat more recent Free Speech TV, Big Noise Productions, Media Island International, Whispered Media, and the Australian project Community Activist Technology.[5] The Minnesota-based Institute for Agriculture and Trade Policy set up a press service for international media, the organization Real Impact set up a live audio- and video-streaming operation to report inside and outside the convention centre. The organizations Public Citizen and People for Fair Trade joined forces to provide radio facilities for Pacifica Radio, for radio host Jim Hightower's syndicated program, and for National Radio Project. EarthJustice Legal Centre produced a daily newspaper, the *World Trade Observer* (Parrish 1999b).

In addition to these more technologically-based media, other grassroots art activists such as puppeteers, banner designers, T-shirt designers, street theatre actors and musicians were energetic in preparing for and contributing to protesting the WTO (cf. Schloss 2000). The drums that consistently reverberated from various points in the streets were equally important to maintaining a sense of momentum, challenge and solidarity.

> November 30 began as a sort of pageant. It was early in the morning. Thousands of people assembled. Most of them wore exotic costumes. One man was dressed as a superhero with a dollar sign across his chest and long johns under boxer shorts. Some dressed as jugglers and clowns. Others were dressed as sea turtles, butterflies and trees. The demonstrators carried colorful banners. They pulled parade floats with giant cartoon puppets representing caricatured aspects of corporate greed (Richmond 2000: Ch.3).

It is difficult to understand the roles of radical media in Seattle as elsewhere unless we link all these forms of communication and expression (cf. Mohammadi and Sreberny-Mohammadi 1994). The point is hard to overstate: a great deal of IMC activity consists of radical counter-information, which is vital, but which absolutely requires a consistent aesthetic approach and effective communications strategies. As the "Situationist" slogan frames it – "All power to the imagination!" – none of us is simply a brain only in need of missing rational-cognitive data.

This linking is true expressively, but also organizationally, which is precisely where the Seattle Independent Media Centre came into play. The IMC was not involved in developing tactics and counter-tactics – others did that. Nor was it even a site for directing the flow of communications. It was, however, the single most significant catalyst for *enabling* communications, perhaps even more so after the event itself. It was the IMC's imaginative deployment of digital media technologies combined with its horizontal organization that in turn captured the imagination of so many activists around the US and other nations. It was its ongoing operation after Seattle that fueled and energized many further challenges to neo-liberal globalism.

## The Seattle IMC during the protest

This chapter explores several points, namely (1) the meshing of multiple media and artistic activities challenging the WTO, and (2) the search for "neo-anarchist" organizational models. This second topic subdivides into (a) recording the details of organizing experience in specific confrontations with the power structure, (b) reflecting on and arguing about those experiences, and (c) developing clear instructions on technical media issues for non-specialists.

*Media Mesh.* The frequent emphasis in both sympathetic and unsympathetic accounts of the Seattle confrontation on what was, at the time, the technically novel utilization of digital technology to prepare and mobilize protest, should not blind us to the extraordinary combination of the most banal forms of communications technology with "whiz-bang" hi-tech. For instance, both in Seattle, and later in the April 16, 2000, World Bank protests in Washington D.C., the IMC organizational record (Blueprint 2000; Sand 2000) urges the use of simple felt pens on whiteboards! Likewise, in subsequent discussions of the future for IMCs and the wider diffusion of their information, voices were heard calling for newsprint versions of information otherwise out of reach to people the wrong side of the digital divide (cf. Arne 2000).

However, the ability to collect audio and video material amassed by independent media activists roving the streets of Seattle, and to edit together this material later into documentaries,[6] was indeed a coup. Webcasting this material simultaneously with the events was also a powerful use of digital technology to convey the reality of the protestors' challenge. But side by side, it is vital to emphasize – in order to keep our feet from sliding off into cyberspace – the mundane materiality of the media mesh.

This includes having enough toner and copiers to handle a crush, and more than one fax machine. It means finding the best rates on cell phones, negotiating a DSL (high speed Internet) line in sufficient time to have it up and running, having a space that worked for recording purposes, having walkie-talkies sufficiently close to the protest zone to function, printing a well-designed card to distribute to demonstrators to let them know of the IMC's function and location, and having people experienced in logging audio and video files. This cookbook list (far from complete) is included here to ram home the point that a media mesh is indeed essential. The walkie-talkie and sound recording problems also illustrate a point that will be more obvious still when we come to questions of organization below; namely that challenges of space and place are absolutely not solved by digital communications technology.

The impact of having a hundred or more videographers on the streets and inside the action was extraordinary in the coverage of the Seattle confrontation. This as opposed to another very large number of mainstream media safely ensconced behind police lines and with their agenda largely pre-set by their employers and their typical routines. The striking difference in costs of the reporting work of the activists (compared to the paid professional teams), combined with the advantage of physical vantage-point, enabled their pictures, sound and written reportage to dispute the mainstream media characterization of the demonstrators as violent, disruptive and uninformed, and to give neoliberalism's global opponents considerable heart and energy.

*Organization: the deepest yawn of all?* The organizational dimension of IMCs may seem the least seductive of all possible topics, but this is arguably a make-or-break issue. One of the intriguing, and indeed most promising features of the growth of IMCs, has been their degree of attention to this humdrum matter.

An historical example can clarify this point. A single model of organizing for radical political change dominated the twentieth century. This model was the Leninist one, a highly hierarchical and quasi-militaristic form of organization forged originally as opposition to the Russian czar and his secret police and the consequent need for clandestine methods and discipline in the interests of survival. Its adoption by the victorious Bolsheviks for all political and media organizing effectively stamped it internationally as the winning recipe, despite the fact that it permitted the indescribable mass repression of the Stalin era.

However, for many – during and after the first half of the century of world wars, the world-wide 1930s depression, fascism, Nazism and the Holocaust, the rape of Nanjing, the nuclear devastation of Hiroshima and Nagasaki – the notion that constructive social change was actually feasible and was taking place in a real country (the USSR) was exceptionally attractive. The alternative seemed to be that there was no way out from the world's disorder. Most people wanted to feel that something was practically realizable before they would sacrifice for it, so Soviet Russia, China, Cuba, became for many the "proof" that capitalism had a workable alternative. For many in the final decades of the twentieth century, the vision of a comprehensive Islamic order, where corruption and exploitation would not be hegemonic, but would be subject to proper punishment, led to a similar idealization of Iran under the late Ayatollah Khomeini.

The two other alternatives that had some play in the twentieth century were socialist anarchism and Gandhian non-violence. The former, however, was largely pushed off the stage after 1917 through the initial success of the Bolshevik revolution, which appeared to prove that the Marxists had won the long battle between them and the anarchists (even though in Spain, Mexico and some other countries socialist anarchism continued to have a presence). Gandhian non-violence was mostly restricted to political movements in two countries, namely the Quit India movement and the civil rights movement in the US, though it was never undisputed in either among those fighting for the same causes. The bulk of the student movements of the 1960s and 1970s, with miniscule exceptions such as the Weathermen in the US or the *rote armee fraktion* in Germany, also took their strategic model from the civil rights struggle. Even those who talked Leninism and Maoism, sometimes incessantly, did not usually read it as a recipe for armed struggle where they themselves lived. While those movements largely subsided during the 1980s, with the exception of feminist, ecological and antinuclear movements, that period could be argued to have been one of recomposition, gradually inserting issues such as race, gender and the environment into the otherwise reductionist framework of economic struggle. In that sense, the Seattle confrontation, with its extraordinary confluence of different political emphases, represented the end of one chapter, and hopefully the beginning of a new one. Reality for the traditional left finally set in during the tumbling of the "iron curtain" in 1989-91 and the June 1989 events in Beijing where law enforcement officials opened fire on student demonstrators. Suddenly there really was no magic place where things worked differently. The most deeply buried ostrich, a number of whom went into terminal political depression could see that. So, as Fukuyama and many others concluded, that appeared to be the end of that.

Except that it was actually, arguably, the crucible – at last! – of fresh thinking, deprived of what had turned out to be the deadening prop of a fairyland far, far away. This thinking could draw upon both socialist anarchist traditions and Gandhian traditions without necessarily being in hock to either, and could seek to respond flexibly and imaginatively to new trends and movements. In an era of triumphant transnational corporate neo-liberal policies, such thinking was more urgently needed than ever and could proceed without the ethical hypocrisy of defending the indefensible in Russia, China, or anywhere else.

This, precisely, is the historical point of intersection between the organizational practice and debates within the IMCs over the year 2000 and since, and the onward march of neo-liberalism. This is why attention to those debates and that experience is so important and why the conscious accumulation by IMC activists of a reservoir of organizing experience, both logistical and political, is such a significant step. Their focus is a combined political and mediatic one, although in practice the balance between those foci remains precarious. For some, the primary goal is grassroots political activism, and for others, radical journalism.[7] The two trajectories – political aims and communication goals – do not automatically dovetail, and their confluence in the IMCs seemed likely to continue to be one of the issues facing these projects (though not necessarily in a threatening fashion).

The organizational watchword over the first year was "consensus decision-making," a notion that many dismiss out of hand as unrealizable and that others love for its ideals while also sporting scars from attempting to make it work! Its importance is both political and practical.

Politically, many individuals were influenced by one or other version of socialist anarchist thought, in some cases by earlier activists such as Emma Goldman[8] or by the Spanish anarchist movement of the 1930s, in others by the more recent argument for Temporary Autonomous Zones advanced by Hakim Bey (1985). The influence of the non-violence strategies of Gandhi and of Dr. Martin Luther King was also in evidence. Negatively, past direct experience of Trotskyist and other Leninist political organizing styles may also have played a role in encouraging a different approach.

Practically, the Seattle demonstrators did represent a hugely varied set of interests and constituencies, and any attempt to germinate a directing centre would have been laughable. In the same way, ordering the hundred or more videographers, photographers and audio-recordists who served to document the demonstrations to hew to a single line would have been equally implausible. The point is the outgrowth of consensus decision-making from the immediate realities of the situation as well as from political principle.

A number of those most intimately involved were convinced that not only did consensual decision-making represent good political sense, but in fact it was the only practical approach as the documents archived under "blueprints" in the Seattle *indymedia.org* site attest. Indeed, a document of fourteen single-spaced pages, entitled *On Conflict and Consensus* (Consensus 2000), was available on the site and spelled out in considerable detail a series of procedures for consensual decision-making, explicitly referring to its objective as providing an alternative to the parliamentary procedure bible, *Roberts' Rules Of Order*. Given the conventional image of the far left as organizationally a shambles – "couldn't organize a piss-up in a brewery" was a favourite self-incrimination among the British far left at one time – the detailed specification of procedures in this fashion initially appears somewhere between surprising and quixotic.

The fact remains that organization is a ventricle of effective political as well as mediatic action.[9] In many instances of radical media, the project could be seen to suffer, sometimes severely, from naïve views of democratic organization. A justly famous article by Jo Freeman entitled *The Tyranny of Structurelessness* was based upon some of the negatives issuing from such naïveté. Additionally, in those cases, the continuing influence of unacknowledged factors such as sexism, or the elitist definition of reporting as prestigious but administrative work, was evident.

Certainly when one considers the massive resources devoted by corporations and states to honing organizational strategies and procedures, it would be senseless and virtually suicidal for the left to avoid putting its intellectual energies into developing its own procedures and objectives. One of the most interesting points made in the Indymedia site discussion of this topic was that using well-thought out consensual decision-making procedures would reduce the impact of planted undercover police sowing internal division and alienation by seemingly radical and insistent interventions that short-circuited the scrutiny of the consensus-building process.[10]

## Year 2000: IMCs proliferate and face new policy issues

As of the end of 2000, there had been a dizzy expansion of Independent Media Centres. In many cases they originated with a particular meeting of some co-ordinating agency of global capital, such as the World Bank in Washington D.C. in April 2000 or of the Organization of American States in Windsor, Ontario, in June 2000. At other times they originated with political conventions, such as the Democratic and Republican presidential nominating conventions of 2000 in Los Angeles and Philadelphia. Their core was typically a group of media and computer activists, normally associated with particular projects but not necessarily permanent political groups or parties, overwhelmingly with a "service-co-ordination" definition of their roles. As of May, 2001 they were operating in Argentina, Australia (Melbourne and Sydney), Brazil, Canada (Calgary, Hamilton, the Maritime provinces, Montréal, Quebec City, Vancouver, Windsor), Colombia, Congo, Europe (Belgium, the Czech Republic, Finland, France, Germany, Italy, Spain, Sweden, Switzerland and the UK), India, Israel, Mexico and the US (Arizona, Atlanta, Austin, Boston, Buffalo, Chicago, Cleveland, Hawaii, Houston, Los Angeles, Madison, Maine, Minneapolis, New York City, the Ohio Valley in Kentucky, Philadelphia, Portland, Richmond, the Rocky Mountain region, San Francisco, Seattle, New York, Urbana-Champaign and Washington DC). Not all of these by any means were at the same phase of development.

At that time, the Seattle site offered its news items in five major European languages (French, German, Italian, Portuguese and Spanish). While this excluded languages from other parts of the world such as Arabic, Hindi, Russian and Mandarin, most Web users would understand at least one. Thus this multilingual aspect of the site was a major contribution toward providing a news service that could week by week and day by day communicate the latest challenges across the planet to free-market fundamentalism. As of December 16, 2000, the Seattle site was logging 16,652 successful requests for pages per day, constituting 746,520 megabytes, serving 18,866 hosts. At that time, its usage rate was steadily increasing (Logs 2000).

This expansion predictably raised a variety of policy issues of which the following will be briefly surveyed here: (1) appropriate links between IMCs and the possibilities for co-ordinated action; (2) questions of free speech and editorial control; (3) how media activists should represent state repression.

*Co-ordination.* Inevitably, within the rapid process of expansion of IMCs inside and outside the US, and given the world-wide interconnected strategies of neo-liberal globalism and transnational corporations, the pressure was quickly mounting for some form of interconnection between IMCs for certain campaigns and confrontations. This was a rather new development in that solidarity campaigns had long been a feature of leftist political movements, but not necessarily globally co-ordinated action against major international institutions such as the IMF, the World Bank and the WTO. It posed a challenge to traditional anarchism too, which has always sought to celebrate the local and has been particularly distrustful of large entities. There did not, surprisingly, appear to be included a discussion of the role of labour unions in this kind of international communication, which despite their sometimes ossified and even corrupt leadership, nonetheless constitute a potential forum for action (Ashwin 2000; Munck 2000; O'Brien *et. al.* 2000: 67-108).

However, there did emerge a major public discussion in the latter part of 2000 about the feasibility of having a (none too elegantly termed) Indymedia Global Spokescouncil to make it possible to "balance both the absolute need for IMCs to make decisions in real life, face-to-face meetings, and...to have a mechanism through which [to] make international decisions" (Spokescouncil 2000). This proposal set out how active IMCs might delegate individuals "empowered to make decisions that affect the whole Indymedia network...via IRC...in very well-facilitated meetings," and how to try to cater to multilingual participation in IRC (Internet "chatroom") debates. An instance of collective action forged this way would be a project for a photo-essay covering the international anti-globalization protests of the previous year. The document sketched out how the proposal could be drafted with international participation, sent out for review and comments from all IMCs, and then finally voted on for endorsement by such a Council. The writer of the document was candid in commenting that he did not "know of any other organization that uses a similar process that combines real life organizing and virtual communication, but that's because Indymedia is a pretty unique happening."

There were also discussions concerning the role of the Seattle IMC in relation to the others. As of the end of 2000, the Seattle IMC – far and away the largest, at that point, with a core of around 15 activists – had effectively asserted its right to accredit new IMCs (cf. So You Want To Be An IMC? 2000). While it was clearly desirable to try to avoid messages running counter to the IMC aims, this in turn raised some issues about authority and centralization that sparked active discussions on the IMC Web sites.

*Free Speech.* Indeed this takes us straight to our second point: the question of censorship and editorial control. No less here than elsewhere is this a hotly contested zone of debate, not least when it comes to the expression of racist or neo-Nazi views (Downing 1999). The debate within Indymedia circles to the end of 2000 veered between dismissal of free speech as a bourgeois slogan associated with philosopher John Locke, the conventional defense of free speech as a gain for the political left that has so often historically been denied the right to circulate its perspectives, and the assertion that a commitment to free speech did not entail offering up the Indymedia sites to racists or other rightist voices, given that they had more than enough space in the public sphere as it was (see Rabble 2000 and the associated hyperlinks).[11] Another contributor argued that Indymedia should only censor "outright calls for violence and hate speech [and that]...All censored materials should also remain accessible to anyone that wishes to see them, and there should always be an explanation as to why something was censored and maybe even who censored it" (Marquis 2000).

However the question of editorial control also produced some interesting contributions. One proposal was for a moderating system for entries based on how highly readers rank them, thereby opening up the evaluation process beyond the decision of an editorial board. In fact a 1-5 reader-ranking procedure was available for postings at the Seattle site and some others. The same contributor added the following remarks as well, which provide a usefully concentrated summary of many of the issues being hashed out in this initial period:

> So. We've stated that we are going to do some editing. Why not do some serious, heavy editing? I feel like it's a bit of a slippery slope: if we agree we'll remove the Nazi posts, why not correct every spelling of America with three Ks [i.e. Amerikkka]? I find them equally offensive. I also think that some of our mannerisms – the KKKs, the substitution of "pigs" for "cops," etc – detracts from our credibility. (I am not going to say we should strive for objectivity; we've been through this before, and we've agreed that accuracy is what we should strive for because objectivity is bunk.) My take on it is that the average person, on seeing such heavily weighted words, is likely to presume that we will also lie about cops to prove our point. Then the icing on our cake: I'm sure most of us would agree that simple proofreading and fact-checking are a good idea (though if we have limited human resources, why bother to make a big deal out of picky details?) (IMC 2000).

As an overall comment on this debate about procedure, of which only some occasional moments have been excerpted here, I observed that tedious as its detailed discussion may become, it really is a fundamental issue. In the previous century the far left either ignored it or – by accepting typical Communist Party practices – sold itself down the river. How to operate an electronic democracy using digital technologies is a topic on which commentators have spent tons of toner, but usually at a level of generality of little applicable use. Easy as it may be to poke holes in bits of the formulations above, the debate is a crucial one and the Indymedia public sphere was a particularly important one for such debate.

*State repression.* The final question is on violence and state repression of protests: in which directions should radical media policy be framed? For the Seattle IMC and for others (Philadelphia, Los Angeles, Prague), as for the video documentaries compiled from the work of media activists, a primary strategy has been to document police violence against peaceful demonstrators, inverting the law-and-order frame of mainstream media and showing the in-shadow side of the moon. It has not been the only strand in the representation. There are plenty of analyses of the WTO and other global economic policy bodies as well. But state violence against the defenseless played a major role in the demonstration coverage and the features. The question is, should Indymedia and radical media coverage of state repression aim to do more than document it and denounce it as anti-democratic?

To answer this pivotal question takes more than a moment. It requires bearing in mind a five-vector relationship between (i) corporate policies and interests; (ii) social movement challenges; (iii) their state repression (police surveillance, arrests, assault, fines, jail sentences) and the roles of both; (iv) radical; and v) mainstream media in framing the repression, its context and its causes. Radical media have a triple agenda: to produce their own accounts from inside the movement, to respond critically to mainstream media versions and, especially in the US context, to challenge the overwhelming hegemony of the law-and-order frame.

In some countries, indeed, the repression will be on a far more vicious level than in Seattle (in Washington DC, during the April 2000 World Bank protests, it was actually less harsh than Seattle). Elsewhere in the world, people do not necessarily reappear from prison, or if they do, they may well have suffered grave abuse while inside. The 1996 hanging of Nigerian environmental activist and writer Ken Saro-Wiwa and eight of his fellow-activists, with Shell Oil piously protesting its impotence and innocence, is only one of many cases in point.

In the US, by contrast, widespread "white" experience of *any* form of jailing had been absent since the civil rights era and the protests against the war in South East Asia that came to a close in 1975. In that context, Seattle marked the baptism of a new political generation – but one that was largely Caucasian and typically not very alert to the already momentous level of incarceration and abusive jail treatment of African Americans and Latinos.

Thus, within the US, there were three gaps in consciousness on the subject of state repression and violence, gaps that radical media and IMCs needed to fill. The first gap was direct experience of repression in large-scale street protests within the US, now partly in the process of being filled as alternative political movements become active again.[12] The second is the overvaluation of state repression of protest within the US, compared to levels of repression in many countries, not least by close US allies such as Turkey, the Israeli occupation of Palestine and Saudi Arabia. The third is the failure to register either the sheer magnitude of racist incarceration in the US or its position within the standard vise of global neo-liberal priorities.[13]

All of this leads us directly to the reigning law-and-order mentality and the responsibility of IMCs and other radical media to attack its hegemony. This public mentality permits the framing of protests like Seattle as a disruption of order, rather than as a protest against the massive disruption of lives on a global scale by free-market fundamentalism. This mentality, equally, has not created, but along with the continuing force of white racism it has permitted the accumulation of a vast prison population, overwhelmingly black and Latino, as well as the arming of the police with potentially lethal riot control technology to repress protests.

These two latter developments may be segregated in American minds from the repression of protest against neo-liberal policies, but that mental divorce is dangerous. People fearful of a recurrence of fascism often look for it to resurface in a Nazi or neo-Nazi format. However, a prime policy of radical media must be to encourage a more alert posture to the fact that neo-liberalism is not just economics and it is not just at work outside the US: it is constituted by repressive power and mediatic power as well, and it is comprehensively global. Neo-liberal policy-makers and corporate elites seem at ease discounting and extruding whole populations of people, using force and incarceration against marginalized publics, arming civil wars in Africa and elsewhere, permitting avoidable agricultural disasters, while the banks meanwhile gorge themselves on gouging debt repayments from developing countries and major banking institutions (the Federal Reserve, the Bank of England, the Bundesbank) make economic policy with no public accountability whatsoever.

Let us pursue the mainstream media law-and-order frame a little further, because radical media critique of it demands more careful analysis than is often offered. US journalistic accounts strongly tended to define the Seattle confrontation in terms of law enforcement and the specifics of physical damage, and thus often seemed to have an uncanny symbiosis with the constricted definition of the issues by...law enforcement personnel.[14] This is not to say that the Seattle police were uniformly happy with their coverage in the confrontation – quite the opposite was the case – but this anger may, realistically, have had much more to do with the frequent cultivation of a barracks mentality within police forces than with a sober assessment of their overall media representation. The ongoing relations between media and law enforcement agencies have been studied from a variety of angles in a variety of countries (eg Chibnall 1977; Ericson *et. al.*, 1989: 91-171, and 1991; Schlesinger and Tumber 1994; Fox and Van Sickel 2000; Entman and Rojecki 2000: 78-93). They are complex, and I am definitely not proposing here an explicit or agreed convergence of perspectives between mainstream media and law enforcement institutions.

At the same time, it is important to single out the various strands within this simultaneous convergence and conflict between the two institutions: (1) the law-and-order perspective has legitimacy and is dominant within both mainstream media and, predictably, law enforcement institutions; (2) law-enforcement labour is often denied rest or refreshment for long periods of time during demonstrations and is, at times, subjected to verbal abuse and taunting, in some instances in physical danger, for spells of eighteen hours or more during protests, producing a resentment that may explode on to demonstrators in a way not publicly condoned by their superior officers, but nonetheless stimulated in part by these working conditions; (3) there is a conservative and mistrustful political subculture normal in police precincts, nurtured by their professional training, working conditions and suburban home locations; (4) the police frequently assume that news media should be on their side and regularly provide copy to journalists that editors, readers and viewers expect, thus helping to keep many mainstream media in business; (5) there are various, sometimes mutually mistrustful, branches of police and law enforcement (for example, in the US, federal agencies like the FBI and CIA as well as state and local police).

Thus a radical media analysis that does not engage with all these multiple and contradictory dimensions, micro- as well as macro-political, and contents itself with talking about "the pigs," offers emotional relief but very little of the needed illumination of the complex and continuing issues involved. Along with the policy issues of free speech and co-ordination, this is a big one.

## Conclusion

Sober recognition of harsh corporate priorities, the multiple dimensions of repression of protest and populations within the US and globally, and the consequent policy responsibilities of radical media, are vital. The Indymedia phenomenon is not the only public sphere where this analysis and debate can take place but, based on now nearly two years of growth, its global potential is very promising. The linkages established between the specific, the organizational, the technical, the artistic, the procedural, the local, the global and the nurturing of radical media policies – *our* policy-making process, not *theirs* – are very important steps.

Structurally, the Indymedia movement is shunning a centralized, transmission-belt, one-way media authority in the Soviet tradition, in favour of a co-ordinated media service role (using "media" here in the sense of communication means of all kinds, including those conventionally defined as "art"). At the same time, while part of their function is that of a global Internet news service, their activism and the immediacy of their involvement in civil disobedience campaigns against neo-liberal globalization represent an interventionist strategy well beyond the purely service offerings of a progressive news service. Their co-ordinating service thus fuses mediatic and organizational engagement.

Toward the end of the discussion above, we examined in some detail certain vital policy issues for IMCs and the radical media they serve. It is to be hoped this will help to forward further discussion and reflection about them, not least the urgent and complex question of the media representations of mass street challenges to neo-liberalism and their attempted repression by the state. Here

IMCs and other radical media have a triple task: (1) to foster effective mobilization of the challenges; (2) to provide reporting and discussion opportunities mainstream media will not normally present; and (3) to respond critically to the hegemonic law-and-order frame dominant in mainstream media concerning both these protests and wider patterns of state repression, such as racialized and class-based incarceration policies.

## Notes

1   Information on the Seattle IMC as on IMC developments around the world is available at www.indymedia.org.

2   These have also been called citizens' media (Rodríguez 2001), popular media, alternative media, etc.

3   It is important to note, although these two topics are beyond the scope of this chapter, that social justice activists in India and elsewhere were very leery of lining up behind some of the demands for fair working standards aired by many Seattle demonstrators, on the ground that they could be used in the short term to deprive "Third World" working families of any source of income at all (Shapiro 1999); and that some ultra-rightists obsessed with threats to US sovereignty also constituted an element, albeit a fringe element, in the Seattle protests (Berger 2000).

4   It seems that for corporate media, only damage to property makes a challenge truly newsworthy, a very significant commentary on their scale of values, which incidentally are also evinced by their frequent moral equation of property damage with violence against human beings. In turn, corporate media usually define police or army violence against unarmed and peaceful demonstrators as somewhere between praiseworthy and regrettably necessary, finding it exceptionally unappetizing to name police riots as such. Radical media do not appear to suffer from this ethical miasma.

5   Information on these projects is available at their respective Web sites: Paper Tiger Television <info@papertiger.org>, Deep Dish Television <deepdish@igc.org>, Radio For Peace International <info@rfpi.org>, Free Speech TV <programming@fstv.org>, Big Noise Productions <web@bignoisefilms.com>, Media Island International <mii@alywa.net>, Whispered Media <com@videoactivism.org>, and Community Activist Technology <cat@cat.org.au>.

6   Such as *Showdown In Seattle* (Indymedia 2000) and *This Is What Democracy Looks Like* (Big Noise Productions 2000), which traveled the length and breadth of the US and Canada, and quite widely in other European and anglophone countries. *Breaking The Bank*, a Paper Tiger TV documentary on the Washington D.C. protest of April 2000, and *The Autumn of Praha*, the Belgian IMC documentary on the Prague confrontation, are two further examples.

7   The Seattle Indymedia site "masthead" states: "Indymedia is a collective of independent media organizations and hundreds of journalists offering grassroots, non-corporate coverage. Indymedia is a democratic outlet for the creation of radical, accurate and passionate tellings of truth."

8   Emma Goldman defined anarchist organization as "based, primarily, on freedom...a natural and voluntary grouping of energies to secure results beneficial to humanity" (Goldman 1969: 35).

9   This is an issue frequently underscored by the case studies in the 1984 edition of my *Radical Media*, and by the longer case-studies in the 2000 edition.

10   Reportedly, in October 1968 the British political police scored one of their all-time coups by having one of their number, posing as a fire-breathing Maoist, elected by spontaneous consent — and probably to his considerable astonishment — to chair the organizing committee for Britain's most significant demonstration against the Vietnam War.

11   Throughout the autumn of 2000, a considerable volume of neo-Nazi "spam" had been posted to the Seattle IMC Web site.

12  Blandly defined these days by government and the manufacturers' sources as "non-lethal" — pepper spray, rubber bullets, CS gas — but a better description would be "less lethal." Rubber bullets, the rubber often being a micro-layer over steel, have killed and seriously maimed many protestors and non-protestors in Northern Ireland, Palestine and elsewhere; the effects of pepper spray, CS gas and other devices are equally very dangerous used intensively at close quarters, which is how a number of police and military actually use them.

13  The US jail population grew five times from 1973-97, and is 6-10 times higher than the percentages in prison in European Union nations; 50 million criminal files exist on 30 million individuals, or one third of the adult male population; a Black male has a one in three chance of spending a year in jail, a Latino male a one in six chance, and a White male a one in 23 chance (Wacquant 1998). The essence of the matter consists of racism and the criminalization of poverty (Wacquant 1998; Parenti 1999; Western and Beckett 1999).

14  See for example the Philadelphia police document (Affidavit of probable cause in support, Search and Seizure Warrant #97382), originating from the run-up to the demonstrations against the summer 2000 Republican Party convention, reproduced by the Philadelphia IMC: http://www.phillyimc.org/articles/00/09/10/2324206.shtml. The same precise critique was made of Czech reporting of the Prague contestation of the IMF and World Bank meeting there in September 2000 (Allnutt 2000; Breyerova 2000), but then with the exception of the Prague Spring of 1968, media and police traditions in the Czech Republic from 1938-89 might serve as some explanation. US mainstream media have no such excuse.

# References

Allnutt, L. 2000. Licking Their Wounds. *Transitions On Line* (October 10). www.tol.cz.

Arne. 2000. Worries/thoughts/ideas Regarding the IMC Network and Local Groups. global.indymedia.org.au/display.php3?article_id=71&group=webcast.

Ashwin, S. 2000. International Labour Solidarity after the Cold War. In *Global Social Movements*, edited by R. Cohen and S. M. Rai. London: The Athlone Press: 101-116.

Atton, C. 2001. *Media At The Margins*. London: Sage Publications.

Bell, D. 1960. *The End of Ideology: On the Exhaustion of Political Ideas in the Fifties*. Glencoe IL: The Free Press.

Berger, K. 2000. Can the Far Right Ever Be Part of the New Anti-WTO and Anti-IMF/World Bank Coalitions? *Seattle Weekly* (April 27). www.seattleweekly.com/features/0017/editorial-berger.shtml.

Bey, H. 1985. *T.A.Z.: The Temporary Autonomous Zone, Ontological Anarchy, Poetic Terrorism*. New York: Autonomedia.

Big Noise Production. 2000. *This is What Democracy Looks Like*. Video.

Blueprint. 2000. How To Make An Independent Media Centre — Blueprint Document. http://process.indymedia.org/blueprint.html.

Breyerova, P. 2000. The Harm Before the Storm. *Transitions On Line* (September 25). www.tol.cz

Chibnall, S. 1977. *Law-and-Order News*. London: Tavistock.

Clarke, T. 1998. M.A.I. Machinations: An Update. *Canadian Forum* 77 (July-

August): 20-22.

Cohen, R. and S. M. Rai (eds.). 2000. *Global Social Movements*. London: The Athlone Press.

Consensus. 2000. *On Conflict And Consensus*. http://consensus.hypermart. net/OCAC/

Couldry, N. 2000. *The Place Of Media Power: Pilgrims And Witnesses Of The Media Age*. London: Routledge.

Davis, J. 1998. The MAI: Multilateralism From Above. *Race and Class* 15.

Downing, J.D.H. 1984. *Radical Media: The Political Organization Of Alternative Communication*. Boston: South End Press.

_____. 1999. 'Hate Speech' and 'First Amendment Absolutism' Discourses in the US *Discourse And Society* 10(2): 175-89.

_____. 2000. *Radical Media: Rebellious Communication And Social Movements*. Thousand Oaks: Sage Publications.

Dunn, T. 1996. *The Militarization of the U.S.-Mexico Border, 1978-1992: Low-Intensity Conflict Doctrine Comes Home*. Centre for Mexican-American Studies, University of Texas at Austin. Austin: University of Texas Press.

Entman, R. and A. Rojecki. 2000. *The Black Image In The White Mind: Media and Race in America*. Chicago: University of Chicago Press.

Ericson, R.V., P.M. Baranek, and J.B.L. Chan. 1989. *Negotiating Control: A Study Of News Sources*. Toronto: University of Toronto Press.

_____. 1991. *Representing Order: Crime, Law, and Justice in the News Media*. Toronto: University of Toronto Press.

Fairchild, C. 2001. *Community Radio and Public Culture*. Cresskill NJ: The Hampton Press.

Fox, R.L. and R. W. Van Sickel. 2000. *Tabloid Justice: US Criminal Justice in an Age of Media Frenzy*. Boulder CO: Lynne Rienner Publishers.

Fukuyama, F. 1992. *The End Of History And The Last Man*. New York: The Free Press.

Goldman, E. 1969. *Anarchism and Other Essays*. New York: Dover.

Gumucio Dagron, A. 2001. *Making Waves: Stories of Participatory Communication for Social Change*. New York: The Rockefeller Foundation.

Haedeman, O. 1998. MAIgalomania: The New Corporate Agenda. *The Ecologist* 28.3 (May-June): 154-61.

Halleck, D. 2001. *Handheld Visions*. New York: Fordham University Press.

Hamilton, J. 2000. Alternative Media: Conceptual Difficulties, Critical

Possibilities. *Journal of Communication Inquiry* 24(4): 357-78.

IMC. 2000. IMC as it is and Ought to Be: Past And Future. http://hamp.hampshire.edu/-gbaF95/imcplan.html.

Indymedia. 2000. *Showdown in Seattle.* Video.

Linder, L.R. 1999. *Public Access Television: America's Electronic Soapbox.* Westport CT: Greenwood Publishing Group.

Logs. 2000. http://logs.indymedia.org/mayday/.

Marquis, S. 2000. *Thoughts on Indymedia, Many Questions As Well,* http://www.global.indymedia.org.au/front.php3article_id=82&group=webcast.

Mohammadi, A. and A. Sreberny-Mohammadi. 1994. *Small Media, Big Revolution: Communication, Culture, and the Iranian Revolution.* Minneapolis MN: University of Minnesota Press.

Munck, R. 2000. Labour In The Global: Challenges And Prospects. In *Global Social Movements,* edited by R. Cohen and S.M. Rai. London: The Athlone Press: 83-100.

O'Brien, R., A.M. Goetz, J.A.Scholte and M. Williams. 2000. *Contesting Global Governance: Multilateral Economic Institutions And Global Social Movements.* Cambridge: Cambridge University Press.

Parenti, C. 1999. *Lockdown America: Police and Prisons in the Age of Crisis.* London: Verso.

Parrish, G. 1999a. Shutting Down Seattle. *Seattle Weekly* (September 11). www.ainfos.ca/99/sep/ainfos00091.html.

_____. 1999b. Getting The Word Out: Alternative Media at the WTO. *Seattle Weekly* (November 25). www.seattleweekly.com/features/9947/features-parrish2.shtml.

Rabble. 2000. On Censorship, the IMC Mission, and Free Speech. http://process.indymedia.org/on_censorship_and_free_speech.php3.

Richmond, P. 2000. *WTO: Investigated, Analyzed, Criticized.* University of Washington Chapter, National Lawyers Guild http://students.washington.edu/uwnlg/wtolegal/report/report.html.

Rodríguez, C. 2001. *Fissures In The Mediascape.* Cresskill NJ: The Hampton Press.

Sand, J. 2000. DC/imc. programming@fstv.org.

Schlesinger, P. and H. Tumber. 1994. *Reporting Crime: The Media Politics Of Criminal Justice.* Oxford: Clarendon Press.

Schloss, J. 2000. Art For Protest's Sake: The Battle of Seattle Lives On at the Intersection of Politics and Art. *Seattle Weekly* (June 15). www.seattleweekly.com./features/0024/arts-schloss.shtml.

Schofield, J. 1997. Trading Insults: Critics Assail a Proposed Treaty on Investment. *Maclean's* 110 (April 28): 46-47.

Shapiro, N. 1999. The Battle Within: WTO's Third World Delegates Say Labor and Environmental Standards Will Hurt the Poor. *Seattle Weekly* (December 9). www.seattleweekly.com/features/9949/features-shapiro.shtml.

Sinking of the MAI. 1998. *The Economist*. March 14: 81-82.

*So You Want To Be An IMC*? 2000. http://global.indymedia.org.au/display.php3 ?article_id=54&group=webcast.

Spokescouncil. 2000. *Proposal for Global Spokescouncil*. http://global.indyme dia.org.au/display.php3?article_id=56&group=webcast.

Wacquant, L. 1998. L'emprisonnement des 'classes dangereuses' aux États-Unis. *Le Monde Diplomatique*. July: 20-21.

Western, B. and K. Beckett. 1999. How Unregulated is the U.S. Labor Market? The Penal System as a Labor Market Institution. *American Journal of Sociology* 104(4): 1030.

# The Politics of Broadband: Virtual Networking and the Right to Communicate

## Bram Dov Abramson[1]

The more bandwidth, the less interactivity. That, at least, was the message from MTVi president Nicholas Butterworth to attendees of the 1999 Streaming Media Europe Conference. Internet users are defined by the richness of their connectivity, explained Butterworth. At the high end, users with broadband connections want high quality but low interactivity. Low bandwidth users, meanwhile (those using dial-up connections of 56Kbps and below), are their opposites; better to sell them on interactivity than empty promises of quality sound and vision.[2]

Research suggests that this typology is oversimplified. Were "broadband" to denote the availability of very high bandwidth all the way from network core to network edge, then features like "virtual presence," the elusive grail of so many virtual environments researchers, might afford very high degrees of interactivity. As a design principle for a world where actual end-users have limited bandwidth (the carrying capacity of communications infrastructure as measured in bits per second) even in the most connected regions, Butterworth's assertion makes sense.

Where low bandwidths or large file sizes forbid casual use of extremely rich media, fewer barriers to entry exist. As bandwidth and compression increase, it becomes possible to push ever more complicated files across the connection. However, more elaborate production is also more resource-intensive and hardware, software, training and time all begin to pose significant barriers to entry. An e-mail is both simple to compose and digitally inexpensive to send. An animated, sound-enhanced video presentation is neither.

Technology design determines the use of many technologies (Norman 1988). Bandwidth indicates network intensity; it is a key part of network technology design. Although the common goal of pervasive broadband access had achieved significant consensus among the industrial and governmental institutions by the year 2000, few had linked the will to go broadband with the conceptual models, constraints, or affordances it implied for emergent genres.

This is not to name access to broadband as the only goal of media policy with respect to the Internet and, more broadly, networked media. Nor are the economics of broadband unpromising. As the dot-com mania died down in 2000, a crackling excitement emanated from those who looked at the separation of physical fibre optic cabling from network capacity. These analysts saw a "dark fibre revolution" that would turn telecommunications infrastructure into a community-owned resource similar to "public infrastructure like roads and sewers" (CANARIE 2000; Cook 2001).

The prospect of a communications infrastructure that is community-owned and benefits the community is exciting. But understanding media does not stop at understanding who owns them. When infrastructure is built, the applications it supports are transformed. That relationship is under-theorized and poorly understood. In too many policy decisions, the relationship between media *infrastructure* policy and media *applications* policy resembles a kind of latter-day scientific Marxism. The media applications' superstructure is treated either as an automatic reflection of the broadband base (eg more bandwidth therefore better media) or as a sphere whose autonomy from bandwidth is absolute. It is as though policy for networks' social implications could be made without considering how bandwidth issues affect our society.

This chapter is not about the development of broadband, however. Rather, it inverts the lens to gaze in at specific use of narrowband, and to consider what happens when – if – narrowband is no more. For six weeks in 1998 an international video and community television non-governmental organization (NGO) called Videazimut convened a virtual conference on the "right to communicate," a concept worth considering as a more sophisticated theorization of the direction of network evolution.[3] The conference was designed to connect Videazimut's traditional constituency with other non-governmental, non-corporate, "third sector" media networks. This combination yielded a group that might variously be described as media producers scattered across 50-odd countries, Internet users with a wide range of network competencies and access levels, and activists accustomed to functioning within English-, French-, or Spanish-language public spaces. Bringing this heterogeneous group into an online discussion, and making that discussion useful, implied a series of design choices.

These design choices are part of an emerging Internet genre, the low-bandwidth online collaboration that has become the tool of an increasing number of virtual networking initiatives. Low-bandwidth virtual conferencing offers myriad possibilities if executed via an appropriate mix of resources, but is designed to the specifications of global narrowband infrastructure.[4] New media technologies such as Internet-enabled networks can be amenable environments for wide distribution of the right to communicate. But they can change, too.

Infrastructure technologies are historically determined processes. These technologies evolve over time and by way of large-scale decisions. The Internet is one set of such processes, and virtual networking intersects with them at several levels. At a macro level, virtual networking enables wide-area political and cultural speech with a velocity that yields new spatial configurations and, potentially, constituencies. At a micro level, virtual networking is a key tool for effective organizing around specific campaigns. As a genre, however, virtual networking is a collision point for policy that shapes media *infrastructure* and policy that shapes media *applications*. With infrastructure in flux, constantly targeted for transformation by the policies of a diffuse and heterogeneous set of institutions, what happens to the asynchronous, low-bandwidth media forms that have characterized the networking of dispersed citizens across different polities around common efforts? And why does it matter?

## Right to Communicate

Addressing these questions requires considering how the right to communicate might guide our understanding of broadband deployment. The articulation is not obvious; in Claire Parnet's video biography *L'Abécédaire de Gilles Deleuze* (1998), for example, the French philosopher attacks the very idea of human rights as an attempt to flatten a series of highly contextual questions into a brittle, universalizing ontology. "I have always been passionate about jurisprudence, about law," he explains. "Had I not done philosophy, I would have done law, but indeed, jurisprudence, not human rights. Because that's life. There are no human rights, there is life, and there are life rights. Only life goes case by case."

Communication rights are a subset of human rights. For both, Deleuze's caution is well-placed. Human rights do not exist separately from individual cases; they are a sociological problem, not a simply philosophical one. But that does not mean that the idea should be jettisoned. Instead we might borrow Felice's (1998: 40) insistence that "[h]uman rights are not utopian dreams, but tools to inform and guide policy" and, to it, add that these tools, like their technological counterparts, cannot be understood except as processes.

Most accounts link the right to communicate with the United Nations' 1948 adoption of the Universal Declaration of Human Rights (UDHR). Though still unimplemented in most national legislation more than a half-century later, the UDHR does act as a codified set of international norms whose relationship to national policy Donnelly has called a "new universalism" (1998: 23; cf. Svendsen 1995): "International human rights, rather than a deviation from principles defining the essence of the 'Westphalian' system, represent a return to a conception of international society that is older and morally much more attractive than the positivist vision of pristine sovereignty."

And, indeed, the UDHR's Article 19, the cornerstone of the right to communicate and namesake of a prominent NGO that lobbies for journalistic freedoms, contains much that is morally attractive. It states that "[e]veryone has the right to freedom of opinion and expression; this right includes freedom to hold opinions without interference and to seek, receive, and impart information and ideas through any media, and regardless of frontiers." The wording merits remark: to seek, receive, and *impart* information. Especially in the English-language context, Article 19 and, more generally, the right to communicate are too often simplified into a concept of entitlement known alternately as freedom of speech, absence of censorship, or the free flow of information. Those elements are important, but they are not enough because they do not address the uneven distribution of the means to impart information.

The political economy of communication – who controls what channels – has always been at the heart of the discussion over the right to communicate. While the UDHR provided the groundwork, the debates would occur later. Hamelink (1994) and Servaes (1998) trace the term itself to a 1969 article by United Nations Information Bureau staffer Jean D'Arcy: "The time will come when the Universal Declaration of Human Rights will have to encompass a more extensive right than man's right to inform, first laid down twenty-one years ago in Article 19. This is the right of man to communicate."

D'Arcy's article was written against the backdrop of a mediascape which, like the one marked by the Internet-oriented transformations of thirty years later, was in the midst of significant change. The International Covenants on Economic, Social and Cultural Rights and on Civil and Political Rights were signed in 1966 – the latter's Article 27(1) pledges commitment to the "right freely to participate in the cultural life of the community," another plank of the right to communicate. It was a full nine years after Sputnik had shocked a world with an incessant orbital beeping, but just two after the founding of Intelsat. The right to communicate was part of an international discussion over how to shape the communications environment, a precursor of sorts to the Global Information Infrastructure (GII) project that former US Vice-President Al Gore would unveil on the world stage in 1995 (Raboy 1997; Winseck 1997).

From the mid-1970s to early 1980s, the focal point of this discussion was the New World Information and Communication Order (NWICO) project, spearheaded by the bloc of non-aligned nations within UNESCO and culminating in the seminal *Many Voices, One World* report stewarded by Amnesty International founder and Nobel Prize winner Sean MacBride (1980).[5] But despite the activism it spawned, the NWICO project failed to achieve implementation through the diplomatic channels it had targeted and the right to communicate debate then lay relatively dormant until the mid-1990s when, just as the GII project took flight and the mediascape began to shift again, it once more showed signs of life. Citizens were confronted by the institutional choices implied by galloping diffusion of innovation in media infrastructure markets. Communication rights were a way of addressing their social implications. This time, however, the proponents of the right to communicate were not government representatives but non-governmental activists concerned with the nature of the Internet's evolving institutional encasements and their policies.

The most publicized activist position of the 1990s evolved through what Barbrook (1998a) has termed the "Californian ideology." This so-called "cyberlibertarianism," catalyzed by groups such as the Electronic Frontier Foundation (EFF), was heavily committed to the text of the US First Amendment and oriented chiefly toward freedom of speech and privacy issues. Unsettled by cyberspace's increasingly obvious lack of immunity to institutional encasement – cyberspace is a mode of spatial production and consumption that overlays other spaces, not a separate plane of human existence – these activists played an important government watchdog function.

A second activist position was staked out by third-sector communications producers whose media philosophy was the opposite of their cyberlibertarian counterparts. They positioned the Internet within an historical sequence of broadcast-capable communications technologies – over-the-air radio, over-the-air television, cable broadcasting, satellite transmission – and, mindful of the dramatic concentration of influence over traditional media in the hands of a very small number of institutional entities, set to work documenting the extension of corporate power to the Internet's workings and evolution, on the one hand, and promoting alternative Internet practices, on the other.

Proponents of the latter position figured less prominently than did advocates of the first. Geographically, the cyberlibertarian position had the advantage of being rooted in US political culture, where US institutions were the key vector for wide deployment of Internet innovation. Philosophically, the cyberlibertarian anti-government position was far more compatible with corporate Internet development than the explicit anti-corporatism of media activists, helping cyberlibertarians hitch themselves to the tremendous infusion of capital and of wealth-seeking energy that played a key role in the Internet's evolution through the late 1990s. Conceptually, meanwhile, the cyberlibertarians' media activist counterparts were handicapped by a lack of wide-ranging and accessible research into the self-reinforcing nature of the World Wide Web's (WWW) linking and searching architectures, or even the Internet's logical infrastructure. This left their position open to retorts that, were corporate influence unwelcome, alternative sites would pop-up elsewhere on cyberspace's unlimited vistas – an updated version of the five-million-eyeballs-can't-be-wrong theory of public interest rendered more compelling by the Internet's apparent de-fanging of the spectrum-scarcity argument.

Research has since confirmed that the WWW is not a self-leveling playing field: choke points exist and economic resources matter. Intense efforts to translate WWW link economies and search engine traffic to inbound money revenues points to the importance of navigational tools in driving traffic (Rogers 2000).

WW traffic is concentrated within a very small proportion of Web sites (Huberman *et. al.* 1998); the top 100 sites remain the same year after year.[6] At the infrastructure level, ten Internet providers operate 80 per cent of the world's international bandwidth.[7] Whether or not the displacement of traditional media activism by cyberlibertarianism has been an important contributor to oligopolization is an untestable hypothesis; the more pressing question is: what does it mean for the right to communicate?

Videazimut's Virtual Conference on the Right to Communicate and the Communication of Rights was meant to address that question. First conceived as lead-in for an international seminar and general assembly to be held in South Africa, the Virtual Conference quickly forged an identity later reinforced by linkage to a second virtual conference held on the same theme immediately afterward by the World Association of Community Radio Broadcasters (AMARC). The rationale for Videazimut's event: though Internet access is in many places difficult, even impossible, Web and e-mail connections – whether on the next street or the next village – remain far more accessible than physical displacement to a Capetown congress.

The Conference played several useful roles in circulating information, promoting linkages, and raising awareness among 300 activists from twenty-odd countries. Various responses and critiques were proposed. But the conference's design and development provided at least as important a lesson in communication rights. As a media activist group, Videazimut's position on the right to communicate bound it to attempt both a critique of the Internet's emerging political economy and the construction of alternative Internet practices. In so doing, the Virtual Conference became an active laboratory for how the right to communicate collides with the affordability of broadband in a wide-area virtual networked environment. Its design is worth considering.

## Media Design

In computer-mediated communication, interface design aims to achieve a series of collaborative human-to-human relationships established in asynchronous time and discontinuous space. The key design challenge is therefore to produce a digital space able to facilitate collaboration between participants who are differently equipped in competencies, connectivities, technologies, time zones and public cultures. This is not the idealized "virtual community" that translates a physical-world conception of community into computer-mediated communication. Virtual conference design means drawing up the architectural plans for a time – and topic – limited community, a temporary zone whose success depends on participant recognition of its ephemeral nature and explicit mission. How are these design goals met in a pre- or non-broadband world?

A number of prepackaged IP (Internet Protocol) applications exist to help with the process. The transformation of the Internet from research environment to multi-use networks via commercial investment[8] was marked by the large-scale attempt to transfer traditional media planning to Internet-compatible business models, a migratory excursion whose trail is marked by cross-over cartographers in the form of Media Metrix, Nielsen//NetRatings, and other television-inspired Web ratings agencies. The meteoric rise of the World Wide Web (its look and feel helped encourage commercial applications and lend the Internet a "home page") caused many to overlook e-mail's status as the so-called "killer app"[9] driving Internet use. Indeed, e-mail's low latency requirements and high infrastructure tolerance[10] make it a central application to virtual conferencing; while these characteristics persisted through Internet investor exuberance of the late 1990s, recall that this exuberance sprang up in the shadow of the World Wide Web, not e-mail. Later, a flurry of popular and trade press articles began to extoll e-mail as a "killer app," leading, ironically, to manuals on e-mail marketing, attempts to wrap HTML (the computer language for creating graphics on the WWW) inside e-mail messages, and other bids to stretch e-mail-as-medium. By then, however, the die had been cast and the genre stabilized; even unilateral graphics extensions placed by Microsoft in its widely-adopted *Outlook* e-mail software failed to trigger significant ferment.

E-mail's centrality to virtual conferencing plays out at the level of user identity. For synchronous applications where standard modes of interaction are conducted in near-real time, the segmented and relatively recent development of most Internet applications is translated for users into an almost-arbitrary identity over which considerable control can be exerted. On the Web, for example, "traceable" attributes such as names tend to be configured within individual applications or sites, and stabilizing agents are often limited to passwords. Many asynchronous, non-real time applications, on the other hand – such as mailing lists or USENET news groups – cite the user's electronic address.

That difference matters. An identity that may refer back to the user's institutional affiliation[11] in physical space, the link between e-mail address and physical identity, is a contested one. During the 1980s heyday of hobbyist-run electronic Bulletin Board Systems (BBSes) – precursors, in many ways, to the virtual networking that would later take place via the Internet – many system operators (SysOps) made a practice of telephoning new users to "validate" them and hence link their online and offline identities. Then, as now, the merits of anonymity remained an open debate. Virtual interaction between individuals without a prior relationship was framed in terms of the ability to explore new identities, on one hand, against the increased responsibility that accompanies a difficult-to-shed offline identity, on the other.

Schuler (1996) terms this "network citizenship." The label is apt insofar as it addresses the individual's cultivation of his or her relationship with a given community in a manner that is both durable and recurring.[12] The term suggests an alternative to the debate's two options – online anonymity or offline identity – by recalling that online identities, too, accrue through an ongoing attempt at self-production which unfolds through what Balibar (1994: 12) has called a process of "subjection and subjectivation:"

> Citizenship is not one among other attributes of subjectivity, on the contrary: it *is* subjectivity, *that form* of subjectivity that would no longer be identical with subjection for anyone. This poses a formidable problem for the citizens, since few of them, in fact, will achieve it completely.

The polarities, online and offline, anonymity and full disclosure, spill over and commingle.

Acting as private agent for inhabitants of public space – its citizens – the virtual conference moderator helps mediate this process. The moderator does not stand alone, of course; moderation is embedded intimately into the socio-technical architecture of the virtual conference itself. Mediation is distributed between the human-computer interface and the human agent, making the choice of which functions to assign to direct human intervention and which to embed in the technology, a key design decision. The virtual conference designer or architect is in this sense a basic arbiter of network citizenship's exercise, trading off automation's scalability for the human's flexibility: reliance upon human intervention is temporally and, by extension, financially costly. Still, it is rare and, probably, unwise for virtual conference design to assign no functionality to the human moderator, a dynamic "gateway" who can adapt constantly to the uses of the virtual conference space that develop diachronically. The moderator cannot control this development process, but can and must help shape its flow, clarify its structure, facilitate its exchanges, and manage its content. In the distribution of net work, the moderator is the community development worker.

In other words, virtual networking is never completely virtual. It demands labour. Videazimut's virtual conference adopted an asynchronous and modest interface resembling that sketched out above, but ultimately relying to a significant degree on volunteer labour. Privileging a textual interface was a design choice made, not as a deliberate reaction to the ramping-up of applications bandwidth and rich media use, but as an in-progress necessity given the Conference's aims and theme and the uneven roll-out[13] of Internet facilities internationally. This translated into a set of mailing lists (discussion groups) managed through a series of simple but widely-adopted scripts called Majordomo, hosted on a machine in Singapore, and a mostly text-based Web site in Montreal with a penchant for reusing simple graphic images. The Web site also acted as an archive and alternative platform for participation.

The goal of wide access made it important that the e-mail and Web interfaces work in tandem, a multi-applications strategy intended to increase the likelihood that, in an applications-limited Internet access environment, most available applications are sufficient to participate in the conference. A store-and-forward e-mail connection might be unable to access the Web, for example, whereas a public library might only offer Web access to its users. The conference addressed these realities in two ways. The first, designed to enable full Web-based participation, demanded ensuring that e-mail messages appear on the World Wide Web and that Web contributions appear via e-mail. This was accomplished using two pieces of public domain software (MailProc and Listserv2WWW) which, because their code was freely available, could be customized as needed. The second, designed to enable full e-mail access to Web resources such as conference archives, was accomplished with the help of a partner organization based in Quito, Ecuador (Comunica) which contributed a Web-to-e-mail gateway to return Web pages as e-mailed text in response to properly structured e-mail requests.

Implementation of this strategy in a low-budget environment was enabled by the availability of modifiable tools and programs to a distributed computing environment, underlining the importance of open source and widely-published software code and, indeed, instruction sets and plans more generally.[14] Eric Raymond (1999), among others, has argued that the software industry's key democratic deficit is in presenting software as a product when it is a service. That the virtual conference's software platform could be achieved swiftly through the presence of source code and unpaid labour, both underlines this tenet and, for non-dominant software providers, suggests a path to profitability through a commitment to open-source principles in conjunction with the supply of labour, whether paid or otherwise compensated.

The portrait painted here is that of a virtual network application implemented with few financial resources but significant human commitment, resulting in a high-yield but relatively unsophisticated platform in an environment rife with technological innovation. This material-limited approach has been used before. The Virtual Conference's form was patterned loosely after a number of analogous efforts (cf. Lawrence and Brodman 2000). During 1998 alone, similarly-designed virtual conferences were held with titles like *Human Rights* (Canadian Centre for Foreign Policy Development), *International Forum on Communication & Citizenship* (Agencia Latinoamericana de Información), *Knowledge and Information for Development* (Panos Institute and World Bank), and *Youth Building Knowledge Societies* (International Institute for Sustainable Development).

That these events shared not only design but thematic and organizational characteristics was more than a coincidence. The design theories and implementations described in this chapter can be understood only by explaining the virtual conference as Internet genre. Generally, media genres are classificatory schemes that help organize the range of likely forms and content for a given communications medium according to a set of well-known ideal-types. For most established media, generic forms are well-established; uncertainty or lack of established media genre may point to a medium that is emergent or that benefits from a disproportionately large community of innovators or that is a historically grounded culture of innovation, such as the Internet.

Media genres are both enabling and limiting. They are enabling because their familiarity allows ideas and concepts to be communicated more efficiently, building upon the prior knowledge that, for example, print communication amounts to a "tacit contract between authors and readers" (Chandler 1997; Livingstone 1994), or that computer-mediated communication "invokes ideas of discourse communities, traditional forms and emerging document types. Users are assumed to base their decisions on movement through information space in part on these attributes of genre" (Dillon and Vaughan 1997: 101). However, that is also what makes them limiting. Genres are habit-forming; they require the user to become "competent in certain forms of knowledge and to be familiar with certain conventions [that] constitute the ground or framework within/on which particular propositions can be made" (Morley 1992: 129; cf. Raskin 2000: 18-20). Because mediated communication is framed by genre, the communicative act creeps up the continuum framed by what Edward T. Hall (1976: 101) has called high- and low-context communication: "high context communication, in contrast to low context, is economical, fast, efficient, and satisfying; however time must be devoted to programming." In so doing, it promulgates an economy of what Bourdieu (1984; 1993) in turn, calls "cultural capital," here the ongoing acquisition of specialized "knowledges" as a measure of participation and, indeed, competition in the use of cultural technologies. In the Videazimut virtual conference, for example, the users focused on its "virtual community" aspect and, in some cases, concentrated almost exclusively on ongoing user interaction. This, despite explicit reminders that, patterned after a traditional conference, production and distribution of knowledge in the form of weekly conference papers was a key conference objective.

Where a wide diversity of genres is absent, an almost oligopolistic environment results making it hard for new genres to bubble forth. The costs of developing these new forms are simply too great. That makes a medium's early days its most important, and that is why the genre expressed through the Videazimut virtual conference's design matters. At a formal level, designers for the medium must fashion genres rather than fall into them. At a political economy level, the medium is organized into institutional structures that have yet to be determined. As an Internet genre, virtual conferencing's value lies partly in its contribution to the network applications ecosystem, as well as to the developing body of design principles that populate it.

Compatibility with low-bandwidth environments and, by logical extension, with the right to communicate, is among these design principles. The genre outlined here evolved to meet them. If narrowband virtual conferencing is designed for wide access, however, it is also resource-dependent, and so its sustainability is affected by its insertion into the Internet's political economy, including policy's broadband bias.[15]

# Network Evolution

Bandwidth is among the Internet's basic currencies; its ongoing growth a staple of network growth. As more users and, to a lesser extent, more intense activity per user, have driven Internet expansion, periodic announcements about growth in backbone and router capacity have become a leitmotif in the marketing discourse of the Internet infrastructure sector. An accompanying anxiety as to lagging adoption rates for broadband local access technologies led to prolonged industry debate on whether the Internet would experience a bandwidth glut. This would result in driving the price of long-haul capacity to near-zero prices and hence threaten the marketplace viability of those wholesalers who had not yet moved to diversify their operations vertically.

What does the future hold? Most conventional histories of the public routed IP network – that is, the Internet – locate its origins within the ARPANET which was first operational in 1968 and whose first international link became operational in 1973. This is in a sense accurate: most of the protocols, architectures and ideas that scaffold turn-of-the-millennium Internet infrastructure are descendents of those developed for use in the university-oriented ARPANET. But another strand of the public Internet is the United States' long quest to install a "free flow of information" as communications policy. For years the US attempted to eliminate state barriers to market entry for media and other communications products and services, through multilateral communications policy fora like UNESCO and the International Telecommunication Union (ITU). In the 1980s and 1990s, US policy finally made substantial progress by shifting "information flow" from a communications issue into a trade issue through establishment of a trade-in-services regime, first in bilateral agreements with Canada and Israel, then multilaterally through what would become the General Agreement on Trade in Services (Hollifield & Samarajiva 1994).

This helped mobilize substantial political, economic, educational and marketing resources to develop a technological platform for processing information both as primary commodity and as a signalling system for more perfect market information.[16] Without this support, Internet development could not have advanced as it did. When the US National Information Infrastructure (NII) and Global Information Infrastructure (GII) projects were first put forward, their architects described the Internet as, at best, a subset of these. As the effort to re-engineer the Internet proceeded apace, however, convergences that from a technical standpoint might have seemed unlikely were embraced and pursued enthusiastically in the marketplace. Upon the Internet were imprinted the GII project's intentions, translating into a full-force effort to rejig infrastructure so as to permit e-commerce-friendly media genres, ranging from carving out a discrete (and trackable) user identity in WWW use (Agre 1999), to creating a robust point-to-mass broadcast content delivery infrastructure (Handley and Crowcroft 1999), to enabling quality-of-service traffic prioritization that facilitates everything from more efficient application-based traffic routing to more easily-implemented price discrimination schemes (Huston 2000).

The push for broadband-driven demand that would intensify per-user bandwidth consumption is part of this direction in network evolution. For bandwidth wholesalers and for their equipment suppliers, continued growth in bandwidth demand is simply a sound business proposition. For those responsible for that demand, however – residential and institutional users of Internet-enabled applications – the chief demand driver is the promise of new media genres or, more prosaically, applications that are more useful or more enjoyable or both. As genre, virtual conferencing does not measure up, because it aims to conserve bandwidth usage, not maximize it. This lends it no more support from the infrastructure sector than it has from the applications layer, from which standpoint virtual conferencing as outlined here, lacks e-commerce capability and must therefore be reengineered.

Genres help define the real world of media practice and do so by binding users together in a discursive field shaped by historical precedent, material conditions, and institutionally-framed activity. By implication, genre's role in organizing a given medium's uses means organizing the social use of that medium itself, making generic definition a key strategic battlefield. Transposing a key plank of international media theory[17] to the study of genre, Neale illustrates this by pointing out (1980: 53, 55) that while the variety of "models in the car industry function to produce diversity, genres in the film industry function primarily to contain it." Genres, therefore, are crucial to the film industry, because they offer "an ordered variety of the discursive possibilities of cinema itself." Little surprise, then, that asynchronous, text-based virtual conferencing – the genre described in this chapter – is dominated by non-profit and under-resourced organizations. It has subsisted via two routes. One is through the indirect effects of explicit policy, in the form of government- or philanthropic-funded organizations that support virtual networking as a civil society technology. The other is the less centralized series of social mechanisms that reallocate non-monetized labour, including elements of what civil society's sociologists call solidarity and shared ideals, and what cybermarketing gurus call "branding" (Braunstein et. al. 2000), what anthropologists of virtual networking call the gift exchange (Agre 1998b), and what observers of organizational communication call the reputation or attention economies (Makino 1998).

In Videazimut's case, the first route provided equipment and some funding through the Canadian International Development Agency (CIDA); the International Development Research Centre (IDRC) and its Singapore-based affiliate, Pan-Asia Networking; and COMMposite, a student-run French-language communications journal with access to public university resources at the University of Quebec in Montreal. The second route helped provide labour. Yet both routes – and, hence, the type of virtual conferencing described here – are threatened by the near-universal international consensus around broadband roll-out as policy's goal, because broadband does not need virtual conferencing.

Nor, perhaps, is there any reason for it to do so. The argument made here is not against high-speed local access *per se*, nor is it in favour of media genres superseded by a better-performing alternative. A world of *universal* broadband access would offer marvelous possibilities. When US policy activism arose around a string of AT&T acquisitions to ensure that widely-installed cable infrastructure built out with the help of regulatory easement not be exploited by its owners to leverage vertical integration of infrastructure and content, this was clearly a step toward, not away from, wider access to the means of communication (Bar *et. al.* 1999). The stated intentions behind policy inquiries such as Canada's National Broadband Task Force (NBTF), similarly, are laudatory; achieving universal access to widely-used critical infrastructure is a basic element of the right to communicate.

But broadband is not simply an enabling technology. It also represents a change in technological conditions, implying different design constraints and abilities. When broadband becomes a policy goal, policies favour broadband applications, and when broadband is an industrial goal, a wide array of resources is mobilized to help create the conditions that require it. It is unsurprising, for example, that almost immediately following the Canadian NBTF's formation in 2001 observers criticized the task force as overly dominated by industry figures with partisan interests in its recommendations.[18] When technology is the driver, the application is too often a passenger, along for the ride but ill-placed to decide on the route.

Technological ferment should be evaluated from the application's standpoint too, then. As genre, virtual conferencing is both highly accessible and a harbinger of the Internet's wider capacity to support diverse genres and innovation more generally. In so doing, its support of the right to communicate is a key feature of its design process. When media policy sets out with infrastructure as its goal, it leaves that process behind.

It shouldn't. Virtual conferencing sits within a matrix of media genres whose low barriers to entry and careful access design optimize them for civil society. As a virtual networking application, it seeks to foster dispersed collaboration via minimally intrusive information flow – the opposite of the direct action attacks which, from "hacktivist" denial of service attacks to the US Army's blasting of rock and roll music at embassy-sequestered Panamanian general Manuel Noriega, mobilize information overload as a weapon. As alternative media form, it complements the Independent Media Centre model which shares its ad hoc nature and low barriers to entry, springing up when dispersed citizens can't come physically together, but don't want to remain apart. But virtual conferencing is also a case study in a larger process of network evolution. Media policy seeks to create an enabling environment for specific conditions, be they widely available broadband or network-enabled health care. That means working with the specific conditions that enable the right to communicate.

These concepts push the right to communicate beyond global media policy and into a media design grammar for researchers, practitioners and policy-makers alike. Earlier we noted the progression of the right to communicate through debate in multilateral fora and, later, media activist groups, and to that contrasted what happens when the right to communicate becomes the goal of interface design. Not just an object of dedicated debate, the right to communicate must also become a key element in the larger question of how network-based media's evolution is to be directed. What do media forms, applications, institutions and environments look like when the right to communicate is a fundamental design principle? When new technologies are available, what do existing applications have to gain from them, rather than vice-versa? Behind these questions are a use-centred policy research agenda. If the right to communicate is to be incorporated into broadband roll-out, that is where it must start.

## Notes

1  The author thanks Michael Gurstein and Leslie Regan Shade for their comments and suggestions.

2  This account of Butterworth's talk comes via an e-mail summary sent by streaming media activist Adam Hyde on 22 November 1999 to several mailing lists.

3  See http://commposite.uqam.ca/videaz/.

4  For an early discussion of these issues, see Hurley and Keller (1998).

5  Though significantly flawed—its emphasis on the nation-state as unit of analysis elided the plays of power that take place within borders and the clustering of elites across them (cf. Miller 1993: 106)—the NWICO focus on co-ordinating efforts to achieve widespread access to public, interactive communications facilities was commendable. The project ultimately failed when the US and UK governments exited UNESCO, reducing the organization to a second-tier player in the international communication policy arena.

6  A January 8, 2001 Nettime posting by Dutch media critique Geert Lovink noted that the Top 100 trafficked sites listing maintained by the "Hot100" Web site was scarcely changed between 2000 and 2001, adding that "[t]he Web has become a world of lawyers and consultants. The overall function of Web design has rapidly mutated. It is no longer demo design for the Web as a whole, if that mythological space of the early days ever existed."

7  Based on TeleGeography research (2000).

8  The nodal point in this process was abolition of the Acceptable Use Policy (AUP) governing usage of the Internet's then-backbone. Until 1991, commercial use of the Internet was limited by an AUP enforced by the National Science Foundation that operated what was then a single Internet backbone. The AUP stated that "NSFNET backbone services are provided to support open research and education in and between US research and educational institutions, plus research arms of for-profit firms when engaged in open scholarly communications and research. Use for other purposes is not acceptable." In 1991, however, the Commercial Internet eXchange (CIX) was formed by General Atomics (later CERFnet, and later AT&T), Performance Systems International (later PSInet) and UUNET Technologies (later acquired by WorldCom) to exchange their commercial traffic and hence completely bypass the NSFNET backbone and its AUP. Noting the Internet's commercial potential, the US judged the time opportune to change its oversight role so as to encourage private finance. On December 23, 1992, NSF announced that it would cease acting as the Internet's backbone operator; two years later, contracts were drawn up for the operation of central Network Access Points similar to CIX, obviating the need for NSFNET.

9  Originally coined to describe Lotus 1-2-3, the first mass-market spreadsheet software program, a "killer app" describes an application whose utility justifies the purchase of its underlying platform in order to use it.

10  Latency refers to network wait time. Applications whose latency requirements are undemanding can be delivered via a greater number of platforms than when such

requirements are stringent, since latency-inducing delays and slow platform throughputs are less threatening to system stability.

11   The evolution of physical world references in standard e-mail addressing, moving from ISP name to corporate affiliation, is a useful index for market Internet take-up.

12   Dibbell's discussion of "A rape in cyberspace" (1993) details a limit-case in this respect.

13   See Abramson (2000).

14   Access to more substantial financial resources might have permitted fax and telephone gateways to conference participation, facilitating an even broader participation; wide publication of access points for computers linked to the conference or of centres at which print-outs of Conference documents could be consulted would have achieved similar aims.

15   On the incorporation of broadband access as a major plank of national communication policy see, *inter alia*, the US Federal Communications Commission's Section 706 Advanced Services inquiry, Canada's National Broadband Task Force, and similar processes at both national and federal levels in Europe and in Asia.

16   The reader will recall that perfect market information is one of the classical model's prerequisites for a properly functioning market under capitalism. A fundamental challenge to this model is the significant role played by transaction costs and other vestiges of imperfect market information in real-world markets. The notion of an information infrastructure capable of "correcting" this imperfection is hence a seductive one; as media theorists from Harold Innis onward have suggested, however, the introduction of any new technology introduces new "biases" into the organization of social life. The view of technological innovation as corrective to existing conditions fails to take into account the new conditions it helps engender.

17   The ontological difference between "cultural" and "other" industries in international trade negotiations is a hallmark of the policy position sometimes referred to as "cultural exceptionalism," and was eventually written into the 1984 Canada-US Free Trade Agreement and, in the 1990s, was championed by French representatives in the hammering out of the General Agreement on Trade in Services. See, *inter alia*, John Sinclair's review of cultural industries (1996: 36). Sinclair juxtaposes Silverstone, Hirsch and Morley's characterization of them (1992) as "doubly articulated"—"meaningful as objects in themselves, as well as being the carriers of meaningful content"—with that of economist Albert Breton for whom cultural industries are distinguished in that they are "not so much about the *stock* of goods that consumers hold as they are about the *flow* of contents that the goods carry."

18   This discussion was held as part of a virtual conference on broadband initiated by communication policy activist, consultant and critic Michael Gurstein as an explicit intervention into the NBTF process.

# References

Abramson, B.D. 2000. Internet Globalization Indicators. *Telecommunication Policy* 24(1).

Agre, P.E. 1999. The Architecture Of Identity: Embedding Privacy In Market Institutions. *Information, Communication and Society* 2(1): 1-25.

Balibar, E. 1994. Subjection and Subjectivation. In *Supposing the Subject*, edited by Joan Copjec. London: Verso, 1-15.

Bar, F., S. Cohen, P. Cowhey, B. DeLong, M. Kleeman, and J. Zysman. 1999. Defending The Internet Revolution In The Broadband Era: When Doing Nothing Is Doing Harm. *BRIE Working Paper* 137. <http://brie.berkeley.edu/

~briewww/pubs/wp/wp137.html>.

Barbrook, R. 1998a. *The Californian Ideology* <http://ma.hrc.wmin. ac.uk/ma.theory.4.2.db>.

Bourdieu, P. 1984. *Distinction: A Social Critique of the Judgement of Taste.* Trans. Richard Nice. Cambridge, MA: Harvard University Press.

_____. 1993. *The Field Of Cultural Production: Essays On Art And Literature.* New York: Columbia University Press.

Braunstein, M., N. Levine, and E. H. Levine. 2000. *Deep Branding on the Internet: Applying Heat and Pressure Online to Ensure a Lasting Brand.* Roseville, CA: Prima Publishing.

CANARIE Inc. 2000. *Around The World, But Particularly In Canada And More Especially In Quebec, A Revolution Is Taking Place In High-Speed Networking.* <http://www.canet3.net/library/papers/ComingRevolution.html>.

Chandler, D. 1997. *An Introduction To Genre Theory.* <http://www.aber.ac .uk/media/Documents/intgenre/intgenre.html>.

Cook, G. 2001. *Cook Report on Internet.* March.

D'Arcy, J. 1969/1977. Direct Broadcast Satellites And The Right To Communicate. *EBU Review.* In *Right to Communicate: Collected Papers, edited by* S. Harms, J. Richstad, and K.A. Kie. Honolulu: University of Hawaii Press: 1-9.

Deleuze, G. with C. Parnet. 1998. *L'Abécédaire de Gilles Deleuze.* Paris: Éditions Montparnasse. [video]

Dibbell, J. 1993. A Rape In Cyberspace: How An Evil Clown, A Haitian Trickster Spirit, Two Wizards, And A Cast Of Dozens Turned A Database Into A Society. *Village Voice.* 23 December. http://www.levity.com/ julian/bungle_vv.html.

Dillon, A. and M. Vaughan. 1997. It's The Journey and the Destination: Shape and the Emergent Property of Genre in Digital Documents. *New Review of Multimedia and Hypermedia* 3: 91-105.

Donnelly, J. 1998. Human Rights: A New Stanford Of Civilization? *International Affairs* 74(1): 1-23.

Felice, W. F. 1998. Militarism and Human Rights, *International Affairs* 74(1): 25-40.

Hall, E. T. 1976. *Beyond Culture.* Garden City, NY: Anchor Books.

Hamelink, C. 1994. *The Politics of World Communication.* Thousand Oaks, CA: Sage Publications.

Handley, M. and J. Crowcroft. 1999. Internet Multicast Today, *Cisco Internet Protocol Journal* 2(3): 2-19. http://www.cisco.com/warp/public/759/ipj_2-4/ipj_2-4_multicast.html.

Hollifield, A. and R. Samarajiva. 1994. The Rise of the Trade Paradigm In

International Communication Policy: Implications Of The National Information Infrastructure. Presented to the International Association for Mass Communication Research, Seoul, S. Korea.

Huberman, B.A., P.L.T. Tirolli, J.E. Pitkow, and R.M. Lukose. 1998. Strong Regularities in World Wide Web Surfing. *Science* 280: 95-98.

Hurley, D. and J. Keller. 1998. *The First 100 Feet: Options for Internet & Broadband Access.* Cambridge, MA: MIT Press.

Huston, G. 2000. *Internet Performance Survival Guide: QoS Strategies for Multiservice Networks.* New York: John Wiley & Sons.

Lawrence, J. and J. Brodman. 2000. Linking Communities To Global Policymaking: A New Electronic Window On The United Nations. In *Community Informatics: Enabling Communities with Information and Communications Technologies*, edited by M. Gurstein. Hershey, PA: Idea Group Publishing.

Livingstone, S.M. 1994. The Rise And Fall Of Audience Research: An Old Story With A New Ending. In *Defining Media Studies: Reflections on the Future of the Field*, edited by M. R. Levy & M. Gurevitch. Oxford: Oxford University Press.

MacBride, S. 1980. *Many Voices, One World: Communication and Society, Today and Tomorrow.* Paris: UNESCO.

Makino, J. 1998. Productivity Of Research Groups: Relation Between Citation Analysis And Reputation Within Research Communities. *Scientometrics* 43: 87-93.

Miller, T. 1993. *The Well-Tempered Self: Citizenship, Culture, and the Postmodern Subject.* Baltimore: Johns Hopkins University Press.

Morley, D. 1992. *Television, Audiences & Cultural Studies.* New York: Routledge.

Neale, S. 1980. *Genre.* London: British Film Institute.

Norman, D. A. 1988. *The Design of Everyday Things.* New York: Doubleday Books.

Raboy, M. 1997. La *Global Information Infrastructure* (GII): un projet impérial pour l'ère de la mondalisation. *Communication & Strategies* 25: 15-32.

Raskin, J. 2000. *The Human Interface: New Directions for Designing Interactive Systems.* Reading, MA: ACM Press & Addison Wesley Longman.

Raymond, E. 1999. *The Cathedral & The Bazaar: Musing On Linux And Open Source By An Accidental Revolutionary.* Sebastopol, CA: O'Reilly & Associates.

Rogers, R. (ed.) 2000. *Preferred Placement: Knowledge Politics on the Web.* Maastricht, Netherlands: Jan van Eycke Akademie.

Schuler, D. 1996. *New Community Networks: Wired for Change.* Boston: Addison-

Wesley. http://www.scn.org/ncn/.

Servaes, J. 1998. Human Rights, Participatory Communication and Cultural Freedom in a Global Perspective. Paper presented to the Virtual Conference on the Right to Communicate and the Communication of Rights. http://commposite.uqam.ca/videaz/docs/jaseen.html.

Silverstone, R., E. Hirsch and D. Morley. 1992. Information and Communication Technologies and the Moral Economy of the Household. In *Consuming Technologies: Media and Information in Domestic Spaces*, edited by R. Silverstone and E. Hirsch. New York: Routledge.

Sinclair, J. 1996. Culture And Trade: Theoretical And Practical Considerations. In *Mass Media and Free Trade: NAFTA and the Cultural Industries*, edited by E.G. McAnany and K.T. Wilkinson. Austin: University of Texas Press.

Svendsen, K. 1995. About International Law. *Clips* 9. http://www.videazimut .org/e/clips/9-5.html.

Winseck, D. 1997. Contradictions In The Democratization Of International Communication. *Media Culture & Society* 19(2): 219-246.

# The Civil Society Challenge to Global Media Policy

## Cees J. Hamelink

## The Conflicting Political Agendas

There is a great deal of serious concern in the world about the possible consequences of global economic integration. Social activists from around the world have expressed this in Seattle, Washington, Nice and Prague. Most news media describe these advocacy groups as the "anti-globalization movement." Many commentators seem to agree with *New York Times* columnist Thomas L. Friedman who has called the protesters "flat-earth advocates" (Kutner 1999). Such opinions put the protesters in the niche of regressive, short-sighted weirdos who want to stop progress. In many news reports there is also the suggestion that the protesters represent narrow-minded nationalist interests. There is something very odd here. If one observes the groups that protest against policies of the World Trade Organization, or the movement against the proposed Multilateral Agreement on Investment, one sees an impressive demonstration of globalization. The groups actively use a global communications medium (the Internet) to build cross-border alliances, show strong global solidarity, and radiate a persuasive cosmopolitan ambiance. To merely claim they are anti-globalization obscures the real issue.

At the core of the recent civil global protests stands the conflict between two divergent political agendas on globalization. There is a neo-liberal agenda that is commercially oriented and market-centred. This agenda proposes the liberalization of national markets, the deregulation of capital flows, the lifting of trade restrictions based on environmental or human rights concerns, and the strengthening of the rights of investors. In contrast to this agenda, in 1996 the Mexican Zapatista movement organized a global conference (with 3000 participants from all over the world) with as title "Humanity against Neo-liberalism." This reflects the sentiment of much recent civil protest. The movement is not primarily acting against forms of global integration per se, but against the neo-liberal political agenda for globalization. Like the Zapatistas, the protesters have their own agenda: a humanitarian approach to globalization. This agenda puts the interests of citizens at the centre of political activity and proposes the regulation of capital flows, the protection of the environment, and fair labour conditions. Basically it aspires to globalization with a human face.

## The Key Issues

These conflicting agendas are also found in the domain of global media policy. In eight major issue-areas, these conflicts are essential in shaping the future of world communication.

*Access.* The neo-liberal agenda perceives people primarily as consumers and aspires to provide them with access to communication infrastructures so they can be integrated into the global consumer society. The humanitarian agenda perceives people primarily as citizens and wants people to be sufficiently literate so that communication infrastructure can be used to promote democratic participation.

*Knowledge.* On the neo-liberal agenda, knowledge is a commodity that can be processed and owned by private parties. The property rights of knowledge producers should be strictly enforced. On the humanitarian agenda, knowledge is a public good that cannot be privately appropriated and from which all people should derive benefit.

*Global Advertising.* The neo-liberal agenda has a strong interest in the expansion of global advertising. This implies additional commercial space in media (mass media and the Internet), new target groups (especially children), more sponsorships (films, orchestras, exhibitions) and more places to advertise (the ubiquitous billboards). The humanitarian agenda is concerned with the ecological implications of the world-wide promotion of a consumer society and the growing gap between those who can shop in the (electronic) global shopping mall and those who can only gawk. Moreover, the humanitarian agenda has a strong interest in defending public spaces against their commercial exploitation.

*Privacy.* The neo-liberal agenda has a strong interest in "data-mining:" the systematic collection, storage and processing of masses of person-related data to create client profiles for marketing purposes. The humanitarian agenda has a strong interest in the protection of people's privacy and the creation of critical attitudes among consumers to guard their personal information more adequately.

*Intellectual Property Rights.* The neo-liberal agenda has a strong interest in the strict enforcement of a trade-based system for the protection of intellectual property rights that provides a large degree of protection for the transnational commercial owners of such rights. Equally these IPR owners have an interest in expanding the period of protection as well as the materials that can be brought under this protection. The humanitarian agenda is concerned that the present system sanctions the grand-scale resource plunder ("biopiracy") of genetic information from poor countries and serves the interests of corporate owners better than the interests of local communities or individual artistic creators. This agenda seeks to protect the interests of communal property of cultural resources and to protect resources in the public domain against exploitation by private companies.

*Trade in Culture.* The neo-liberal agenda has a strong interest in the application of international trade law to the export and import of cultural products. Under these rules, countries are not allowed to take measures restricting cultural imports or other forms of protection as part of their national cultural policy. The humanitarian agenda would like culture exempted from trade provisions and latitude for national measures to protect cultural autonomy and local public space.

*Concentration.* The neo-liberal agenda has a strong interest in creating business links (acquisitions, mergers and joint ventures) with partners in order to consolidate controlling positions on the world market and wants to create a sufficiently large regulatory vacuum in order to act freely. The humanitarian agenda is concerned that today's global merger activities have negative consequences for both consumers and professionals in terms of diminishing diversity and creating the loss of professional autonomy.

*The Commons.* The neo-liberal agenda wants the private exploitation of common assets such as the airwaves and promotes the auctioning of these resources to private parties. The humanitarian agenda wants to retain the public property of the human common heritage so that public accountability and community requirements remain secured.

Summing up the concerns of the humanitarian agenda for global media policy: shall human rights in global media policy be taken as seriously as property and investment rights? The key challenge of this agenda to global media policy makers is that they are asked to not only advance the interests of transnational corporations but also the interests of citizens. In so far as the policy makers are public functionaries, the humanitarian agenda seeks to remind them that they were elected by citizens and not by business firms.

## The Substantial Challenge

Why does human rights activism pose a challenge to a political agenda controlled by the interests of corporate capitalism? On the surface it would seem as if human rights and free markets go well together. Usually the reasoning to support this assumption is as follows: a society that respects the defence of human rights is a democratic society; democracy is a political arrangement in which people's needs and aspirations are freely expressed and the market is an economic arrangement by which people's needs and aspirations are satisfied. Thus democracy and the free market are a marriage made in heaven! The market is the perfect tool for a democratic social order.

The trouble with this argument is that the market only caters to the needs and aspirations of those people who can pay for their satisfaction. The market is selective and exclusive in its treatment of people whereas a human rights inspired democratic order should be inclusive and egalitarian. Moreover, the market does not meet all needs and aspirations equally well. It prioritizes some needs and aspirations over others. Priorities are not determined by substantial moral standards such as human security but by monetary value. Those needs and aspirations that can be defined in hard monetary terms are at an advantage.

Characteristic for "free market" societies is the "money culture" that judges all human activity in terms of its monetary value. Everything is provided with a price tag: even basic resources, such as water, air, maternal care, security, time. Everything can be acquired through money and be traded against more money. In this culture people engage in contractual and calculating relations with each other. Its greatest problem is the totalitarian nature of the money culture; it is world-wide the most prominent model for the organization of societies. As a result the relations that people have in the marketplace spill over into domains such as education, health care, care for the elderly, science and culture.

In the marketplace people have the greatest advantages if they are good at calculating. However, this attitude is disastrous for the quality of human relations when affection and trust are required, such as in health care. In caring institutions the key principle is solidarity between the various parties. As the principles of the market are introduced in more and more countries, solidarity disappears. In the market, the primary motive is self-interest. Choices people make are tested against the yardstick of "what is in it for me?" As health care institutions introduce the rules and standards of commercial operations, all decisions are tested against their stockholder value.

The money culture has winners and losers and is therefore unsuitable for the caring professions and institutions. Most people would probably find it unacceptable that some people should be excluded from health care, even if this is due to their own faults. When the notion of profit begins to dominate health care, however, the aim to provide care to as many people as possible is rapidly eroded.

The money culture has also begun its devastating journey into the domain of science. Science shows a tendency of becoming like professional sports. It increasingly is a ruthless game in which competition is more important than co-operation. Quantity is more important (numbers of quotes, numbers of students) than intellectual quality. The essential academic assessment criteria are fundraising, top ten lists, production output and money flows.

By applying market principles in more and more social domains, people are not merely calculating consumers, but they become calculating citizens. This poses a serious obstacle to the implementation of human rights. In the marketplace, people entertain contractual relations because they expect to gain from these exchanges. Within this mental map, human rights are only considered if they yield a profit.

The choice to respect human rights is, however, largely based upon a form of empathy with the conditions experienced by others – even people one does not know. This is to a large extent a non-rational choice inspired by a strong sense of disgust against avoidable suffering. This revolt is not motivated by social contracts or well understood self-interest and cannot be legally enforced.

The most powerful motive for the protection of human rights is "compassion." Respecting human rights requires an altruism that does not thrive within the money culture. In a culture where the accumulation and expansion of private property has the highest priority, human rights do not stand much of a chance. They need a very different point of reference: a culture of compassion.

The effective implementation of human rights demands a democratic structure of society (with civil participation and public accountability) and a culture of compassion, whereas corporate capitalism is basically undemocratic and based upon a culture of calculation. Those who pursue the humanitarian agenda face a formidable task precisely because they pose a fundamental substantive challenge to the dominant world order.

## The Strategic Challenge

At present, the battle between the two conflicting agendas is fought with inequality of arms. The commercial agenda is supported by a strong constituency of the leading members of the World Trade Organization and powerful business lobbies (such as the Business Software Alliance and the Global Business Dialogue). The humanitarian agenda, although increasingly active in the economic arena, is still in search of an active constituency in the world communications arena.

Although civil advocacy would be up against formidable opponents, a global movement could pose a serious political challenge. It would represent the interests of democratic citizenship and thus present a stronger claim to legitimacy than business firms. As its inspiration would spring from fundamental notions such as universal human rights, it would have a moral authority that is superior to those who are driven by commercial interests. It could use the court of public opinion more effectively than corporations and use this to get major concessions from their commercial opponents. A global civil movement would be made up of citizens who are both consumers and clients of the media industries, making them a forceful lobby.

On December 20, 2000, *The International Herald Tribune* used the following lead for one of its articles: "Small Advocacy Groups Take Big Role as Conscience of the Global Economy." In the same way, it should be possible to state: "Small Advocacy Groups Take Big Role as Conscience of Global Media Policy" (Small Advocacy Groups... 2000).

However, before global media advocacy could pose a serious challenge to global media policy, the movement itself has to confront some very complex strategic challenges.

These challenges include the question of how civil society organizations (CSOs) can effectively impact (inter)national governance.

## The Lack of Co-ordination

One of the key problems that affect the capacity of the CSO community to influence international governance is the lack of co-ordination. In many different areas of social activism, organizations often operate at cross-purposes to one another, spending more time and energy on competing with fellow bodies than on achieving their own mandate. The problem of co-ordination is often complicated by the fact that CSOs may differ greatly in the power they can wield.

It seems obvious enough to call for the mobilization of civil society in order that the public interest be effectively represented. In much of the literature and debates one finds the tendency to "romanticize" civil society by viewing it as inherently good and homogeneous. In reality, civil society is neither. We have to realize, for example, that ordinary members of civil society have committed the pervasive crime of genocide. Moreover, the civic sector of most societies is composed of a heterogeneous collection of – often mutually exclusive – interests. There are strong divisions and antagonisms among the members of civil society.

Some of the implied issues for the media advocacy movement are:

*How can the movement link up with social activists who may not perceive themselves as part of a communications/culture movement, but who are in fact, involved in communications and cultural projects?*

A special problem to be mentioned here is that although many civil society associations know very well how to manipulate the media in order to get public attention for their causes, they are not necessarily sensitive to the larger political issues in the "info-com" arena. The question remains: how can we sensitize and educate them?

The fundamental challenge is still whether a sufficiently large number of people can be made aware of how communications affects their daily lives and how vitally important it is that they take action. The confrontation with this challenge should have the top priority on the agenda for the realization of human rights in global media policy.

*Who are pertinent allies with whom to form coalitions?*

Because of heterogeneous interests it may be necessary to establish changing ad-hoc coalitions that focus on specific issues. This would fit well with the observation that many social advocacy movements seem to focus on a single-issue concern. However, this raises the much bigger question of how to move from a focus on a single-issue commitment to a broader sustainable political participation. This is increasingly complex as many countries are experiencing the simultaneous development of growing political activism (in matters of environment, human rights etc) but diminishing participation in formal political structures (such as political parties or elections). Therefore, we must further wrestle with questions like how crucial is the institutionalization of political processes and can informal activist politics ally with formal institutions such as national parliaments?

The latter question actually raises the intriguing issue of the role and significance of national parliaments. In much of the contemporary debate the focus seems to be on the confrontation between civil society and state, and civil society and market forces; national parliaments are seemingly omitted. This is odd as these are national lawmakers who can, in principle, considerably influence global policymaking of their national delegations. As the members of national parliaments are often uninformed about their own governments' global policies (the secret negotiations surrounding the Multilateral Agreement on Investment provided an excellent example), they could benefit from information provided by civil society organizations. At the same time they could provide civil advocacy movements with a pertinent access to political power (by way of lawmaking).

Different fora and different issues require different modalities of intervention. The ad-hoc coalitions should be cross-border in nature. Not only in the geographical sense, but also in terms of discipline and orientation. They should involve not only civil movements that are active in the info-com field but stretch beyond this community to include public interest groups in human rights, environmental concerns, peace and security matters, etc. Actually, since the political and business domains are divided themselves, there could also be alliances – on certain issues – with representatives from business and diplomatic communities.

There are several instances of negotiations in the recent past in which interest-communities could be formed across conventional borders. For example, the World Intellectual Property Organization (WIPO) conference was convened in 1996 to debate the adequacy of existing copyright regulation for the digital age. At the conference the US government proposed – with the support of the European Commission – that making temporary digital copies (as is commonly done when surfing the Internet) should be considered a violation of copyright. This position was backed by a lobby from the music and entertainment industries including the Motion Picture Association of America, the International Federation of Phonographic Industry, the Federation of European Publishers, and the Business Software Alliance (with, among others, Microsoft, Apple, and IBM). A coalition of telecommunications and Internet firms including AT&T, Philips, British Telecom, France Telecom, Netscape, as well as libraries and private users of the Internet, successfully challenged this lobby. One could also take the illustration of the debate around surveillance and the need for encryption. Here civil privacy watch groups may ally with business firms who want to secure the confidentiality of their electronic commerce against the interests of law enforcement agencies, intelligence services and tax authorities.

Coalitions may also be possible between social activists and the academic community. In other social domains (like the environment, world trade or human rights) there are often so called "epistemic communities" of scholars that provide a solid background of facts and analyses for political activism. So far the communications research world has often been absent from the arena of global media policy making. For effective civil advocacy in global media policy, a research agenda must be formulated to systematically explore the issues of major conflict as well as the political priorities and the above-mentioned question of civil intervention.

## Representation: Which constituencies are represented by whom?

A vital issue for all civil society organizations is the question of whom they represent. Can they speak on behalf of a constituency? Do members of that constituency recognize the organization(s) as legitimate representatives? Is there a democratic process by which constituencies can channel their concerns? Do CSOs account for their operations vis-à-vis their constituencies? These are critical questions because the civil institutions that represent the public interest are not necessarily paragons of democratic governance.

Some of the implied issues for the media advocacy movement are:

- How can the constituency for the movement be defined?

- How can this constituency participate in the movement?

- Who should be accountable to whom, why and how?

## Targets for Lobbying and Access to Decision-making Bodies

Much of the lobbying activity of CSOs has traditionally been directed towards governments and state institutions. Is this still relevant in the present international reality where transnational businesses make most of the decisions that affect people's daily lives? There have been important recent cases where social activists have directly targeted major companies for their campaigns.

In past decades, the CSO community has achieved some success with its involvement in the decision-making process of major intergovernmental organizations. International NGOs have managed to get observer and advisory status in many of the UN special agencies.Therefore, some of the implied issues for the media advocacy movement are:

- Should the movement address policy-makers in state bodies or go directly to the private media and their owners?

- Should the lobbying effort be mainly national or global?

- Should the movement aspire towards influencing such decision making fora as the United Nations, or the World Trade Organization?

- Should the movement do this through the creation of its own representative procedures or through co-ordination with those NGOs that already hold a status with international bodies?

- Should the movement strive towards the formal adoption of an intergovernmental agreement on communications and cultural issues?

## "The Ombudsoffice"

Intervention by public interest coalitions, the presentation of alternative policy proposals, and effective publicity around such action, will not come about spontaneously. These actions demand organization and mobilization. A modest beginning has been made to achieve this through the Platform for Co-operation on Communication and Democratization, established in 1995 (and transformed, in 2001, into the Platform on Communication Rights; see Platform 1995). Members of the platform have agreed to work for the formal recognition of the right to communicate. They emphasize the need to defend and deepen an open public space for debate and actions that build critical understanding of the ethics of communication, democratic policy and equitable and effective access.

The right to communicate is also the central concern of the so-called People's Communication Charter (PCC). The People's Communication Charter is an initiative that originated in 1991 with the Third World Network (in Penang, Malaysia), the Centre for Communication & Human Rights (Amsterdam, The Netherlands), the Cultural Environment Movement (US), the World Association of Community Radio Broadcasters (AMARC), and the World Association for Christian Communication (WACC). The Charter provides the common framework for all those who share the belief that people should be active and critical participants in their social reality and capable of governing themselves. In connection with the Charter, a series of international hearings and tribunals have been organized such as the International Hearing on Languages and Human Rights in 1999 (at The Hague) and the International Tribunals on Global Advertising (in 2002) and on Media Concentration and Cultural Rights (in 2004) (People's Communication Charter 1999).

These events should, in time, develop into a permanent institution such as an "Ombudsoffice" for communication and cultural rights. The UNESCO World Commission on Culture and Development chaired by Javier Pérez de Cuéllar also recommended this kind of institution in its 1995 report, *Our Creative Diversity*. The Commission recommended the drawing of an International Code of Conduct on Culture and—under the auspices of the UN International Law Commission—the setting up of an "International Office of the Ombudsperson for Cultural Rights" (World Commission 1995: 282). As the Commission writes:

> Such an independent, free-standing entity could hear pleas from aggrieved or oppressed individuals or groups, act on their behalf and mediate with governments for the peaceful settlement of disputes. It could fully investigate and document cases, encourage a dialogue between parties and suggest a process of arbitration and negotiated settlement leading to the effective redress of wrongs including, wherever appropriate, recommendations for legal or legislative remedies as well as compensatory damages (Ibid: 283).

Ideally the proposed Ombudsoffice would have full independence from both governmental and commercial parties and, as an independent agency, it would develop a strong moral authority on the basis of its expertise, its track record and the quality of the people and the organizations that form its constituency. Given the growing significance of the global info-com arena and the urgency of a humanitarian agenda for its governance, the building of this new global institution constitutes one of the most exciting challenges in the 21st century!

## References

Friedman, T. L., quoted in Kutner, R. 1999. The Seattle Protesters Got it Right. *Business Week*. December 20 : 11.

People's Communication Charter. 1999. www.pccharter.net.

Platform for Co-operation on Communication and Democratization. 1995. www.comunica.org/v2.

Small Advocacy Groups Take Big Role as Conscience of the Global Economy. 2000. *The International Herald Tribune*. December 20.

World Commission on Culture and Development. 1995. *Our Creative Diversity*. Paris: UNESCO.

# A Global Movement for People's Voices in Media and Communication in the 21st Century

## Voices 21

*V*oices 21 is an informal association of media activists and concerned individuals. It was founded in March 1999 with a view towards building a new social movement around media and communication issues. Its concerns and proposals for action are outlined in the following statement.

*Voices 21 members are involved in a range of initiatives, but as an umbrella association, Voices 21 speaks only for the individuals whose names appear at the end of the statement and not officially for the organizations whose names are included for purposes of identification only. The association's short term objective is to build a network of support for the goals described in the statement and, through that, to create appropriate mechanisms and organizational structures for achieving these goals.*

## Summary

This proposal calls for civil society and NGOs to form an international alliance to address concerns and to work jointly on matters around media and communication. We believe a new social movement in this field is needed, and is ready to act internationally.

Uniting civil society organizations that today use media and communication networks in their work for social change is:

An awareness of the growing importance of the mass media and communication networks for the aims they are trying to achieve;

A concern about current trends in the field of information and communication toward concentration of ownership and control into fewer hands;

A concern that state censorship is giving way only to more subtle censorship, through subjection to commercial exigencies and maximizing shareholder gain;

An awareness of the lack of public influence on these trends, in both developed and developing countries, in democracies and under dictatorships.

The central focus of the movement would be to tackle problems and find solutions to one of the greatest challenges of our time: To ensure that the voices and concerns of ordinary people around the world are no longer excluded!

A two-fold approach is required.

First, strategic level cooperation amongst NGOs must build common agendas, joint funding proposals and exchange and cooperation mechanisms. Gathering, analyzing and dissemination of information will be a key aspect of this. Second, concrete cooperation could begin through joint activities of the people and organizations participating in the movement, under the following suggested themes:

> Access and Accessibility
> Right to Communicate
> Diversity of Expression
> Security and Privacy
> Cultural Environment

Concrete targets and actions around these themes are suggested. This proposal will be spread widely among media and communication organizations, in order to initiate discussion on the most effective means to collaborate.


## Full Statement

This is a call to build a Global Movement on Media and Communication for the 21st Century. At its core is the demand that the voices of ordinary people around the world are no longer excluded from media and communication.

It is drafted, and continues to be refined, by a group of concerned media and communication practitioners, academics and NGOs, coming together under the banner of Voices 21. It is associated with the People's Communication Charter (PCC), a civil society initiative that promotes the rights of people in media and communication and which in the last few years has been endorsed by many thousands of organizations and individuals; and has close links with a number of other current initiatives.


## 1. A Common Concern

NGOs all over the world have long worked in the field of media and communication: creating and supporting community radio and access TV networks, bringing the Internet to civil society, using video for local development, attempting to influence media and communication policy, and through a variety of other means. Others have grown expert in the use of media and communication to pursue their development and empowerment strategies, whether through electronic networking, effective media influencing or media-based educational campaigns.

Increasingly, however, concerns are being expressed regarding the major trends in global media. While technological progress, and political and regulatory changes, can potentially benefit many of those in need, the scales seem increasingly tipped in favour of the already powerful. There is genuine and growing concern that global trends in media and communication are leading us into uncharted territory, and that those at the helm have no particular interest in the needs of the majority of the world's people. Civil society organizations, in general, share the following:

An awareness of the growing importance of the mass media and communication networks for the aims they are trying to achieve;

A concern about current trends in the field of information and communication toward concentration of ownership and control into fewer hands;

A concern that state censorship is giving way only to more subtle censorship, through subjection to commercial exigencies and maximizing shareholder gain;

An awareness of the lack of public influence on these trends, in both developed and developing countries, in democracies and under dictatorships.

## 2. An Emerging Movement

For some years now, NGOs such as the World Association of Community Radio Broadcasters (AMARC), Vidéazimut, Association for Progressive Communication (APC) and World Association for Christian Communication (WACC) have been building international organizations to promote the interests of their members and more generally to focus on the media needs of civil society. Others, such as the Platform for Democratic Communication, People's Communication Charter, MacBride Round Table and Cultural Environment Movement, are concerned from the outset with democratization of the media domain, spreading the message sometimes to thousands of people and their organizations.

More recently, these have embarked on what is in effect a process of global mobilization, seeking common ground, joining forces around specific issues, and developing proposals for cooperation. Alongside and supporting this have been numerous international events, in every region of the world and organized by a great variety of organizations and coalitions, where civil society voices are calling for a fundamental review of the media and communication domain, including global governance structures.

## 3. The Perceived Threats

The potential impact of current trends, especially given the absence of significant public influence upon them, are enormous, with ramifications spreading into the ordinary lives of people everywhere. Fears can be summarized as follows:

## *A Threat to Media Diversity in Form and Content:*

"Dumbing-down" of news and educational programming forms, with "infotainment" and "edutainment;"

Reduction of real content diversity, displaced by multiplication of homogenized programming.

*A Threat to Public Understanding and the Democratic Process:*

Undue influence of commercial imperatives on news, current affairs and educational content;

"Media Moguls" controlling the political slant of their publications, and directly biasing the information available;

Growing global electronic surveillance, by government and private interests.

*A Threat to Global Equity of Access and Economic Development:*

Growing disparity of access to information and communication technologies and applications globally, between urban and rural, and between groups in society;

A proliferation of advertising globally, perpetually delivering distorted messages of lifestyle expectations;

The imposition of a single dominant set of cultural values, promoting values that implicitly and explicitly advocate commercial over human relationships.

*A Threat to Cultural and Social Forms:*

The subjection of sport and all forms of entertainment to purely commercially driven criteria;

Domination of a single language in the new media content, and consequent loss of linguistic diversity;

Ubiquity of advertising, interrupting and deforming other social and cultural information, visually and aurally;

A considerable body of academic research, and the real experience of numerous NGOs, confirm that these threats are real and merit the urgent attention of international organizations, governments, and organizations everywhere that claim concern for our future. It is imperative that people, and civil society, everywhere begin to understand the nature and dynamics of these changes, and mobilize the means by which democratic accountability can be introduced.

## 4. Purpose of the Movement

The central focus of the movement would be to tackle problems and find solutions to one of the greatest challenges of our time: To ensure that the voices and concerns of ordinary people around the world are no longer excluded! Despite all the solemn declarations about information societies and communication revolutions, most of the world's voices are not heard. In today's reality most people have neither the tools nor skills to participate in social communication. Nor do they have a say in communication politics. The preamble of the People's Communication Charter goes: "All people are entitled to participate in communication and in making decisions about communication within and between societies." In spite of all the developments and innovations in the field of information and communication, this standard is far from being realized.

## 5. What to Do

We believe that a two-pronged approach is needed, one at the level of strategy development, the other at the level of cooperative action. These two are complementary, and can proceed any distance only by joining together hand in hand.

On the one hand, building a movement will require planning, strategic thinking, resources and the space to explore common ground and build strategies. On the other, organizations committed to democratization can, under a common banner, begin to plan and implement cooperation on practical activities that will help build the movement and tackle the issues.

## Building A Strategy Together

Building a movement in which all can feel part of and play a role, but yet which is coherent and focused, takes time and effort. There is also a major information and educational challenge, to ensure civil society is adequately informed on local to global trends, and opportunities to influence agendas. Voices 21 seeks only to build bridges, not to displace existing initiatives and organizations which have carried the issue to the brink of a movement.

Voices 21 began as a proposal to initiate a World Congress or Summit on Media and Communication. This intention remains as a future milestone in cooperation. In the meantime, however, as steps towards building a movement, we are encouraging participation in the following range of activities.

## Activities within the movement

Networking and concrete cooperation could, for example, begin around five campaigns, described below by Theme, Concerns, Targets and Actions.

*Theme 1: Access and Accessibility.*

## Concern:

Participation in social communication presupposes access: to big media, to community media, to computer networks, to information sources and to other tools. However, physical access is right now for many neither sufficient nor affordable. Most people in the world are denied access to such basic tools as a telephone. As a result, a social gap grows between those who can afford access to information and those who will be excluded. This must be changed.

## Targets:

International donor institutions that demonstrate in their policy and practice an enormous gap between words and actions: There is much rhetoric about the right to communicate, but totally inadequate supportive funding and support.

The international trade negotiators, particularly at the WTO, who enact policies that are not conducive to universal access and accessibility of communication infrastructures and information networks.

## Action:

Collaborate on building media and communication access where needed; for example telecentres, low-cost radiowires.

Use modern techniques where local infrastructure doesn't exist, such as solar energy, satellite and radio communications.

Find joint ways to finance access-building work.

Lobby meetings of the WTO and other multilateral institutions.

## Theme 2: Right to communicate

### Concern:

Around the world, old and new forms of state and commercial censorship are rampant; they threaten not only the independence of conventional mass media, but also the right to communicate through new channels like the Internet. Universal access to media and networks means little in the absence of adequate public space where information, opinions and ideas can be freely exchanged and debated. State censorship and providers' self-censoring of social debate, copyright rules, laws on business defamation, are all complex matters where rules need to be defined not to hinder, but to support, political debate and exchange on socially important matters.

### Targets:

Governments and cultural industries, broadcasters and Internet providers.

The emerging international regime for the protection of intellectual property rights at fora such as the WIPO and the WTO.

The European Union and Internet providers world-wide.

### Action:

Support and facilitate distribution of censored voices and material.

Build security systems for civil society organizations.

Provide cross-media services for international and simultaneous radio, TV and Internet broadcasting.

Provide support to various anti-censorship campaigns around the world.

Widely publicize examples of commercial censorship.

Lobby forthcoming meetings of WTO, WIPO, and the E.U. Commission.

## Theme 3: Diversity of expression

### Concern:

The commercialization of media and concentration of media ownership erode the public sphere and fail to provide for cultural and information needs, including the plurality of opinions and the diversity of cultural expressions and languages necessary for democracy. This occurs not only in the conventional media business, but is also beginning to affect the Internet.

### Targets:

WTO.

European Commission.

Mergers & Acquisitions Commissions in different countries.

### Action:

Build independent media and communication channels for civil society.

Create a civil society media economy to make non-profit media channels sustainable.

Develop concrete proposals for anti-cartel regulation.

Mobilize local consumer actions against media mergers.

Joint promotions of alternatives where they exist.

## *Theme 4: Security and Privacy*

### Concern:

Electronic communications through such media as the Internet have become targets for surveillance by governments without public debate on the consequences for communication on social matters. Across the world, 24 hour ubiquitous electronic surveillance is expanding (for example through the Echelon program of the US National Security Agency), including employee monitoring, and widespread commercial data-mining. Internet service providers are made liable for contents they carry, and the bigger ones have begun collaborating with the security police. This forces forms of self-censorship upon the ISPs, making the Internet an unsafe place for those living under dictatorships or political oppression. This must be changed.

### Targets:

ILO, OECD, European Commission/Parliament, governments,

Internet service providers and their networks.

### Action:

Build secure systems for social movements and defend them together when threatened.

Develop legislative proposals.

Design protective measures against privacy intrusion.

Mirror and broadcast material unfairly threatened.

## *Theme 5: Cultural environment*

### Concern:

The global media foster a culture of violence, discrimination, exclusion and consumerism. Most public interest NGOs strive toward the creation of a culture of peace, solidarity environmental awareness.

### Targets:

The global media industry, CEOs of TNCs like Time-Warner/CNN .

Bertelsmann, Disney/ABC, News Corporation (Murdoch), gGovernments and Parliaments, and media consumers.

### Action:

Educational campaigns to foster critical media awareness.

Children's editions of documents like the People's Communication Charter.

Create media and communication channels that offer positive alternatives.

Encourage mainstream media to offer positive alternatives.

Consumer media boycott/advertiser boycott.

Arrange and participate in tribunals and hearings.

Media monitoring.

To begin mobilization across these five themes, Voices 21 hopes to shortly launch a Debate and Discussion List. In addition, we are seeking to generate joint proposals for funding, to foundations, agencies and others, to further both strategy development and concrete activities, which could include:

preparation of educational resources around the issues discussed in this document;

creation of a "Virtual Centre for Media and Communication Democracy," conceived as a central repository for information and analysis and a hub for civil society networking;

a "Global Media Monitoring Project;"

an "International Ombuds Office on Media and Communication."

## 6. Interim Organizing Group

The following comprise the Interim Organizing Group for this evolving proposal. The associated proposal for a World Congress on Media and Communication has been endorsed widely, including at the International Forum on Communication and Citizenship in October 1998 in San Salvador, the MacBride Round Table in Amman in November 1998, and the Vidéazimut Congress in Cape Town in November 1998. It has also been endorsed by numerous civil society organizations.

The Organizing Group is in the process of expanding to ensure better regional and gender representation, and broader civil society participation.

Alain Ambrosi, Vidéazimut, Canada. ambrosia@web.net

Michael Eisenmenger, Deep Dish TV, USA. eisenmen@rci.rutgers.edu

George Gerbner, Cultural Environment Movement, USA. ggerbner@nimbus.temple.edu

Bruce Girard, Delft University of Technology, The Netherlands. bgirard@comunica.org

Cees Hamelink, People's Communication Charter, The Netherlands. hamelink@mail.antenna.nl

Wolfgang Kleinwächter, MacBride Round Table, Denmark. wolfgang@imv.au.dk

Cilla Lundstroem, Association for Progressive Communication, Sweden. cilla@apc.org

Robert McChesney, University of Wisconsin, USA. rwmcches@facstaff.wisc.edu

Kaarle Nordenstreng, University of Tampere, Finland. tikano@uta.fi

Marc Raboy, University of Montreal, Canada. raboym@com.umontreal.ca

Seán Ó Siochrú, Platform for Democratic Communication, Ireland. sean@nexus.ie

Pradip Thomas, World Association for Christian Communication, UK. pradip@wacc.gn.apc.org

Karen Thorne, Vidéazimut, South Africa. ownnat@wn.apc.org

Rick Vincent, MacBride Round Table, USA. rvincent@hawaii.edu

Lynne Muthoni Wanyeki, EcoNews Africa, Kenya. wanyeki@iconnect.co.ke

# Appendix I

The global communications policy environment

(Selected Examples)

| ISSUE AREAS | SITES |
|---|---|

### Global

| | |
|---|---|
| -Telecommunications:<br>    technical standards<br>    international rates<br>    frequency allocation | ITU |
| -Media content monitoring,<br>    media training and development | UNESCO |
| -Informatics development | UNESCO |
| -"Culture," cultural aspects of<br>    cultural industries, cultural<br>    policies, cultural diversity | UNESCO |
| -Information flow, development issues | ITU, UNESCO,<br>World Bank, UN |
| -Satellites | ITU, INTELSAT |
| -Intellectual property rights | WIPO |
| -Human rights | UN |
| -International data flow, protection of<br>    privacy, internet regulation | To be determined |

### Multilateral

| | |
|---|---|
| -Global Information Infrastructure | G7/G8 |

| | |
|---|---|
| -Market liberalization (telecom) | WTO |
| -Market liberalization (cultural industries) | WTO (GATT, GATS) |
| -Trade-Related Aspects of Intellectual Property Rights (TRIPS) & Agreement on Trade-Related Investments Measures (TRIMS) | WTO |
| -Multilateral Agreement on Investments | OECD |

### Regional

| | |
|---|---|
| -Cultural exception | NAFTA |
| -Television quotas | EU |
| -Principle of public broadcasting | EU |
| -Media concentration of ownership rules | EU |

### National (Canadian examples)

| | |
|---|---|
| -Information highway policy | Industry Canada |
| -Broadcasting/telecom/internet regulation | CRTC |
| -Cultural policy | Canadian Heritage |
| -Public cultural institutions | CBC, NFB, etc |
| -Cultural industries subsidies | Federal & provincial governments |
| -International co-productions | FAIT |

### Transnational corporate sector

| | |
|---|---|
| -Technical standards development | ISO (ITU) |
| -Telecom pricing | ITUG (ITU) |
| -Infrastructure development | GIIC (G7/G8) |
| -Investment | OECD input |
| -Ownership, mergers, acquisitions, market access | WTO input |
| -E-commerce | GBDe |

-Direct lobbying of national governments and international organizations

## *Civil society*

| | |
|---|---|
| -Issue monitoring | MacBride Round Table |
| -Research | IAMCR |
| -Grassroots media | AMARC (radio)<br>Vidéazimut (video)<br>APC (Internet) |
| -Networking<br>Communication<br>Voices 21 | Platform on Rights |
| -Mobilization | Cultural Environment<br>Movement |
| -Right to communicate | People's Communication<br>Charter |

## *"Transversal" / "Homeless" issues*

-Transnational media regulation
      -access requirements
      -tax on benefits
      -obligations
      -performance evaluation
      -offensive content

-Transnational public service media
      -financing
      -access
      -accountability

-A "WTO for culture"

# Appendix II

## Charter for Media Freedom

The participating States of the Stability Pact for South Eastern Europe, drawing on the valuable preparatory work done within the framework of the Royaumont Process for the elaboration of this Charter for Media Freedom;

hoping that the whole area, including the FRY, will soon be included in the Stability Pact and will implement the principles of this Charter; recognizing that lasting peace in the region based on stable democracies is crucial for peace in Europe in the 21st century;

acknowledge that freedom of the media, free flow of information and ideas and open discussion, without the interference of public authorities, play a fundamental role in the development of free, stable and democratic societies; are prerequisites for the establishment of mutual understanding and good relations among states and their peoples; and deserve the full support of interested governments and organizations;

reaffirm their adherence to the principles of freedom of expression, the media and free flow of information as laid down in Article 19 of the Universal Declaration on Human Rights, the International Covenant on Civil and Political Rights, OSCE principles and commitments and, as applicable, Article 10 of the European Convention on Human Rights and Fundamental Freedoms and case law related thereto, and other international conventions and agreements including those of UNESCO and the Council of Europe;

emphasize that the promotion of mutual respect, cooperation, stability and democracy requires respect for the interests, values and cultures of all communities in the region and for international commitments relating to democracy, human rights, fundamental freedoms and the rule of law; consider that there is a need for a more active and better informed public debate in order to achieve the objectives of peace, stability and mutual understanding that underpin the Stability Pact; believe that cooperation among media professionals from the region contributes to enhancing mutual confidence and reducing the risk of tension in South Eastern Europe;

The Participating States of the Stability Pact, and the interested parties and organizations associated with the Pact, will endeavor to cooperate to protect freedom of expression and encourage observation and implementation of the following principles in the region.

The Governments in the region will:

1 defend and promote freedom of expression, information and comment and act in accordance with the rule of law and international commitments relating to the above freedoms;

2 keep under review media and other relevant laws, including defamation laws, and take steps to identify and remove obstacles to media freedom and to the exercise of independent journalism, consistent with international standards and commitments, including removal of powers of censorship or suppression of the press or radio and TV programs;

3 encourage and actively support the development of pluralistic and accessible electronic and printed media which are professional and independent, and encourage the development of regional cooperation schemes to facilitate the flow of information;

4 facilitate the ability of media organizations to control their own means of production and distribution; recognizing that economic independence has a central role to play in the development and maintenance of free and pluralistic media;

5 remove by democratic process obstacles to free access to sources of information and facilitate the unimpeded flow of information;

6 recognize that the public interest is served by the right of journalists to protect their sources of information; any restrictions to this right must serve a legitimate interest in a democratic society and must be narrowly defined by law;

7 support the development of media networks which facilitate the free flow of information between neighboring states and which bring journalists together, in particular through the exchange of young journalists;

8 ensure an appropriate legal framework for Public Service Broadcasters and state news agencies, which should serve the interests of the public and not the parties in power or special interest groups;

9 facilitate the establishment of independent broadcasting regulatory bodies, where they do not already exist, charged with implementing the internationally recognized standards of transparency and accountable administration of broadcasting;

10 recognize the key role of media professionals in matters of media ethics and support self regulation and the establishment of appropriate

structures independent of government in order to encourage professionalism, high quality and diversity in broadcasting and publishing. These structures should inter alia set standards and deal with complaints;

11 promote tolerance by facilitating access to the media for persons belonging to minorities;

12 apply, or where necessary enact, laws relating to the use of the media to incite unlawful acts of racism, xenophobia or violence. Such laws should be narrowly and clearly defined, requiring a direct connection between the incitement and an unlawful act;

13 give every encouragement to the media to promote the highest standards of professional journalism and to facilitate sources of independent and diverse information and opinion;

14 encourage media professionals in the region to develop their own code of ethics, taking into account standards developed by independent media organizations of democratic societies and principles and norms enshrined in international law and practice. These codes should take into consideration the special circumstances of the region and the need to respect human rights and minority rights.

15 encourage the independent media bodies referred to above to develop and apply standards appropriate to open and democratic societies, respecting fair business practices and political impartiality as well as international agreements on intellectual property rights.

*From:*
*http://www.stabilitypact.org/stabilitypactcgi/catalog/view_file.cgi?prod_id=247&pro p_type=en*

# Biographical Notes

*Bram Dov Abramson* studied communications at Concordia University and Université de Montréal, and is currently research director for international Internet infrastructure with TeleGeography, Inc., the research arm of London-based bandwidth exchange Band-X. His group's work on transborder IP topology, traffic flow, and institutional structures appears in *Hubs + Spokes: A TeleGeography Internet Reader* and in *Packet Geography 2002*, the group's first annual publication.

*Alison Beale* received her Ph.D. in Communication from McGill University in Montreal, Canada, has taught at the Université du Québec in Montreal and is currently Associate Professor at Simon Fraser University, Vancouver, Canada. Her publications include *Ghosts in the Machine: Women and Cultural Policy in Canada and Australia*, edited with Dr. Annette van den Bosch (Garamond, 1998), and book chapters and articles for journals including *Media, Culture and Society* and *MIA/Culture and Policy*. She is currently working on a book on cultural policies and globalization.

*Stuart Cunningham* is professor and director of the Creative Industries Research and Applications Centre (CIRAC), Queensland University of Technology, Brisbane. He is co-editor (with John Sinclair) of *Floating Lives: The Media and Asian Diasporas* (Rowman and Littlefield, 2001). Recent publications include (with John Sinclair and Elizabeth Jacka), *New Patterns in Global Television: Peripheral Vision* (Oxford University Press, 1996) and (with Graeme Turner) the standard Australian media textbooks, *The Australian TV Book* (2000) and *The Media and Communications in Australia* (third edition, 2001).

*John D.H. Downing* is the "John T. Jones Jr. Centennial Professor of Communication" in the Radio-Television-Film Department of the University of Texas at Austin. He is author most recently of *Radical Media: Rebellious Communication and Social Movements* (Sage, 2000).

*Terry Flew* is senior lecturer and head of Media Communication, and a researcher with the Creative Industries Research and Applications Centre at Queensland University of Technology, Brisbane. He is the author of *New Media Technologies: An Introduction* (Oxford University Press, 2002, forthcoming). and co-author of *The Business of Borderless Education and New Media* and *Borderless*

*Education: A Review of the Convergence Between Global Media Networks and Higher Education Provision.*

*David Goldberg* was formerly senior lecturer at the School of Law, University of Glasgow, Scotland. He now runs deegee Research/Consultancy, specializing in media and communications rights, law and policy. He is the co-editor *of Regulating the Changing Media: A Comparative Study* (OUP, 1998).

*Ben Goldsmith* is a research fellow at the Australian Key Centre for Cultural and Media Policy (CMP), Griffith University. His research interests include comparative media regulation, and the internationalization of cultural policy. In mid-2001 he took up a postdoctoral fellowship at the CMP. His current research focuses on international trends in production and finance in the film industry, with a particular emphasis on studio developments and runaway production.

*Cees J. Hamelink* is professor of International Communication at the University of Amsterdam. He is also the editor-in-chief of the international journal for communication studies, *Gazette*. Most of his research work is in the field of human rights and information/communication technologies. He has authored fifteen books, most recent of which is *The Ethics of Cyberspace* (Sage, 2000).

*John Hannigan* is professor of Sociology and associate chair, Graduate Studies, at the University of Toronto. His text, *Environmental Sociology: A Social Constructionist Perspective* (Routledge, 1995), has been translated into Portuguese and Japanese and was recently cited by the International Sociological Association on its "Books of the Century" list. His most recent book, *Fantasy City: Pleasure and Profit in the Postmodern City* (Routledge, 1998), was nominated for the John Porter Award given by the Canadian Sociology and Anthropology Association.

*Wolfgang Kleinwächter* received his Ph.D. in International Communication from the University of Leipzig in 1982. Since 1998 he has been professor of international communication policy at the University of Aarhus in Denmark. He is a member of the International Council of the International Association for Media and Communication Research (IAMCR). His recent research activities have been concentrated on ICANN and in 2000, he was a member of ICANN's Membership Information Task Force (MITF). His latest book, *ICANN: The Long Road Towards Self-Regulation of the Internet*, will be published by Beck Verlag in the fall of 2001.

*Robert W. McChesney* is a research professor in communications and library science at the University of Illinois at Urbana-Champaign. He is a co-editor of the socialist magazine *Monthly Review*. He earned a Ph.D. in communications at the University of Washington (1989) and is the author of seven books and some one hundred journal articles and book chapters. His work has been translated into 12 languages. Specializing in media history and political economy, McChesney's most recent book is *Rich Media, Poor Democracy: Communication Politics in Dubious Times* (New Press, 2000).

*Tom O'Regan* received his Ph.D. in screen studies from Griffith University in 1985, returning in 1999 to take up his current position as Professor and Director of the Australian Key Centre for Cultural and Media Policy. His research interests straddle cultural and media policy. His books include *Australian National Cinema* (1996) and *Australian Television Culture* (1993).

*Monroe E. Price* is founder and co-director of the program in Comparative Media Law and Policy at the University of Oxford and professor of law at the Benjamin N. Cardozo School of Law in New York. He received his law degree from Yale University and his field of research involves national responses to media regulation.

*Marc Raboy* (Ph.D., McGill, 1986) is full professor and head of the Communication Policy Research Laboratory in the Department of Communication at the University of Montreal. He is the author or editor of books, articles and research reports on various aspects of media and communication and has been a consultant to a range of organizations including UNESCO, the European Institute for the Media and the Policy Research Secretariat of the government of Canada. He is a member of the International Council of the International Association for Media and Communication Research, where he also heads the Global Media Policy working group.

*Katharine Sarikakis* is a doctoral candidate in Media Policy at Glasgow Caledonian University and is a lecturer at Coventry University in International Communications and Media Policy. Her research interests include the role of transnational organizations on communication policies and the socio-economic and political dynamics of new technologies. Currently, she is working on a book on the international dimensions of national media.

*Julian Thomas* is director of the Electronic Policy Project at the Institute for Social Research, Swinburne University of Technology. His main interests are in new media, information policy and cultural policy. Prior to taking up his current position, he was inquiry research manager on the Australian Productivity Commission's Broadcasting Inquiry, and was a senior research fellow at the Australian Key Centre for Cultural and Media Policy at Griffith University for several years. He is currently working on a book-length study of information policy and public computer networks.

*Daya Kishan Thussu* teaches transnational communications at Goldsmiths College, University of London. He is the co-author (with Oliver Boyd-Barrett) of *Contra-Flow in Global News* (1992), published in association with UNESCO, editor of *Electronic Empires – Global Media and Local Resistance* (Arnold, 1998) and author of *International Communication – Continuity and Change* (Arnold, 2000).

*Voices 21* is an informal association of media activists and concerned individuals founded in March 1999 with a view towards building a new social movement around media and communication issues. Voices 21 members are involved in a range of initiatives, including preparation for an NGO intervention in the

World Summit on the Information Society, planned for 2003 under the auspices of the International Telecommunication Union (ITU).

*Dwayne Winseck* is associate professor at the School of Journalism and Communication, Carleton University, Ottawa, Canada. Before arriving in Ottawa in 1998, he lived and taught in Britain, the People's Republic of China, the Turkish Republic of Northern Cyprus, and the United States. His research focuses on the political economy of communications, media history, communications policy, theories of democracy and global communication. He has authored and co-edited three books on these topics: *Reconvergence: A Political Economy of Telecommunications in Canada* (Hampton Press, 1998); *Democratizing Communication: Comparative Perspectives on Information and Power* (Hampton Press, 1997); and *Media in Global Context* (Edward Arnold, 1997).